# THE
# PSYCHIC
# WORLD
# OF
# PETER
# HURKOS

# THE
# PSYCHIC
# WORLD
# OF
# PETER
# HURKOS

## by *Norma Lee Browning*

DOUBLEDAY & COMPANY, INC.
*Garden City, New York*

# Contents

# Foreword

Psychic phenomena have probably existed as long as man himself. As cofounder of the Mind Science Foundation, I have been associated with research projects for many years which have delved into almost the entire spectrum of these most unusual occurrences, which many people never experience, some experience one or more times during their lifetime, and others, such as Peter Hurkos, are able to experience almost at will. I have known Peter for more than ten years, both as a personal friend and as a man who has always been willing to subject himself to all types of research study programs. In the many tests I have seen conducted with Peter, he has always been much more accurate than would be possible under the laws of probability. Time after time I have seen him perform feats such as those recounted in this book, feats for which there is no known explanation of how such clear mental pictures of the past, present, and future could be developed within his mind.

The author has done an excellent job in selecting some of the most interesting situations with which Peter has been associated, and in this book the reader will find full documented descriptions of the fascinating accounts of Peter Hurkos' psychic ability. I don't think there is any question that this ability developed within Peter's mind as a result of his fall from a ladder in his native Holland. Within the Mind Science Foundation we have studied many persons who have had certain psychic abilities, and in almost all cases the ability developed after either experiencing a fall or being hit on the head, or after having an extremely high fever. This seems to imply that suddenly a person is able to use another part of the brain—more or less the same as suddenly fusing two wires—because of either the pressure from the blow on the head or the heat of the high temperature.

I think it is obviously only a matter of time until the scientific world will discover how such a phenomenon is achieved, and perhaps it will then be possible for anyone to have this added "sixth sense."

*The Psychic World of Peter Hurkos* explores the many achievements of Peter Hurkos and the famed Edgar Cayce in dimensions of the past, present, and future. It offers a challenge to us better to understand psychic phenomena, and it deserves the attention of everyone who is concerned with the better understanding of the human mind. For whether or not one agrees with the views it presents, *The Psychic World of Peter Hurkos* offers the kind of stimulation that is germane to any serious thought of our future involvement in the areas of psychic phenomena, and that is a large achievement for any book.

C. V. Wood, Jr.

. . . He had never heard such music as this, never dreamt such music was possible. He was conscious, while it lasted, that he saw deeper into beauty, the sadness of things, the very heart of them, and their pathetic evanescence, as with a new inner eye—even into eternity itself, beyond the veil.

*Trilby*, Part I

—George Louis Palmella Busson du Maurier
(1834–1896)

THE
PSYCHIC
WORLD
OF
PETER
HURKOS

# · 1 ·
# *The Beginning*

When Peter Hurkos first asked me to write his book, I thought he was joking.

"You know better than to ask *me* to write your book. Remember? I'm the one who exposes people like you," I said.

"Ya. But you know me long time now. Do you ever hear me make lies?" he demanded in his guttural Dutch accent.

Well, no, I hadn't heard him make lies, as he put it. But I hadn't tried very hard either. I thought back to the time I first met him, when I tried to trap him and expose him as a fraud, and failed. But that, I had decided, proved only my own incompetence or Peter's expertise at psychic trickery.

As an investigative newspaper reporter, I had specialized in exposing charlatans and quacks. Over the years I had investigated many of the world's famous so-called psychics, sensitives, occultists, and ESP experts and had concluded that in most cases their alleged supernormal powers appeared genuine because of either deliberate fraud, trickery, or the human urge to *believe*—and sometimes a combination of the three.

I had a researcher's familiarity with such flamboyant fakes as D. D. Home and the marvelous Madame Blavatsky, and a nosy newshen's knowledge of how many of today's successful "sensitives" come by their "supernatural" powers—via gimmicks from a mail-order house in Columbus, Ohio. Its owner once told me, "The world wishes to be deceived, so I deceive it."

To be perfectly honest, I too started out wanting to believe. I have always been fascinated with psychic phenomena, as nearly everyone is, and I must admit that at one time I had great faith in what is now popularly known as (but I think is misnamed) "extrasensory perception," and in the psychic abilities of some persons I knew. But in my quest for self-enlightenment, as I delved deeper I became more disenchanted. Though I tried to remain objective, and even hopeful (wishful thinking!), eventually I realized that for me, at least, ESP simply hadn't lived up to its golden promise, and in my opinion most psychics were phonies. This was my position when Peter Hurkos asked me to write his book.

Let me hasten to say that in spite of my skepticism, I did indeed have a healthy respect for the unique and awesome abilities of the human mind to perform marvels that certainly must be accepted even if they are not yet explained.

How does one explain, for example, the power of suggestion that can cause the primitive aborigine to will himself to die? Or the power of mental self-discipline that can develop superhuman strength in the yogi? Or the power of faith that creates immunity from burns for the Fijian firewalker? Having lived for brief periods among the aborigines of Australia, the Yogis of India, and the Fijians, I am well aware that there are many things betwixt heaven and earth of which we know neither the wherefore nor the why.

How does one explain the extraordinary human sensitivity among primitive peoples and religious mystics? How explain the actual phenomena of age regression under hypnosis, of *déjà vu,* the eerie feeling of having been there before, of the storing of memories in the brain, or of Mozart, an infant prodigy who could compose minuets and sonatas before he was seven and an opera at twelve?

I would be the last to deny the factual existence of these fascinating riddles of the mind.

But who could ever make me believe that Peter Hurkos had

acquired psychic powers after falling on his head from a ladder? Utter nonsense department.

I liked Peter very much. You couldn't help liking him. He was a big, bumbling Dutchman, simple, unsophisticated, untutored. He had been in this country since 1956, but he still had trouble with the language, and he had a charming childlike naïveté that made him seem genuinely incapable of perpetrating the usual psychic hocus-pocus. Though he was sometimes moody and impetuous, I had always known him to be an extremely kind and gentle man, and far too generous for his own good.

Yes, I liked him very much. But I didn't believe in him. I didn't want to hurt his feelings, but I had to tell him the truth.

"Look, Peter, I love you madly," I said, "but let's just stay friends, O.K.? You'd better get someone else to do your book. I don't have time."

"You think I'm phony, like all the rest, don't you?"

"Well . . ."

"I prove it to you I'm not."

"How?"

"I bring you all my files, records. . . ."

"Hospital records from your accident?"

"Yes."

I wasn't convinced, and I told him so, I'm afraid not too gently.

"Don't lie to me, Peter. Do you really expect me to believe you became psychic from falling on your head?"

"That's how I got my gift." He insisted on calling it his "gift." "Well, you can say it is God's gift," he said, "but that is not all the answer. There are many things we do not know yet. I remember the time I was falling and I didn't want to die. Then everything was black. And when I wake up I had no mind of my own. And then I got my gift. I was in somebody else's mind, and I was scared because I didn't know what was happening. My father and mother said it's not the same Peter any more. They said he died and I came back with two minds. You can ask my father, I swear it. He will tell you his real son Peter died and I come back with two minds. There are two minds here, dear, two minds, you understand?"

He had worked himself up to a feverish pitch trying to convince me. He was tapping his head with his big fingers. His black eyes blazed. "It's God's truth," he said, "I came back with two minds."

There was no doubt of his sincerity. Obviously, that's what his parents had told him and he believed it. "You know there are people with two characters?" he asked. He meant, without knowing it, split or multiple personalities. "Well, I have two minds. My father was right when he said it's not the same Peter any more. He died, and he came back hearing the voice and seeing the pictures . . ."

Hearing voices? Seeing pictures? . . . Hmmm.

There are those who would have insisted, I'm sure, that Peter Hurkos belonged in a mental hospital. Was he truly psychic—or psychotic? Was he possibly a schizophrenic (split personality) or even a true multiple personality? (As in the authenticated and celebrated Sally Beauchamp case and *The Three Faces of Eve*?) Was he really "reborn" a clairvoyant because of a brain injury, as Bridey Murphy had been reborn under hypnosis? Did he really have a sixth sense, or was he a mental case?

The questions intrigued me. If Peter's story of his accident could be checked out, some light might be shed on his so-called psychic powers. I have always had a theory that much of what we know as psychic phenomena is natural rather than supernatural, physical rather than metaphysical, physiological rather than psychological. I am convinced that one day all so-called psychic experiences—everything from dreams to *déjà vu*, from age regression to reincarnation—will be proved to have a physical basis within the electrical-chemical components of that most marvelous of all computing machines, the human brain. And I was beginning to think that the brain of the man sitting there on the other side of my desk might be worth probing, and with something more than the routine ESP card and dice tests, which really hadn't proved very much.

In my previous research and investigation into psychic matters, I had had a report from Henry Belk, the man who put up the money to bring Peter to the United States to be tested by Andrija Puharich at the Round Table Foundation laboratories at Glen Cove, Maine. Belk, a chain department store magnate in

Miami, had his own psychic research foundation. Here is an excerpt from his findings on Peter:

". . . The damage apparently was to the mid-brain disturbing tissue in the medulla area. His brain has been compared to a telephone exchange, wherein somehow the wires became crossed or shuffled in a different fashion, thus changing a normal man into a psychic who could transcend the laws of time and space. Outwardly, Hurkos recovered, with a big knot on the rear of his head. Inwardly, these reports state that the injury was inflicted on the pineal, hypothalamus, and brain stem area, resulting in a form of schizophrenia, disorientation of reality, loss of free choice, ability to make decisions, concentrate, and resulting in a mental age under ten, according to reported opinion. Nonetheless, he has been known to:

1. Perform telepathy at will, fairly consistently.
2. Recite forgotten events in people's lives.
3. Report on people or objects without reference to distance intervening. . . ."

Belk believed that Peter's mysterious gift was the result of a purely biologic physical brain injury, but he also believed that his injury had left him a zombie, "controlled by a discarnate spirit." He felt, as Peter's parents did, that the real Peter died the day he had his fall.

"I have come to the conclusion," Belk once told me in an interview, "that Hurkos is a zombie and have often wondered if he didn't die the day he fell on his head and is controlled by some other spirit. I don't say this as a fact." But he did believe it strongly. (Webster defines zombie as "the supernatural power or essence which it is believed may enter into and reanimate a dead body.")

The whole idea, of course, was preposterous. Yet as I sat there looking at Peter, I knew that here was a tormented man, a man possessed of something—I didn't know what. In a sudden flash I felt the desperate yearning within him for answers to things he did not understand. I asked him, "Peter, why is this so important to you? Why do you want to tell your story in a book?"

He answered simply, "Because I want to find the key to what is wrong with me."

We were sitting in my study, with its windows overlooking a wide green canyon and ridge of hills beyond, the hills of Bel-Air. We were in the heart of movieland, with its lush homes and lavish pools and fabulously rich movie stars. Many of them were clients of Peter's. In the entertainment world it is simply taken for granted that anybody who is anybody naturally has his own astrologer, analyst, guru, or crystal gazer of one sort or another to turn to for advice and guidance. And Peter was doing private readings—or consultations—for rather hefty fees.

"Tell me the truth," he asked suddenly, "do you think I'll lose my gift if I use it for money?" Many are convinced that a genuine psychic should not use his gift for commercial purposes, and Peter was constantly being reproached by friends and critics alike, but most of all by psychical researchers and self-styled experts, for using his gift to earn money. Apart from his private readings, he was best known and highly paid for some of his work as a psychic detective on murders and missing persons cases, though on some of these, notably the missing Stone of Scone and the case of the Boston Strangler, he worked without a penny of pay. He has frequently offered his services *gratis* to local police departments. But he was very well paid, for example, for his work on the case of the missing American millionaire Thai silk king, Jim Thompson. And he was haunted by the fear that he was going to lose his gift because he was using it for money.

"But who pays my rent, buys my food?" he asked. "I have my family, my father in Holland, my kids. We have to eat. I have offered my gift for research, but who pays the bills? I don't know any other work. All I have now is my gift." Yet when I asked, "Would you rather have your gift and be rich and famous, or would you rather be the way you were before your accident?," he surprised me by replying promptly and with passion, "I will give all the money in the world, I will give up everything, if I could have my own mind again, to live and think the way it was before. No, I'm not happy, dear. How can anyone be happy with two minds?"

In many ways Peter reminded me of another great psychic, Edgar Cayce, who had died before my time. My biggest regret in my travels into the realm of psychical research was that I had missed meeting Cayce, the psychic healer from Hopkinsville, Kentucky, whose career was one of the most baffling in the annals of American medicine. He was probably America's greatest and certainly its best-loved mystic. He still lives in his deathless legacy of prophecies and in the indestructible web of enchantment he spun even among skeptics. No one was ever able to expose Edgar Cayce as a fraud—or explain how his subconscious mind could peer into the past and the future and "see" or *know* the unseen and unknown.

Nor had anyone yet been able to expose or explain Peter Hurkos. In fact, the more I thought about it, I had to admit to myself that of the whole kit and kaboodle of tantalizing psychics who have paraded across the pages of history, all but two had left me totally unimpressed, and those two were Edgar Cayce and Peter Hurkos. I'm sure some of the Cayce cult will think me brash and presumptuous to utter the names of these two men in the same breath. Peter's forte is not prophecy or psychic belief in reincarnation in the same sense as Cayce's—the belief that the soul is eternal, appearing again at intervals in other bodies.

When Peter told me that his parents said he had died and come back a different person, I asked him if he believed in reincarnation. He didn't know what I meant. When I explained, he then said, "Oh, definitely. Because my father said Peter he died and he come back." In other words he understood only that he was "reborn." Unlike true reincarnationists, he didn't go into flights of fancy about previous existences. He was only a simple Dutch house painter before his fall, hardly knowing what the word "psychic" meant, much less "reincarnation."

One day early in our meetings I asked Peter if he had ever heard of Edgar Cayce.

"Sure. I met his son in Miami. It's when I was working in Belk's department store. There was Cayce and his wife and Morey Bernstein [author of *The Search for Bridey Murphy*] and Belk and me. We had lunch in the coffee shop. It was in the summertime, and that's when Cayce's son told me his father said I was going to carry on his work."

It seemed highly improbable that Edgar Cayce had said anything of the kind, but because of Peter's language difficulty he could honestly have misinterpreted what Cayce's son said.

"What did you tell him?" I asked.

"I tell him I am not a healer. I do not prescribe medicine. He tell me, that's what my father say, someone is coming from Europe to take his place."

"What was his son's name?" I asked. He didn't remember. Since his fall Peter has had practically no memory for names. I told him that Edgar Cayce had two sons, and I named them—Hugh Lynn Cayce and Edgar Cayce, Jr. Which one was it? I asked. Peter didn't know. But he told me to write down both names on separate slips of paper, hold one in each hand, and he would tell me which son he met by touching my hand. Any Cayce fan would of course know that it had to be Hugh Lynn Cayce if the story checked out, as he is the more active son in carrying on the work of his father through the Association for Research and Enlightenment, known usually as the A.R.E., at Virginia Beach, Virginia.

Peter knew nothing about the A.R.E. or Hugh Lynn Cayce, and very little about Edgar Cayce himself other than through hearsay. He admits that since his fall he has not been able to concentrate enough to read a book. But because he was brought to America for psychical research and has spent most of his time here traveling in the psychic set, it can be assumed that Edgar Cayce's name must have left an impression even on his faulty memory. Beyond this, though, I'm sure that when I asked him he knew very little about Cayce or his career.

I wrote the names Hugh Lynn Cayce and Edgar Cayce, Jr., on separate slips of paper, crumpled them, and switched them back and forth behind my back from one hand to the other until it was impossible even for me to know the name either hand was holding. Then I held my closed fists out to Peter, saying jokingly, "if you're really psychic, you know, you'd better pick Hugh Lynn."

"I don't know his name," he said, "but this is the man I met." He tapped my left fist, I opened it, and it was Hugh Lynn.

Later, I checked out Peter's story with Hugh Lynn. Yes, he had met Peter in Miami on the occasion Peter had described. And he had been very impressed with him. "He is undoubtedly a gifted person," Hugh Lynn told me. "I think he has real sensitivity. And he is very sincere." As for carrying on the work of Edgar Cayce, Hugh Lynn said, "No one is coming forward to take Dad's place, though many have claimed to be able to do the same thing. In fact, Dad insisted that we all have a certain amount of psychic ability, and if we would only bother to develop it as he did, a great many people could do what he did. As for Peter Hurkos or any other one person taking his place, there is no reference to this in my father's readings, although he did say there would be others in other countries, India and Europe, who would be able to give readings similar to his."

This could account for Peter's misinterpretation. Certainly he has never made public claims of taking over for the great sage of Virginia Beach (as others more cunning than he blatantly do), who could diagnose illnesses he had never studied and outline medical treatments that he had never heard of. Peter's area of specialty is crime cases. Yet, curiously, he has a remarkable degree of accuracy in medical and anatomical matters and quite possibly could have done as well as a psychic healer if he had chosen to—and if he had lived in a different era. Edgar Cayce was arrested only once for practicing medicine without a license (and also once for fortune telling), but today with the powerful whip of the American Medical Association, as well as more stringent state laws governing the practice of medicine, he probably would not be permitted to operate as openly and successfully as he once did.

Even Hugh Lynn Cayce was astonished by Peter's accuracy in medical matters. And like many others, he tried to persuade Peter to give up his work on crime cases and to lend himself to something of more far-reaching importance, such as research with long-range objectives.

"No one realizes better than I the problems of the psychic," Hugh Lynn told me. "I lived with it with my father. There were always the materialistic pressures of earning a living, supporting a family, and the conflicts that came with using his gift for money. I met Peter in the early days, soon after he came to this country, and I think that then he had a remarkable gift. But I was disturbed at all his bouncing around on crime cases. My father's early attention to things that had to do with crime got him into a lot of difficulty and trouble. And frankly, I'm afraid this has hurt Peter, too."

Cayce cultists who scorn commercialism of psychic powers point with pride to the fact that in all his life Cayce rarely made more than seventy-five dollars a week. Few of Peter's friends or critics know that at one point in his career he could have had great riches and fame as a stage telepathist in Europe. He could have combined a few magic tricks with his "sixth sense," sprinkled them with the supernatural, and exploited his talent as an entertainer, a performing psychic, much in the manner of the run-of-the-mill phonies who get rich quick at it. Instead, he chose to come to America and offer himself as a research guinea pig in the hope of finding out what was wrong with his head.

This is not the ordinary pattern for the run-of-the-mill psychic. But then the more I learned about Peter, the more I realized he was no ordinary man. Like Edgar Cayce, he was a simple, humble man who believed that his "gift" should be used to help people and not for material gain—except that, unlike Cayce, he had arrived in this country with no knowledge of English, to become a pawn in the hands of ambitious men trying to exploit him. (Some did a pretty good job of it.) Like Cayce, he gave readings free—and still does—to people who could not afford to pay or who for some reason felt they didn't need to. I have been on many cases with Peter where he received no fee for his services. Like Cayce, he could help others become richer by exploring for gold or oil, or advising them on business ventures. But like Cayce, he was most inept in handling his own business affairs, and he gave away more than he earned with his readings.

The truth is, as I came to know him better in preparing this book, I was more and more impressed with the eerie parallels between Peter Hurkos, the Dutch psychic, and Edgar Cayce, the great American mystic, whom Jess Stearn calls the "sleeping prophet" (*Edgar Cayce, The Sleeping Prophet*).

Many of Edgar Cayce's earthshaking prophecies and remarkable medical cures came to him either while he was in a trance or while he was asleep. And he had an unusual flair for imparting the messages from his subconscious mind by talking in his sleep.

Similarly, some of Peter's most spine-chilling revelations on the Boston Strangler case came while he was talking in his sleep. One of the first things that ever impressed me about Edgar Cayce, when I started reading about him years ago, was that as a schoolboy he learned his lessons by sleeping on his books! Peter's astonishingly accurate descriptions of the Strangler's victims came from sleeping with some of their clothes.

Both Edgar Cayce and Peter Hurkos were psychic awake as well as asleep. But both were literal dreamers—that is, they dreamed voluminously, and their dreams frequently had psychical interpretations.

Though Edgar Cayce was far more famous for his remarkable prophecies, many of Peter's prophecies were equally remarkable if not as spectacular. Precognition was not his specialty, although many of his predictions came true.

And though Peter never went in for psychic healing, Cayce's specialty, the term "psychic diagnostician," which Cayce was known as, would apply equally well to Peter Hurkos. In the Glen Cove research laboratories in Maine some of his most remarkable records were scored in readings that dealt with disease or illness or anatomical details, according to Dr. Andrija Puharich.

As boys, Edgar Cayce in Hopkinsville, Kentucky, and Pieter van der Hurk in Dordrecht, Holland, both were very poor students, sixth-grade school dropouts, and both spent a great deal of their childhood outdoors, in the woods or in seclusion, lonely and brooding, dreamy and introverted, prone to fantasies and "visions."

Cayce was deeply religious all his life, even as a boy. Peter became religious only after he had acquired his gift through his accident.

"My father say, 'Look at him. He is not the same Peter. He gets religious!' Because I buy a secondhand Bible for two guilders in the market. And my mother thought I was crazy, and my father laughed at me because I sit all the time studying the Bible. I wanted to find the key to what is wrong with me."

Strangest of all are the physical parallels between Edgar Cayce and Peter Hurkos, the peculiar circumstances of their birth, and their accidents. Cayce was born with "milk on the breasts" (later cured by being pricked with a needle), and Peter was born blind, with a veil over his eyes (literally). Both were constant crybabies the first months of their lives.

Peter fell on his head; Cayce was hit in the head by a thrown baseball. In a semistupor he told his parents to prepare a special poultice and put it at the base of his brain. They did as he instructed, and the next day he recovered. That was his first health reading. A few years later, in 1900, following a severe cold, he contracted laryngitis and lost his voice, seemingly for good. Then a vaudeville hypnotist playing at the local theater claimed he could cure Cayce's condition by putting him to sleep and giving him suggestions. Under hypnosis, Cayce's voice returned loud and clear, and in addition, it took on a strange new quality of authority. "This body is unable to speak due to a partial paralysis of the inferior muscles of the vocal cords . . . this may be removed by increasing the circulation to the affected parts by suggestion. . . ."

From then on Cayce seemed able to diagnose and treat every conceivable kind of disease with incredible accuracy, even though he had never gone to medical school, never studied pathology or anatomy, never worked in a hospital.

It was as though a Great Healer had taken possession of his body, much as that zombie took over Peter's body after he fell on his head.

After acquiring their gifts, both Edgar Cayce and Peter Hurkos could speak in alien tongues while asleep or in a trance. Both had an uncanny way with plants and flowers, talking to them as though they were people, making them grow, keeping them alive. . . .

Both had an incredible ability to look inside everything, to "see" or know the unseen and unknown through subconscious channels. Cayce's gift was known as a "universal mind," which seemed to draw from a subconscious register of everything that had ever happened or was going to happen. In experiments with Peter, Dr. Puharich declared that he had obtained the best evidence on record for telepathic interaction between two minds, but like Cayce, Peter seemed able sometimes to pierce the past, present, and future by means of something more than simple telepathy.

Curiously, and perhaps significantly for future researchers, both Edgar Cayce and Peter Hurkos were known—at different times and places—as "the man with the X-ray eyes." In Europe, Peter was also sometimes billed as "the man with the radar brain." Curiously, both became subject to blinding headaches, apparently related to the physical strain of their psychic forces at work. And they shared certain personality characteristics, such as a volatile temperament—easily hurt or disturbed—and mercurial moods.

Both were fundamentally frightened of their gift, of delving into things they didn't understand, of controlling the lives or the actions or the health (as Cayce did) of others. Both viewed their gift with misgivings. *Was* it a gift? Or a curse? Certainly it was a burden that weighed heavily on their conscious minds.

Cayce once said, "I honestly don't know what this power is and why it was given to me. I've been giving these readings since 1901. I'm told they've helped a lot of folks that were in serious trouble. So I think it must be from God. Sometimes I'm afraid of the power. Sometimes I wish it hadn't been wished on me. It's brought me and the wife and the family a heap of troubles. But I can't bring myself to turn down folks that are sick and need help."

It might be that other psychics share many common characteristics in their physical, mental, and emotional makeup, but in my own experience and research, I have found none with more similarities than Edgar Cayce, son of a struggling tobacco farmer, and Peter Hurkos, son of a peasant Dutch house painter.

In fact, one final vignette, almost too spookish for belief, raises the haunting question, Why were the stars in their subconscious heavens so much the same? For although the two men never met, their psychic paths crossed briefly on a cold Sunday in New York on February 8, 1964. Peter had just finished working on the Boston Strangler case and had flown to New York. The newspapers were full of his exploits. And suddenly he was roused from his sleep at 3:30 A.M., arrested for allegedly impersonating an FBI officer, and hauled off to jail. He spent only a few hours there. The incident turned out to be a political move to discredit him—

or to embarrass the public officials who had permitted a soothsayer to work on the case. Queen Juliana of the Netherlands dispatched her own private attorney, Baron von Haimstraff, whom
Peter had never met, to represent him, although this turned out
to be unnecessary. A quick-witted judge sensed the political
hanky-panky, and the case was quickly dropped.

But by some strange and eerie coincidence—or was it only coincidence?—the jail in which Peter spent those few hours was the
very same jail in which Edgar Cayce was briefly incarcerated
when he was arrested for fortune-telling thirty-three years earlier, on November 8, 1931. And on that occasion a kindly judge
had listened intently to the simple recital of his work by a simple
man, who candidly admitted that he himself wasn't sure how he
functioned or how much good he did. The judge recalled a line
from Shakespeare, "There are more things in heaven and earth,
Horatio,/Than are dreamt of in your philosophy," and dismissed
the case.

Is it possible that in some other world, perhaps in one of
Cayce's previous reincarnations, the American mystic and the
Dutch psychic were kindred soul spirits?

Or is their psychic kinship due to a physical brain injury?

It seems that if scientists and medical men would stop scoffing
long enough to take a serious look at the physiological brain
processes of a man like Edgar Cayce or Peter Hurkos, we might
one day know the answers to some of the mind's hidden mysteries.

# · 2 ·

# Show Me

I remember vividly the very first time I met Peter Hurkos. It was a balmy night in North Miami in December, 1960. I hid in a car and stalked him outside his home in his own front yard, when he was just returning from a two months' stint in Hollywood.

And I didn't like him at all. I had come wholeheartedly prepared not to like him.

For months I had been trying to locate the great Peter Hurkos because I had an assignment from my editor at the Chicago *Tribune* to do a story on him. But the great Peter Hurkos was being infuriatingly elusive, unavailable, unapproachable, incommunicado, and all that sort of thing. I was to learn later that this was not Peter's fault. None of his assorted associates had bothered even to tell him that I wanted an appointment with him. This was early in his career in America and at a time when he was surrounded by phalanxes of exploiters who didn't know quite what to do with him, except to keep him under wraps, or at least away from the press.

Peter was new to this country and its ways. He didn't understand the language (he still doesn't), and he was a very trusting soul. He had been brought here for research into his psychic powers, and in good faith had turned himself over to a succession of pseudo-ESP experts, some of whom involved him in a little cosmic clique of so-called business managers, agents, and all the latchers-on one acquires when one is about to become a huge commercial success, and especially if one happens to be a gifted but guileless Dutchman with no experience in the great American con game of success.

I knew none of this at the time I was trying to locate Peter Hurkos, whose psychic specialty, I had heard, was locating missing persons. Having no psychic abilities myself, I couldn't locate the missing Hurkos, and I was getting nothing but the runaround from his flock of protectors.

I finally learned through friends (not through clairvoyance) that he was living in North Miami, and so I went there well armed with my own tests to prove or disprove his psychic powers.

I had a pretty good track record as an investigative reporter. I could usually smell a quack a mile away, and I had a special inverse affinity for phonies. I was given no special instructions on my Peter Hurkos assignment other than the usual write-it-like-you-find-it. But I had a preconceived idea that what I would find in Miami was a Peter-Hurkos-Is-a-Fraud story. How could it be anything else when a man claimed he had got his psychic "gift" through falling off a ladder and landing on his head? Absolutely preposterous, I thought, as I knocked at the door of his modest white suburban bungalow. That name on the door was his real Dutch name, Van der Hurk. Few of his neighbors knew he was Peter Hurkos.

A woman answered the door and told me that Peter had been in Hollywood and was expected back momentarily. I decided to wait for him outside. Surprise attack. I wasn't going to take another chance on telephoning him and getting another runaround. I didn't have to wait long. He drove up in the dusk, and as he climbed out of his car, I leaped out of mine. Of course, we clashed, right off the bat. The great Peter Hurkos obviously didn't like being surprised by reporters in his own front yard.

"I am very busy and very tired, and my wife is waiting dinner," he said.

I told him I was very busy and very tired too. "But if you're as good as you're cracked up to be, why aren't you willing to prove it to a newspaper reporter?" I asked.

I could see that he didn't care much for my approach, but it got results.

I have always maintained that it is possible for a woman to be a good newspaper reporter—as good as a man—and still be a lady. But Peter Hurkos was trying my patience. After all, in my work I had met a few VIPs—Presidents, other politicians, and royalty. And frankly it annoyed me to be standing there arguing with a so-called psychic who was playing as hard to get as Garbo.

"All right," he boomed. "I prove it to you if it take me two days. Be here noon sharp tomorrow. Bring an object. I need object."

I already knew what. Ha! Just wait until he saw the objects I'd bring. Just wait until he read all about himself in my exposé.

"Why can't we start tonight after you have dinner?" I asked. I didn't want to take a chance on his calling Chicago and checking up on me. I needn't have worried.

He repeated that he was very tired, and he admitted that he didn't work well when he was tired. I realized too that it was rather brash of me to expect him to spend his first evening at home, after being gone for two months, trying to convince a skeptical newspaperwoman of his psychic powers. Looking back now, I think Peter was a very patient man that night.

I told him that I had been trying to contact him for months. He said this was the first he had heard about it, and he apologized.

When I went back at noon the next day, he answered the door himself and ushered me into a small, sunny den. He seemed refreshed and relaxed. I had to admit to myself even on that first meeting that he wasn't exactly what I had expected. He seemed very serious, sincere, unassuming, and, I thought, terribly naïve about himself. He told me he was just a "working man" in Holland, a "house painter," and that he didn't have much schooling.

"I do not know what you call ESP," he said, "but everybody say that's what my gift is, ESP. I don't know."

I was thinking, *Well, O.K., Pop, come on and prove your ESP. I'm from Missouri. Show me.*

I was surprised at how ruggedly good-looking he was, with piercing dark eyes peering intently from a craggy face. His eyes are his dominant feature. They sometimes look directly at you or through you with searing penetration, or they are sometimes fixed in the far-off, impenetrable glaze of a hypnotic trance. But they are never shifty or sly. I could detect none of the conman's hanky-panky in either his manner, his looks, or his approach. I was surprised at his cleanness (I don't know what I expected), his openness, and yes, his gentleness.

But when he said he didn't use his gift for "good," it was too much.

*So he doesn't dabble in the stock market, horse racing, or gambling, he tells me, because he doesn't want to lose his gift. What sort of nut is this?* I ask. *Big fat fake,* said I. I was positive he was no more psychic than I was.

With mixed feelings about him I started putting him through the tests which I knew would trap him at his own game, whatever it was.

For a warm-up I gave him a pair of cuff links that had belonged to my father, who had died in August of that year. Peter claims to operate best through psychometry—occult for the divination of facts by touching an object belonging to someone. He rubbed the cuff links between his palms and described certain details of my father's death, as though he had been there. Creepy. But I rationalized to myself, *Oh well, they could probably apply to anyone.*

He missed on some points. He doesn't claim to be 100 per cent accurate—only 87 per cent.

I next gave him a pen that was a Christmas gift to my husband from a friend.

Peter started out: "This is not paid for by the person who owns it. He did not buy it himself."

Certainly not an earthshaking observation, but why did it have to be so accurate?

He then went on to describe my husband precisely and accurately, from physical appearance to personality traits, work and hobby interests, even to his car trouble and shoulder pains.

Score on this one—100 per cent.

But, said I to myself; *I don't believe it. He's got a gimmick. Why can't I figure it out?*

I gave him my wristwatch, which had been in the repair shop for a thorough overhaul.

He started with, "It's a good watch, but I see a repair in the spring." I thought; *Sure, Buster, you'd be safe to say that about anyone's watch.*

Then he launched into so many uncomfortable accurate "visions" of my personal life—including a detailed description of my Chicago apartment—that I cut him off for the more important business at hand.

I now presented him with my *pièce de résistance*. Of the objects on which he could psychometrize, I had brought with me from Chicago, a city of unsolved crimes, an envelope containing seven pictures copied from those in our newspaper files.

I took them out, one by one, and placed them face down, as Peter requested, so that he could not see the picture. The first was that of a girl who had lived not in Chicago but in LaCrosse, Wisconsin. Her name was Evelyn Hartley. In October, 1953, at the age of fifteen, she was kidnaped and presumably murdered in what was later to become known as the classic Baby Sitter Mystery.

The case is still unsolved. Evelyn's body was never found. For a while police thought it probably lay somewhere in the depths of the Mississippi River.

In 1953, the year the crime occurred, Peter Hurkos was still in Europe. And during his years in this country he had not lived in the Midwest. It might be reasonable to assume that even if I had given him the name Evelyn Hartley, it would have meant nothing to him.

I had worked on the case—in the middle of winter when it was icy cold. Police were planning to dredge parts of the Mississippi for the body—after the spring thaws.

When I gave Peter the picture, he turned it face down, rubbed his fingertips across it, broke out in a sweat, excitedly thrust it back at me, and cried, "No! No! I don't see this. She's like ice —cold. No! It breaks off. There's no contact."

He grabbed the picture again, fingertipped it, and asked, "Who gave you this picture?" I shrugged and said nothing. "It stops. There's no feeling. I'm scared. It's so fast. Here I am, and now I'm nothing anymore. I'm sorry. It's too much for me."

He thrust the picture back at me, shuddered, and just glared at me with his piercing black eyes. That was all. But it was enough. I wondered how much more he could have told if he had been given the tennis shoes and the jacket, the principal clues in the case, to go on.

I was making notes on everything he said, but I refused to give him any assurance or assistance by so much as a yea or a nay. I told him nothing, said nothing, and throughout the entire session I was careful to keep a poker face, not raising an eyebrow, nodding my head, or batting an eye. But by now I was thinking, *Hmmmm. Not bad. But how does he do it?*

I then gave him two pictures that many Chicagoans would recognize—pictures of the Grimes sisters, Patricia and Barbara, who left home to see an Elvis Presley movie on December 28, 1956, and never returned. Their frozen bodies were found nearly a month later. The crime has never been solved, and Peter didn't solve it either. But from their pictures he came up with specific details of their personal lives and family background that tallied uncannily well with police findings.

My next test was a picture of Orja G. Corns, Jr., Chicago's most baffling missing persons riddle. On July 2, 1948, Corns went nightclubbing on North Clark Street, then drove home to Winnetka, left eighty dollars on a bedroom dresser, and drove off in his dark green 1947 Oldsmobile four-door sedan. He hasn't been seen since. Neither has his car.

How Peter could tell merely by fingering the back side of a picture of Corns that he even owned a car, I'll never know. How did he even know it was a man?

He said, "This man is not around anymore. Nobody knows where he is. He was in trouble. He went out with his car. It was a dark colored car. His last contact was at home, and then he left with his car. I don't see a body in the United States. I see him in Mexico or Caracas.

"This man isn't what people thought he was. Outside he was a nice guy, but he was a tough character. I see a gang and crooks, gambling, shooting, horses, money in restaurants, nightclubs. He was in trouble. He was with bad people."

If Peter Hurkos had known I was coming with a picture of Orja Corns, he could have made a quick trip to Chicago and checked the files. He would have found that Orja Corns was from a prominent family and lived a life of respectability on the outside but that he liked entertaining customers in bars, bistros, nightclubs, and strip tease joints, that police found he had a tendency to become belligerent when drinking, that he sometimes went to the horse races with bartenders, that an old address book of his was found later in a South Side Negro district.

How could Peter Hurkos sense all of this? Your guess is as good as mine.

By now I was beginning to feel a bit squeamish about putting him through my last picture test.

Somewhat reluctantly I pulled out two photographs and sat holding them on my lap, trying to decide which to give him first.

One was a picture of two boys, John Schuessler, thirteen, and his brother Anton, Jr., eleven. The other was a picture of a good-looking, smiling youngster, Robert Peterson, fourteen. Their bodies were found on October 18, 1955. They had been beaten and strangled in one of the most brutal of Chicago's unsolved murders.

Peter Hurkos reached over, took the Peterson boy's picture from my hands, and placed it face down. He ran the tips of his big fingers over it, then suddenly, with a look of horror on his face, tossed it back in my lap and cried, "No! It's too much."

I said nothing. His forehead and palms were perspiring. He asked me quietly, "Do you know this boy?"

I shook my head—no.

He took the picture again and said, "I am sorry to say it, this is horrible. He was a very fine boy, no troublemaker. Someone grabbed him in the back and hit him in the head, awful."

Peterson, the largest of the three boys, was the most brutally beaten. Police believed that the killer or killers, in an effort to keep him under control while handling all three boys, grabbed a hand rake of a clawed type and struck him savagely several times on the left side of the head. Marks and bruises on all three bodies testified to the viciousness of the beatings.

Peter went on: "This did not happen recently. It happened about five years ago. I see two houses. The family must have two houses, or there are two families. This boy was not alone; he was with somebody else.

"This is in the woods, not in town, but in a lot of woods, past trees, in a shallow spot about fifty-five or sixty feet off a little side road. That's where the body was found."

He drew me a diagram to illustrate.

The boys' bodies were found in a shallow weedy ditch near a parking lot in the Robinson Woods forest preserve, about five miles west of their homes.

Peter told me the crime had been committed by a sex degenerate. That was also the police theory.

I was fresh out of tests for Peter. He seemed surprised. Our session had lasted two and a half hours, and though he looked rather well wrung out from the ordeal, he was willing to keep going. It wasn't necessary. I'd had enough. I asked what his fee was. No charge. It was my turn to be surprised. I had heard that he charged fantastic fees.

But he obviously hadn't liked my cynical show-me attitude and was intent only on proving himself, and then, I suspect, getting rid of me. He didn't even ask whether he had been accurate on any of the readings—and I didn't tell him. I thanked him politely and he thanked me politely, and we parted. I never expected to see him again.

In retrospect, I still couldn't believe him.

True, he had astonished me with his accuracy, but he had not made a convert.

True, he had made metaphysical mishmash of my feeble efforts to prove him a fraud, but he could never convince me that he had become psychic from a blow on the head. I checked this out with medical experts at the time, and they said it was impossible. (The medical experts, however, may need to do some expert explaining after they read this book.)

I also checked with some of the researchers and police officers who had worked with Peter, and some gave him eloquent testimonials. Dr. Puharich told me, "I would stake my professional reputation on Peter Hurkos. I have screened two hundred persons for extrasensory perception in the last twelve years. I have found only six who could be considered to have genuine ESP—and of these Peter Hurkos' abilities were the greatest."

Well, I still wasn't convinced of ESP, even though Dr. Puharich was. . . .

As I looked back on that first meeting with Peter, I gradually convinced myself that it couldn't be true: it had to be trickery, certainly the most expert psychic trickery I had ever encountered but nonetheless trickery. I knew a little about the *modus operandi* of stage mentalists, mediums, magicians, their talking and silent codes, their "cold readings," sealed-message readings, and hidden mirrors.

I also knew that intellectual competence, in itself, is not sufficient for the unerring detection of psychic fraud. Harry Houdini, modern history's greatest mystifier, put the idea in these words:

"The scientific mind is usually helpless against a trained trickster. Because a man has mastered the intricacies of chemistry or physics is no qualification for him to deduce how the Chinese linking rings, for instance, seem to melt into each other, passing solid metal through solid metal. Only a knowledge of the rings themselves can reveal the secret. The scientific mind is trained to search for truth which is hidden in the mysteries of nature— not by the ingenuity of another human brain."

If great scientific minds could be deceived by the techniques of psychic trickery, why couldn't mine? And I assumed it had been.

I might have been more impressed with Peter's performance if I had not once had a similar baffling experience with that amazing master mentalist, the Great Dunninger.

I am fully aware, of course, that Dunninger and Hurkos are in completely different categories. Dunninger is strictly a magician and doesn't claim to be psychic. Though he calls himself a "mindreader," it's only part of his magic act, and he does not pretend that his mystifying feats are the result of any supernatural or supernormal gift. Moreover, to his credit, he did not hop on the ESP bandwagon; and for that matter, neither did Peter Hurkos, though there are many who believe that his gift is genuine extrasensory perception. And there are others who think it is simple magicianship or trickery under the guise of a so-called psychic gift.

Personally, I belong to an old-fashioned school that is reluctant to attribute a psychic explanation to a phenomenon just because I don't understand it. I didn't understand how Dunninger did his marvelous magic "mind-reading" feats, and I didn't understand how Peter Hurkos did his. But my lack of knowledge didn't prove he was psychic.

Peter moved to Milwaukee, and I began seeing him again occasionally. He was then spending a great deal of his time working with various research groups, demonstrating his "gift" for them, and submitting to endless tests, most of which he didn't understand. But he seemed genuinely interested in cooperating with anyone who could help him find clues to his strange hypersensitivity. I was beginning research on my own book on psychic phenomena at the time (*The Other Side of the Mind*, with W. Clement Stone) and so had reason to keep Peter under observation, so to speak. On several occasions I was present when he gave readings with such embarrassing candor that I cringed for those who had requested them. He didn't mean to embarrass anyone, but he has always had difficulty controlling his psychic valve and is apt to blurt out whatever he sees.

I saw him come up with some remarkably accurate psychic readings, and some not so remarkable. Sometimes he missed completely.

Meanwhile the research for my book on psychic phenomena took me around the world and into some fascinating areas—from the laboratories of Leningrad to the banks of the Ganges, seeking answers to such mind mysteries as hypnosis, telepathy, autosuggestion, faith healing, extrasensory perception, cybernetics. It was in the course of this research that I met many of the world's best-known clairvoyants and present-day Nostradamuses and became disillusioned with them.

But it was through comparison with all the others that I began to wonder more and more about Peter Hurkos. He was the only one of them all who still had me baffled, whose "gimmick" or *modus operandi* I couldn't figure out, and whom I could not neatly pigeonhole with the phonies, fakers, or frauds. He was the only one who *seemed* to me to be genuinely sincere—and note I said *seemed* to be. I still wasn't sure. But he seemed too unsophisticated, too unwise to the ways of the world, to play the con game, and besides, I really didn't believe I could be that easily conned.

Peter intrigued me if for no other reason than that he had stood the test of time with me. Maybe I didn't believe in him. But I had found no valid reason to disbelieve him, either. Just as in all my research I could find no reason to disbelieve Edgar Cayce. And at times when I really let myself go and permitted myself the pastime of pondering, a niggling question reared its head: Could it be that I was wrong and that Peter Hurkos and Edgar Cayce really had something? And why did I, who didn't believe in any of this psychic hogwash, have a hangup on these two? Probably because I didn't know how to explain them, and it bugged me.

So forget it. I finished my book and went on to other assignments and forgot about them.

On a smoggy evening in April, 1967, Peter and I literally bumped into each other on the dance floor at one of *those* Hollywood parties. . . . Dean Martin was there, and Marlo Thomas, and Barbara Stanwyck. The place (I've forgotten where) was loaded with celebrities, and I was following the flashbulbs like a magnet. I had been transferred to the West Coast to cover the Hollywood beat for my newspaper.

I was pleased to see Peter again, and I wasn't particularly surprised to find him making the scene on the Hollywood celebrity circuit. He told me he then lived in Hollywood, and I mused to myself, this was where he belonged, really—with all the other phonies. But I was somewhat taken aback when he whirled me off into a corner to let me in on a "secret"—his latest assignment. He was very excited about it. He was leaving next day for Bangkok, he told me, and on a "confidential" mission to Malaysia, to help in the search for the missing American millionaire Thai silk king, Jim Thompson. I had known Jim Thompson personally, so I had more than a passing interest in the case. And confidentially, I was amazed that a psychic would be called in on a case of such importance. This, I thought, was really straining credulity too far. Peter had to be kidding or mistaken or maybe stretching the truth? Anyway, tongue in cheek I wished him luck.

And the next thing I knew, Peter Hurkos was in the headlines again—from Bangkok—with his reports on the case of the missing Jim Thompson. . . .

After Peter returned, I saw him occasionally around Hollywood-land. In December I invited him to a party in my home which nearly turned into a fiasco and which was to influence my decision about writing his book. Naturally, I would not invite Peter Hurkos to a party with the thought of entertaining my guests with crystal ball gazings any more than I would invite my doctor with the expectation that he would dispense free medical advice. Anyone who wanted readings or consultations by Peter, I thought, really should make a business appointment with him rather than taking advantage of a social affair.

But human nature being what it is, most people simply cannot resist testing the powers of a psychic if they get the opportunity, and quite a few of my guests were grabbing at the opportunity. Peter, as I have said, is moody, impetuous, and unpredictable. Usually, at parties he is somewhat subdued and taciturn. Sometimes he will go all evening without "seeing" anything for anybody, and I have known him to refuse people brusquely, almost to the point of rudeness. If he's not in the mood, you can't budge him. On the other hand, I've heard him blurt out things suddenly, spontaneously, uncontrollably to complete strangers who didn't ask him. And anyone who *does* ask him, I might add, should be prepared to take the consequences.

He happened to be in rare form the night of the party. He was most obliging to everyone and was hitting with such accuracy that a couple of the guests left abruptly, in shock. Among my guests was a young college professor with his wife and also his mother, recently widowed. The professor watched from behind the bar with obvious displeasure (and with too many bourbons under his belt) as Peter gave his wife a reading, at her special request, from a small color photo she pulled from her wallet. Though I wasn't eavesdropping, I could tell from the expression on her face that she was scared out of her wits (she told me later in private that he was so accurate it frightened her), and I could also tell from the expression on her husband's face that he was seething.

Peter had barely finished with the wife when the mother removed a watch she was wearing, thrust it at him to "feel," and challenged him: "Now, tell *me* something."

He "felt" the watch, then hesitated. "No," he said, "I better not tell you what I see."

"Go ahead," she urged him. "Tell me."

What he "felt" and saw turned into a very painful experience for the lady who had asked for it.

"This was your husband's watch," said Peter. (Correct) "Your husband was a big man, he walked like this. . . ." And like a man possessed, Peter jumped up and limped across the room like a cripple, holding his right side as though in pain. He rushed on with all the unpleasant details, proceeding to describe her late husband's ailments, the circumstances of his death, and even the precise location of his grave, to the horror of all the guests within hearing. Some raised their voices in chatter and laughter to draw attention away from Peter and the woman. Some pretended not to hear or see. I was circulating among the guests trying to herd them over to the buffet table—or anywhere away from the scene. Once he had started, there was no stopping Peter.

The poor widow was in tears, but she seemed almost to be enjoying her grief when it was interrupted by a commotion at the bar. Her son, the college professor, scathingly announced, "This is ridiculous. The man is obviously a charlatan. How can anyone possibly believe in this sort of rot?"

He was, of course, concerned for his mother, and you couldn't blame him. But he also clearly conveyed the message that I was an idiot for inviting this fraud into my home, and especially for inflicting him on my friends. His outburst nearly broke up the party. At least it put a damper on Peter for the rest of the evening.

It was only a few weeks after this that he came to me and asked me to write his story. As a friend, I had begun to accept Peter without probing or analyzing, and I liked it better that way. What if his story didn't check out? Deep down I was afraid it wouldn't, and I didn't want to take a chance on it.

But he was so insistent and so willing to submit himself to any kind of double-checking, cross-examination, or investigation to help support or confirm his story that it became a challenge to me. *Peter Hurkos is a charlatan. Peter Hurkos is a fraud.*

The words were still ringing from the night of the party, and from my own vacillating but still lingering doubts.

And yet, as William James once observed, the limits of the powers of the human mind are unknown, the range of its potential abilities virtually unexplored territory.

Was it possible that Peter Hurkos was not a fraud or a charlatan? And if not, then what was he? A zombie? Come, come now.

But somehow finally, for my own peace of mind, I had to know.

And so began my search for the real Peter Hurkos.

# · 3 ·

# The Accident

On May 21, 1911, in the small industrial town of Dordrecht, Holland, Pieter Cornelis van der Hurk was born.

It was no ordinary birth. He was *wet-de-helm-geboren*—"born with the helm." The more colloquial expression in Holland is "born with the fleece." There is a very old superstition in Holland that anyone born with the helm can see into the future.

The more familiar expression in America is "born with a veil"—commonly denoting a "sixth sense" or psychic powers.

The word "veil" itself is enshrouded with mysterious connotations. It usually refers to a gauzy, diaphanous mask or net that covers or hides the face. It is often used in a religious sense, *i.e.*, to take the veil, meaning to become a nun. And in a mystical sense it is commonly used with reference to the beyond, the next world, as in the memorable words from Du Maurier's *Trilby:* "He saw deeper into the beauty, the sadness of things, the very heart of them, . . . as with a new inner eye—even into eternity itself, beyond the veil. . . ."

I had always thought that being "born with a veil" was merely a symbolic figure of speech, until I checked it out with medical authorities. To my surprise I learned that whether called the helm, the fleece, or the veil, the phenomenon is more than psychic folklore. It has its origin in a very real, though extremely rare, medical phenomenon which occurs during the miracle of birth

—being born with a veillike membrane or velum over the head. This is known medically as a "caul"—defined as "a membrane enveloping the fetus, which sometimes covers the head of a child at its birth."

In normal birth the filmy membrane known as the "bag of waters" ruptures at the time of delivery. But sometimes a portion of it—the caul—is wrapped around the head of the child at birth. It is as thin as onion skin and like a wet piece of tissue, and it must be punctured and removed immediately so the baby can breathe.

Some refer to such a birth as being born with a *capote*—a shield or hood over the head. The Dutch use the word *helm*, meaning a head covering or helmet, and the word *fleece* to indicate the thin, woolly fibroid quality of the membrane.

The word "caul" also has some interesting and ancient non-medical definitions: Gossamer threads forming a kind of film on grass; the web or cocoon of a spinning caterpillar; a net, a spider's web, a netted cap worn by women. Thus in some ways the caul shares the gauzelike mystery of the veil, which has always had a symbolic meaning.

And it is part of the medical folklore in many countries that anyone born with the caul is regarded as lucky. In ancient times the caul was believed to be a preservative against drowning. In some of the Scandinavian countries the membrane, after being removed from the baby's head, was preserved in alcohol and given to the Viking sailors for good luck.

Apparently similar beliefs prevailed in America. One theory was that the veil-skin membrane must be pickled (preserved in some way) and kept, and that the well-being of the gifted one would be assured so long as nothing happened to the veil. A friend's mother told me of a case that she heard of as a child, involving such a birth, in this instance twins. One was born with the veil, the other without. The one with the veil was quite bright, gifted, and died suddenly after some other children (not knowing what it was or the superstition connected with it) were playing with the jar containing the veil and broke it and did nothing about saving the veil.

Among some people the caul is an omen of bad luck rather

than good. But among most of them—and especially in Holland where people seem to be more psychically attuned than in other countries—the caul—or the helm, as it is called there—is commonly accepted as a "gift."

Ask any Dutchman, and he'll tell you, "Anyone born with that —the helm or the fleece, the skin over the head—can see into the future."

The Dutch rarely refer to such a person or his strange powers as "psychic." In fact, I'm not sure they understand the word. They say simply, "Wet-de-helm-geboren", and they mean simply, but unquestionably, that such a person is gifted with strange and inexplicable powers. Sometimes they call him a telepath or a clairvoyant. More often they avoid calling him anything and refer only to his "gift." And frequently those so gifted also become faith healers—who are very big in Holland.

Many will remember the widely publicized reports of Queen Juliana's daughter, the Dutch Princess Marijke, who was treated by a faith healer, Miss Greet Hofmans—until Prince Bernhard became disenchanted and ordered her to go.

And another famous Dutch psychic, Gerard Croiset, is probably even better known in Holland as a faith healer than as a psychic detective.

Practically all fakers in the occult arts, from faith healers to fortune tellers, from common garden variety seers and soothsayers to gypsy tea-leaf readers, claim to have been "born with a veil"—to use the most familiar term.

The astonishing paradox is that of all this cult I have known, Peter Hurkos is the only one who has never claimed that he was born psychic, and yet he is possibly one of the few who actually was born with the caul, the part of the amnion membrane wrapped around his head.

And because of it he almost died at birth.

And because of it he was born blind and remained blind for the first six months of his life.

And because of it he lived a great deal of his childhood in the darkness . . . in dark places . . . a morose and brooding child.

Peter himself has always insisted that his "gift" came to him only after his "accident" (which was much later in life), but is it possible that it actually had its physiological beginning at the moment of his birth?

Amazingly, he didn't even know that the caul and the helm, the fleece and the veil are all symbolically one and the same, signifying that he was born with his "gift."

Throughout all our sessions he emphatically denied that he had had any unusual psychic powers as a child. But his family remembers otherwise. His brother Nico says, "Yes, yes, Peter was a very strange boy. He was born with the fleece over his head. He saw things which we couldn't see, we couldn't understand. But he could."

His sister Allie remembers: "As a child, when he got upset he would run off to the woods or get in the little canoe and ride down the river and stay away for four or five days. He liked dark places. He didn't like to be with people. Then after the fall he said strange things and he saw strange things. . . ."

Shortly after we started this book, Peter went back to Holland to gather up some of the records and documents we needed. He also brought back his eighty-five-year-old father, Jacobus van der Hurk, an utterly delightful and sprightly *pater familias*, with twinkling eyes, twinkly toes, and a courtly flair with the ladies. He still liked his daily nip of gin, and he was still nimble on his feet. When he wasn't glued to the television (which he didn't have in Holland), he occupied himself with doing Irish jigs and singing Italian operatic arias in his native Dutch. He was once a part-time opera singer, and he still had a marvelous resounding tenor voice which would take off at the drop of a hint, and sometimes he didn't need even that to burst into song. We called him Father, and Father and I had a mutual-admiration society going. He couldn't speak a word of English, nor I Dutch, but somehow we managed to communicate. And we could always find a friendly family interpreter.

"Ja, Ja, he was born blind with the fleece," Father said. "The doctor didn't give him much hope. Completely blind, not enough oxygen. He was too small and tender baby, about four and a half pounds. Dr. Bos took the skin off his eyes. Otherwise he be blind for life. And always those drops in his eyes and crying, crying all night. . . . The *froetvrouw* [midwife] took the skin but she damage his eyes."

In checking out with medical authorities the peculiar circumstances of Peter's birth, it appeared that the *froetvrouw* who delivered him had difficulty removing the caul part of the amnion membrane. Other doctors were called in. After several hours they had removed all the membrane—or fleece—except that which covered his eyes. It took about six months of treatment before the doctors were able to remove the remaining "skin" over the eyes. The operation was finally a success, and Peter could see, for the first time, though his eyes would never be normal.

Peter's parents were people of simple means. His father was a painter, an artist—as well as an unemployed opera singer. He didn't care about money at all. At the time Peter was born, his father was earning about nine guilders a week—or the equivalent of three dollars.

The brick house where Peter was born, at Vondel-Str. 66 in Dordrecht, is still standing. It is about seventy years old. Peter remembers that downstairs it had a living room, kitchen, and one hideaway bedroom with *bet-see*—the built-in baby shelf or crib directly above the built-in, no-springs feather bed. At least his mother didn't have far to go to give him his eye drops. He slept on the shelf—or plank, as he calls it—for most of his first year, although he actually slept very little. Most of his first year in this world was spent in sleepless terror and darkness, sick and sightless in a cold and drafty crib *bet-see*.

Although Peter's eyesight was restored, he had eye troubles continually throughout his childhood. His eyes had a tendency to cross. Even today, as he puts it, "My eyes are not standing straight."

He was a sickly child and a poor student whose academic sojourn ended when he hurled an ink pot at a teacher and he was thrown out of school.

He ran away from home and went to sea, signing on his first ship as a cook's assistant—and as the youngest member of the crew. He was only fourteen years old, but he looked about eighteen. He was almost six feet tall. He had broad shoulders and black curly hair and was growing into a handsome young man.

The sea gave him a sense of peacefulness that he had not found before. It was to be his home for many years.

On one of his home leaves, he met and fell in love with a beautiful Dutch girl, Bea van der Berg, and they were married in 1937. They had a small home near Peter's parents, and Bea gradually weaned him away from the sea. She presented him first with a son, Benny, and then a daughter, whom they named Bea because she was the image of her mother. . . . And so in 1939 Peter came home from being a sailor to settle down with his family. He went to work for his father as a house painter.

Though life at home was blissful, the world outside was in turmoil. Hitler's Germany was boasting that the Germans would soon become the rulers of the world. England had declared war on Germany on September 11, 1939. . . . The Dutch people hated the Germans so much that they formed an underground army to fight them. About 70 per cent of the Dutch people became members of this movement, and Peter was one of them.

The Van der Hurks' painting business had dropped off because of the gathering war clouds. They were forced to paint buildings for the Germans. . . .

### *7/10/1941 to 8/5/41*
### *July 10, 1941 to August 5, 1941*

These are the dates on the official records of the 'S-Gravenhage Zuidwal Hospital for patient Van der Hurk, Pieter Cornelis, *geboren* [born] 5–21–1911. The records show that he was admitted to the hospital on July 10, 1941, and released August 5, 1941. He was then thirty years old.

July 10, 1941. Elsewhere in the world, a communique from the German High Command said that German troops were progressing relentlessly on the Russian front. . . . British planes raided Naples, Syracuse (Sicily), and Cherbourg. . . . German planes bombed Hull, England. . . . Another group of German planes sank five merchant ships in a convoy at the mouth of the Bristol Channel. . . .

On July 10, 1941, Pieter Cornelis van der Hurk was helping his father paint a four-story building on a street in The Hague. His father was painting the hall inside. Peter's job was to paint the outside, starting at the roof and working down. His father gave him the upper stories of the building to work on because, as Peter put it, "Who cares about the roof if it looks nice from down below? The roof they don't see. Down below it had to be nice looking. My father paint down below. He give me high only."

To save time and in order not to have to move his equipment and heavy ladder twice, Peter assembled the ladder and placed it between two windows set rather far apart, barely within arm's reach. But by stretching his big six-foot-three frame and his long arms, he could lean precariously first one way and then the other to reach both windows and cover the space between them with his paint brush. His gallon pot of paint hung on a hook to his right.

Peter remembers reaching over and grabbing for the paint bucket. And then it happened—the long fall and his whole life spinning before him.

"I can never forget this," he said to me. He spoke haltingly at first, as though he didn't want to talk about it, but once he began, it was like a torrent bursting from the floodgates of memory. A physical change came over him. He seemed unaware that anyone else was in the room. He didn't look at me. He sat like a man transfixed in aloneness and pain, reliving every frightful detail of that fateful moment.

"So I remember this, how I hang over, and then I slip over and the ladder falls. And that moment I was falling, I saw my whole life pass before me, and I didn't want to die. I want to live. I was fighting, fighting, from the moment I was falling down from the ladder, because I didn't want to die. And then I fall down and everything was black, and I remember when I tried to get up because I want to live, I want to live! But then it was black, for a long time black. I was in darkness."

Witnesses who saw Peter fall agreed that what saved his life was that he fell on his shoulder, thus breaking the impact of the fall. His shoulder was broken. There are different versions of what happened to his head. He was told later that there was "a crack in it" from the fall. His family thought it was a skull fracture. But the hospital records, which I obtained with the help of a Los Angeles physician, show it to be a brain concussion, with all the primary symptoms of severe neurological damage.

The report lists the symptoms as "unconscious, vomiting, amnesia." According to neurologists whom I consulted, these are the three cardinal symptoms of severe brain injury or irritation and can cause "cerebral disorientation."

The actual hospital records and reports indicated that Peter had been wrong on a few minor details, which accounts for some inconsistencies in previously published stories about him. He had thought that his accident occurred in 1943. The hospital records show that it was 1941. (He also couldn't remember the date of his marriage to Bea, and his later divorce, or the birth dates of his children; we tracked down the records in Holland.) He had always thought that he was unconscious for only three days in the hospital; actually it was four days. Although the doctors who treated him at the time were no longer living, some of the current hospital staff—doctors and nurses—remembered him and helped translate the old records for us. They also revealed something that he had not previously known—that the accident had required an operation on his head in order to save his life. Apparently neither Peter nor members of his family had ever been aware of the operation, and though the present hospital staff was most cooperative, it was difficult to interpret all the details or the exact nature of an operation that occurred almost thirty years ago. Peter has a good-sized scar—about three inches long—a little lower than midway down on the back of his head, though he doesn't know whether it is from the operation or from his head's "cracking open" when he hit the ground.

Peter lay unconscious for four days in the Zuidwal Hospital. The doctors agreed there was no hope for him. When he regained consciousness he was amnesiac. He had lost his memory for many things, including names and faces and dates. For a while he could recognize his family only by the sound of their voices. He didn't know even his closest friends. He still can't remember names or dates or even his own telephone number. He carries the number on a card in his wallet. . . .

In trying to recall and relive the accident that changed his life, his memory was as faulty in some areas as it was remarkable in others. He apparently had days of lapsing into semicomatose stages . . . and there were days that blurred one into the other. He remembers his four days of unconsciousness as no more than a fleeting five minutes.

"But everything was so beautiful, the flowers, the mountains, the music. Like people singing far away. And when I come out conscious, there was no color. It was all dirty, gray, one color, and I couldn't stand the light, it was like a knife in my head."

He remembers waking up and hearing people talking, but it was as though they were a thousand miles away. Their voices were like echoes. He remembers seeing the nurses and doctors in their white uniforms, moving close to him, then far, far away, like shadowy distorted images. He could feel someone hold his hand, but he couldn't talk. . . . He remembers the tremendous headaches and pain: "Like knives in the head, and then I went out again. . . ."

He remembers waking up and seeing planks around his bed and realizing that he was tied in bed. "I wake up and I see there are planks around me on the bed. I am like a wild man. They have tied me up with both arms and legs, and I couldn't move. I get panicky. I'm not a criminal. Where am I? Why have they tied up my arms and legs with ropes? First, when I am falling, I didn't want to die. Now, when I come out conscious and I didn't die, I want to go back to unconscious, where it was so beautiful. Here there is no color, no happiness, I want to go back. . . ."

Peter doesn't remember how long it was after he regained consciousness that he was able to begin swallowing food again—he thinks it was about four days—but he does remember how delicious that first taste was, a drink of raw eggs with orange juice.

He remembers the first time he recognized his wife's voice. He can't explain what happened, but it was also the first time he was able to use his own voice after the accident. . . . And this was the beginning of his "gift."

He couldn't see her, but he could hear her voice, and he cried out angrily, "Bea, what are you doing here? Where's Benny?"

Bea said she had left their son with a neighbor while she came to visit him at the hospital. Peter suddenly lashed out at her, "You belong at home with Benny. You shouldn't be here in the hospital. You're not a good mother. You go now and get Benny. Quick! Now! Oh, God!" he screamed. "The whole room is burning with Benny!"

Only his timing was off. It wasn't happening at that moment. It happened five days later. But firemen broke down a door and rescued Benny.

This was the first indication Peter had of his new "gift." Others were soon to come.

He remembers the day he awakened to find that the planks had been removed from his bed. He was no longer tied. And there was the nurse in a white uniform beside him, straightening his pillow.

"Where am I?" he asked.

She told him that he was in the Zuidwal Hospital in The Hague, and she introduced herself as Nurse Zelda.

Suddenly he grasped her hand and said, "You better be careful when you go on the train, or else you lose your valise."

She looked at him strangely, then started to walk away. She stopped and asked hesitantly, "But how did you know?" Again his timing was off. She had lost her suitcase that morning on the train.

His head was echoing with noises. He asked the nurse what was going on in the hallway, why he was hearing all the noises. She did not reply. He thought perhaps he only had a bad headache.

After the nurse left, he looked around the room again and found someone in the bed to the left of him. "You are a bad man. . . . Your father died recently and left you a gold watch. . . . You have already sold it," Peter told him. He didn't know why he said this; it just came out. The man said he was right.

Peter knew something had happened to him; he didn't know what. "I felt I had no mind of my own."

He called for the doctor and told him he needed something for his head. It was only then that he was told that he had fallen and injured his head. Peter told the doctor that he kept "hearing things." He asked for something to take these sounds away. The doctor said he was going to make a series of tests and that soon he would be able to tell Peter what was wrong with him.

One day a stranger stopped in his room to wish him a speedy recovery. The instant they shook hands and said good-bye, Peter knew that he was a British agent and that he was going to be killed by the Germans in a few days. Shocked by what he "saw," Peter gripped the man's hand so hard that he bewilderingly struggled to free himself, and as he left the room Peter shouted, "Stop him! Stop him!" A nurse and doctor, hearing the disturbance, rushed into the room. They calmed Peter down by giving him an injection. Soon he went to sleep.

Two days later the doctor came into his room with a newspaper which he showed to Peter. The man had been killed. How did Peter know? Was he working with the Germans? He tried to explain.

"I didn't know what I was saying. I just heard it. . . . It just came to me. Doctor, what's wrong with me? . . ."

The doctor told him he would have someone come in to check him over the next day.

What was this new and strange thing that had happened to him? Whatever it was, he didn't like it. He wanted to get rid of it. He was afraid to go to sleep, afraid of the darkness. "I thought I was crazy sometimes. My life was like a nightmare. I didn't want to see all these things, these pictures and voices. . . .

"Sometimes it didn't matter if I saw a person or not. If I touched an object like the water pitcher next to my bed, I would hear sounds. When I touched the wall I would hear sounds and see things. Sometimes I would put the pillow over my head to cover my ears and eyes, but these pictures and sounds always came to me. And even when I slept, my mind would travel to places I had never seen before. . . ." (So did Edgar Cayce's "sleeping" mind.)

From the time Peter told Nurse Zelda that she was going to lose her valise, he was regarded with more than the usual doctor-patient interest by the hospital staff. And also with a considerable amount of skepticism.

One day he was visited by a number of doctors, including a Dr. Peters, director of a mental hospital, and some of his staff. "I know what they think. They think I am nuts. They think they sign papers and put me in mental hospital with lot of nuts people," Peter recalled. "They ask why I sleep with the lights on and what kind of pictures I see and what kind of voices I hear. I try to tell them, they start laughing, and I say, 'Listen, doctor, are you playing games with me?' "

A couple of the doctors asked Peter, tauntingly, what he could "see" about them. Nothing, he said. He didn't like their attitude. Then the head medic said in a supercilious manner, "Tell me, what do you see in me?"

Peter looked at him closely, then said, "Give me an object."

"Why do you need an object?" the doctor said, sneering.

"You ask me what I see, give me an object," Peter snapped. The doctor gave him his pencil. He had been making notes.

Peter rubbed his fingers over the pencil and began, "I see you have a pajama—"

"Yeah, everybody has pajamas," one smart alec interrupted.

Peter said, "Doctor, I see you have pajamas with stripes that look like a tiger. . . ."

"You're right," the doctor admitted. "But many people have pajamas with stripes, you know."

"But your pajama, sir, has the initials G and D in designs. G D, sir. Now, can I talk with you alone? Or do you want me to tell it here in front of all these people?" Peter asked.

Dr. Peters, who by now had lost some of his superciliousness, seemed more than willing and ready to let Peter continue the confrontation in private.

Peter told him, "If you think I am crazy, sir, I am not, and I will prove it. You are the one who is nuts. If I was crazy I would hurt you.

"This pajama was given by your girl friend who is a nurse, and you have a child from her and you are still married. And your wife asked you where you got this pajama, and you told her you bought it yourself. But the design G D was done by your girl friend."

The doctor didn't say no, and didn't say yes. When the other doctors asked him what Peter had told him, he brushed them off with, "Nothing important." But instead of recommending that Peter be committed to a mental hospital, he recommended two months' more rest—which meant two months' more money for Peter from his insurance company.

In a couple of weeks Dr. Peters came to see him again.

"Remember what you told me about my pajamas? Do you think I'll get into trouble with my wife? Will she find out?" he asked Peter.

"Well, someday, but not right away," said Peter.

"Will she find out about the baby?" he asked.

"Not right away."

"Does she know that I go once a week out in my bungalow or somewhere? Do you think she knows? Will she find out?"

Peter said, "No, she won't find out. That's God's truth, sir. I don't know how I know, but I do. So you think I am nuts, doctor? Then tell me when will this thing in my head go away?"

"I don't know," the doctor said. "Maybe it will go away, maybe not. You will have to learn to live with it. But you are a very lucky man to be alive. You have suffered a very severe head injury and lost a lot of blood. We can't explain these things you see and hear, because we do not know much about the mind yet."

Peter was finally discharged from the hospital. But at home, things seemed to go from bad to worse. Everything had changed. Or rather, Peter had changed. He couldn't stand the noises of his own children, the tensions of his family, the curiosity of his friends. He didn't want to see anyone. He was still afraid of the darkness and could sleep only with the lights on. He spent nights pacing the floor, or sometimes he would stay in bed until the early dawn, then quietly dress and slip out of the house to wander for hours through the deserted streets of the city.

Four days after he came out of the hospital he bought a secondhand Bible in the market for two guilders and began reading it from cover to cover. He even slept with the Bible, and he found he could sleep better with it, even in the darkness.

But it didn't give him the answers he was searching for, and he still spent many long lonely nights in Holland, wandering the streets aimlessly . . . walk, walk, walking . . . trying to run away from this strange other mind that possessed him.

One night he went out walking the streets for miles and miles until finally, exhausted, he came to a cemetery. He decided to stop and rest. The dead were dead, he thought. They could not talk. He would not hear the voices. He sat down on a bench near a gravestone marked with the name William Hendricks. He remembers it distinctly.

As he gazed at the stone in the misty moonlight, he was suddenly gripped with fear. What was he doing here in a cemetery in the middle of the night? What if someone should come along and find him here? Then it happened. . . . He heard a woman crying. He looked around. He saw no one, nothing. He got up and walked among the tombstones, stealthily, following the sound of the woman's muffled sobs. He was coming closer and closer. . . .

Then he saw a gravestone that had the picture of a man engraved on it, and beside it was one single red rose, still fresh, as though placed there only recently. Peter bent over to pick up the rose, and then he heard the woman's voice, first soft, then strong and clear, "Darling . . . why did you have to leave me like this . . . I loved you. . . ."

Peter dropped the rose and began running, running, and it was as though all the voices from the graves were running after him. His head was bursting with all the sounds of the dead. He ran and ran until he reached his home. He locked himself in his room and hit his head on the wall, and still he heard the voices. When daybreak came and the city awakened and stirred, he slipped out of the house and started walking again. Walking, walking, then running, running. He was like a crazed man when he pushed his way into Dr. Peters' private office and cried out, "Doctor, what is wrong with me? Am I going crazy? Can't you stop these sounds and pictures? I need help. Oh, doctor, please help me!"

The doctor gave him a shot for his nerves and tried verbally to calm him. He was the same doctor who had once laughed at Peter's "gift." But he didn't laugh now. He talked to him soothingly, gently, trying to explain his condition in such a way that might help relieve him from worry.

"Peter, it is possible that what you have is something all of us have in limited degrees. In your case it is more highly developed apparently because of your accident and your brain injury.

"There are many things we do not know yet about the human mind and its capabilities. It is possible that your injury damaged certain functions of the brain and stimulated others, at least temporarily. And it could very well be that when you are fully rested and recuperated, you may stop having these . . . ah . . . hallucinations—"

Peter interrupted him. "You mean this thing I've got could go away?"

"No, I didn't exactly mean that," the doctor said cagily. "I cannot give you any guarantee that what you have will go away, but perhaps it could. . . . We just don't know. . . ."

Whatever it was he had about cemeteries didn't go away. Peter gets some of his strongest vibrations at gravesites and from clothing or objects that have belonged to dead people, especially when he works on murder cases. If the body is buried in the ground, he is usually taken to the gravesite. "But I don't like to go in cemeteries," he says. "Not that I'm afraid, but if I walk in cemetery for half an hour I'm completely exhausted, as tired as if I worked fourteen days. Even when it is cold, I am sweating like hell when I go in a cemetery. Because I get the vibrations, and then comes the mental picture and then the voices."

During the Nazi occupation of Holland, every able-bodied man was shipped off to camps to work for the Third Reich. Peter escaped en route and returned home to join his countrymen in working for the Dutch underground. He, of course, carried forged papers. This was when he became Peter Hurkos.

Hurkos is not a Dutch but a Hungarian name. When anyone

asks Peter about his name, he usually replies, "Peter Hurkos—it was my underground name."

As an active member of the underground, he did whatever work was given to him. But he was assigned mainly to the explosion and bombing detail. "Blow-up" he calls it. He did the blow-ups on bridges and railroads carrying prisoners and food from Holland to Germany. Working at any job now was not easy for him because he had lost his ability to concentrate for any period of time. But he didn't mind risking his life in the underground, because in the back of his mind he was hoping he would be killed and all his troubles would be over.

Peter's "gift" has never been of much help to him personally. He admits, "I cannot even find my own shoes." But occasionally it came in handy in his underground work, as when the voices or pictures told him the best day of the week and the hour for blowing up a bridge. But his "gift" could not save him from being shipped to a concentration camp. He was arrested for cutting trees for firewood to keep his family warm, and after the usual brutal Nazi interrogation, he was sent to Vught, one of the worst punitive labor camps in Holland, somewhat comparable to Buchenwald in Germany.

Strangely, during his questioning by the German officers, one of them, a bald-headed, iron-jawed man who was notorious for his brutality and sadistic assaults on prisoners, kept eyeing Peter coolly but did not touch him. Even the guards told Peter later, "You're lucky to get away from that one without a broken jaw or mashed nose. He has iron knuckles. He loves to beat up people."

But Knuckle Fists only glared at Peter and snarled. "You are a liar. You are a liar. I am sending you to the camp." Then aside and under his breath he muttered to Peter, "There is something wrong with you. I don't know what is wrong, but when I look in your eyes, I couldn't beat you up. You know this? I couldn't beat you up. There is something wrong with you. . . ."

When the war was over, Peter, along with several other members of the Dutch underground, was notified to appear at the Royal Palace to receive a commendation from Queen Juliana. All were presented to the Queen, and she, in turn, presented each of them with a gold medal and a scroll commending them for serving her as well as the Netherlands.

It was Peter's shining moment, and his hand was shaking when it reached out to greet the Queen. Realizing that he was nervous, she smiled and said, "Thank you."

For Peter it was all unreal and unbelievable, reading about himself in the newspapers. He remembers buying a dozen or more papers to take home to his family and friends. . . .

And then? . . . What was there for him to do?

He took a part-time job in a coffee shop in The Hague and began giving "readings." . . . He and Bea drifted apart. They were living in different worlds. Peter was trying to rebuild his life and to understand this thing that everyone called his new "God-given gift."

One morning about three o'clock, he was awakened by the ringing of the doorbell. He went to the door to find a woman crying, "Herr Hurkos, Herr Hurkos. Please help me! Please! My husband has disappeared!" The police had not been able to find him, she said, and she promised Peter any amount of money if he could locate her missing husband.

Peter said he could not do anything without some object that belonged to her husband—a coat, a watch, anything that was his. She left and returned a few hours later with her husband's coat. Peter touched the man's coat and said, "What happened to the football? I see a football—and also a uniform."

"That's right, that's right," the woman cried. Her husband had been a famous football player. He was now in the army.

The woman became hysterical. She kept screaming that she wanted her husband back. Peter tried to calm her, but at the same time the words came rushing out of him. "The police told you, madame, do not worry about your husband. He is probably out with some friends. I am sorry to tell you, madame. . . . He has fallen into an ice trap. . . . He decided to take the shortcut through the woods . . . not the main road. . . . As he is walking down the street toward the outskirts of town, he stops. . . . Yes, he is thinking which way to go, and he decides to take the short-cut through the woods. . . .

"As he is walking, he trips and falls into a ditch. . . . No, it is a tank trap, and it is filled with water. . . . He struggles, but he is too weak . . . He had drunk bad booze. . . . He freezes to death in the water. . . . I am sorry, madame, your husband is dead, I am sorry. . . . Here, I make you a sketch where you find his body. Go and tell the police. Show them this. . . ."

The woman looked at him in shock and continued her hysterics until she was exhausted. Then she left.

The police laughed at her story. But she insisted that they come with her to the place Peter had described. Finally they agreed to look. They found nothing.

"I knew it all the time," the police captain gloated. "This Peter Hurkos is a fake."

The next day the woman went back to Peter and persuaded him to come with her to the police station. The captain and three policemen finally agreed to go with them to the place called the Maljebaan in The Hague where Peter "saw" the body. They found the dead man's cap in the bushes, then a pencil, and after seven days of digging and dredging they found the body.

A postmortem showed that he had been suffering from an illness of a paralytic nature. He was despondent because he knew that he would never again be able to play football, and he had begun to drink heavily. He had been drinking with friends at a café and started back to camp late at night. He had taken a shortcut and was somewhat high—from bad booze, as Peter had said—when he fell into the ice-covered trap. . . .

It had happened almost precisely the way Peter "saw" it with his extraordinary "sixth sense."

His fame spread. He became known as the man with the "radar eyes" and the "X-ray brain."

He soon was in demand throughout Europe to work on cases of missing persons and crime, and for lectures, demonstrations, and private consultations.

Many of his most accurate "visions" were spontaneous. Once, for example, he abruptly told two friends he was visiting "a farm near here is going to burn tonight. The farmer's name is Janson, and his place is over by the small canal. It is going to happen at nine o'clock."

It was almost nine o'clock at the time. The three men drove

hastily over to the small canal, inquiring their way to the Janson farm, but as they approached they could already see the red glow from the flaming wooden buildings. The police, who had been plagued by a rash of fires somewhat reluctantly called on Peter for help. He took a padlock from a shed where the fire had started and then asked the police to provide him with photographs of everyone in the district—identification photos, school pictures, snapshots, anything they could get.

At police headquarters next day he pored over scores of photographs, face down, placing the scorched padlock on each and concentrating so hard that perspiration rolled down his face. Finally he turned up a photograph and exclaimed, "This is the one!"

The police were unimpressed. "That boy," they informed Peter, "is one of the best and brightest boys in the neighborhood, and his father is one of the richest and most respected men in the country."

It was Peter's turn to be unimpressed. He was adamant. "Take this boy in, and there'll be no more fires, I promise you."

Grudgingly, the police complied, and when questioned closely, the boy tripped himself up and finally admitted his guilt.

How could Peter know about the fire, and how could he name the boy?

The case reminded me of a far more famous and authenticated one of a couple of centuries earlier. It has become one of the classics in psychical literature as an example of spontaneous clairvoyance.

The subject was Dr. Emanuel Swedenborg, the Swedish scientist and philosopher, who one day while in Göteborg (in 1759) described a fire blazing in Stockholm, three hundred miles away. He gave a detailed account of the fire to city authorities, named the owner of the burned house, and even stated the time when the fire was put out. The accuracy of his clairvoyant vision was confirmed several days later by royal messenger.

As any student of psychical literature knows, there are too many well-documented cases of such spontaneous "visions" to ignore the possibility that mind transcends time and space. The important question to be answered is, How?

# · 4 ·

# *Psychic Detective*

Once while Peter was working in the small coffee shop in The Hague, a woman came in and asked him to help her locate a missing manuscript. He told her to look *behind* her husband's file cabinet, not *in* it, as both had done, searching the files thoroughly. The manuscript, Peter said, was caught at the back between two file drawers. And so it was, as the woman later discovered. It was only one of thousands of small, comparatively insignificant, certainly less than earthshaking, episodes in the incredible career of Peter Hurkos. But it was so characteristic!

For when the woman started to reach into her purse for the money she had set aside for him, he said, "Madame, please, you need your money. But if you please, I would like the chocolate which you have there next to the money."

The woman was goggle-eyed. Her purse was not open. It was as though Peter could see right through the purse to the piece of candy. She gave him the candy, thanked him, and left.

Peter wanted the candy more than the money because at that time candy was hard to come by and very expensive. It was a real treat for his children. . . .

Peter left Holland to work in Belgium and then Paris. He was sent to Spain by a rich Belgian businessman to try to tie up some loose threads in a long strewn-out will. While in Madrid and seeing bullfights for the first time, he had a dream—cows and other animals and people drowning. Two days later in Holland the rains fell, the dikes broke, and thousands of people drowned.

In Madrid, Peter received a call from the Dutch embassy, asking him to do a benefit performance to help raise money for the Netherlands flood victims. Twenty-five dollars a head. Top social and political personages were there, as well as some of Spain's most famous bullfighters. All the proceeds went to the Dutch embassy. First, a film was shown of the flood disaster in Holland when the dikes broke. And after the film, Peter gave a demonstration. He spoke in Dutch, and a secretary from the embassy translated for him in Spanish. (Although Peter had picked up a smattering of several languages, Spanish was not one of them.)

Peter did not know until after the performance that Señora Franco, wife of Generalissimo Franco, was in the audience that night. She was very impressed with Peter's performance. The next day he received a telephone call from Franco's secretary saying that the Generalissimo requested Peter's presence at the palace to give a demonstration. Peter said he would think it over and call back in half an hour. He did not know how his own Dutch embassy officials would feel about his performing for the Fascist Generalissimo. And furthermore, nothing had been said about inviting Peter's wife. He had recently remarried, after his divorce from Bea.

"And if my wife is not invited to the palace, the hell with Franco," he said.

First, he called the Dutch embassy and learned that there was no objection to his giving a demonstration for Franco. Then he called the Generalissimo's secretary and asked whether his wife could come, too. The secretary explained politely that of course his wife was automatically invited.

They arrived at the palace and after being searched for guns by two soldiers wearing tall hats and red capes, they were ushered into a large, luxuriously decorated room where about seventy persons had assembled for Peter's demonstration. Among them was the Minister of War and several doctors, including Franco's own private physician, Dr. Blanco-Solero. And of course the General and Señora Franco.

Peter astonished them by giving accurate readings from the

objects presented to him. One of the doctors gave him a cap from an inner tube of an automobile tire.

"You know what, you blow up a tire," Peter told him. "And this tube save your life. It is at the time of the revolution and you escaped and are driving to Valencia but you get a flat tire, and you are lucky because if you get to Valencia you be dead. The republicans [or Rebels?] have took Valencia, so you get a flat tire what saved your life and you stayed in a farm house. Is this correct?"

It was absolutely correct. And everyone seemed shocked by the reading—except the Generalissimo, who maintained a stolid expression on his face throughout the one hour demonstration.

In recalling the incident for me later, Peter still could not forgive Franco for not speaking to him in German but instead commanding that everything be translated into Spanish.

"He is hard, hard like a rock," he remembered. "He can speak perfect German, but he wouldn't talk German to me. He wants to have it translated. The translator speaks in Spanish. You know, if I talk in German, maybe I will say too much to him, I don't know. So after the lecture, they went separate, man and wife (Spanish custom), and I can feel the tension from Franco, and then the guard came and said Mr. Franco wants to talk to me alone, and two soldiers came over to take me to him, and I think maybe I say too much in the lecture, I don't know. You never know. I only say what I see.

"So the guards take me into a beautiful study, and there is Mr. Franco waiting for me, and he comes over and shakes hands with me, and he say, 'I thank you very much.' Then he give me a key and ask me what I see. I tell him, 'You think something is stolen. It is not. It is taken by accident by the Minister of War. You will get it back in twenty-four hours.'"

The key was, indeed, the key to a filing cabinet from which some important documents were missing. The Minister of War had taken them by accident. They were returned within twenty-four hours.

Peter received no fee for his performance, but his wife received an elaborate silver coffee service from Franco, which the Hurkoses later sold for five hundred dollars.

On Christmas Day, 1950, a bulletin flashed around the world: The Stone of Scone had vanished! The Scotch Coronation Stone, which had been in England for 664 years, had been stolen from its resting place beneath the Coronation Chair in Westminster Abbey, before Elizabeth II's coronation.

Peter was in Dordrecht spending the holidays with his parents, his ex-wife and children, when he heard the news. He followed the day-by-day happenings during the search. It was reported that Scotland Yard was dredging the Thames for the Stone. Other reports stated that the Yard was combing the streets and alleys for the Stone. Many reports and leads were coming in to Scotland Yard from people who thought they knew where to look for the Stone.

And Peter was being urged by friends, and by hundreds who by now had heard or read of his psychic abilities, to go to England and help find the Stone of Scone.

His first response was, "I have not been asked by them [Scotland Yard or the English people] to come. I do not go on a case unless I am asked."

But letters began to pour in to him from the English people— though at that time he had never worked in England and in fact had never even been in that country.

The Stone of Scone, upon which the Scottish kings were crowned, was taken from Scotland by Edward I and moved to Westminster Abbey, where it laid beneath the Coronation Chair, which stands in the Confessor's Chapel in the Abbey. Since the time Edward I brought the Stone to England, the English kings and queens have been crowned upon it. The Stone, though of Scottish origin, is traditionally identified with Jacob's Pillar at Bethel, and Peter, watching the daily developments of the search, became increasingly aware of how much its recovery would mean to the English people.

Meanwhile, a close friend of Peter's had been in contact with an Englishman who said that arrangements were being made for Peter to go to England. Peter was told that he would get full cooperation from Scotland Yard and that the Yard, in fact, would welcome his assistance. This information did not come directly to him from Scotland Yard, and indeed the Yard later tried to discredit Peter's work on the case.

Characteristically, when Peter decided finally to go to England to try to help find the missing Stone, he decided to go *at his own expense.*

At that time he did not speak English, so he asked a friend who spoke both English and Dutch to accompany him and act as his interpreter.

On Tuesday, January 16, 1951, he left Holland for England. He was nervous about the trip because it was to be his first flight in an airplane. No sooner did he step off the plane at London Airport than he was whisked off by Scotland Yard detectives and taken in a police car directly to his hotel on Dolphin Square. It all happened too fast, as in a cops and robbers game, and his interpreter friend was left at the airport to find his own way to the hotel.

At the hotel, Peter was escorted to his room and the police immediately began flashing questions at him. Since he couldn't understand a word they were saying, he merely looked at them in bewilderment, although his "gift" told him they were highly skeptical of his abilities to help solve the case. Finally, his interpreter arrived, and through him Peter explained his mission, said he was anxious to begin working, and asked to be taken to Westminster Abbey.

Once inside the Abbey, he searched around haltingly, trying to make contact with something that would give him a clue. Then he went to the Coronation Chair under which the Stone had lain, knelt down, and touched the chair to get its vibrations.

Pictures began to flash at a rapid pace through his mind. At first they were blurred. Then he saw them more clearly, and many, many images. In them he saw much of the history revolving around the Stone. He worked feverishly, trying to sift out the historical events that he saw and concentrate only on the theft itself.

After about thirty minutes of intense concentration, during which he seemed to be in a semitrance state and was perspiring heavily, he began talking in short, rapid phrases:

"I see five people were involved. . . . Three breaking in . . .

two waiting outside . . . in a truck. . . . [He then called out some sets of letters which spelled out Lower Thames Street, then Fashion Street, Earl Street, and Pennington Street.] I see an old church near a river . . . a bridge, and also a cemetery. . . . It's blurred, but I see something that looks like the ruins of a church."

He then asked for a pencil and paper and drew a rough sketch of the position of the streets that he saw in the pictures in his mind. He also drew a sketch of the position of the church and river.

When Scotland Yard checked his sketch of streets with a map of the Lower Thames Street area, they found that it corresponded exactly—even though Peter had never been in London before and had not seen a map of the city. Moreover, subsequent investigation proved that Peter had even spelled the names of all the streets correctly.

The next morning, Wednesday, January 17, Peter was given the jemmy (crowbar) that had been used to break into Westminster Abbey, a strap of a watch found near the Coronation Chair, and a plaque found at a nearby bombsite on Tufton Street.

He spent two full hours concentrating on the objects, handling them, trying to call forth the visions—or pictures, as he called them—that would help find the Stone of Scone. He was able to confirm what he had divined the day before from the Coronation Chair. He was now able to see also the routes that he felt the thieves had taken. On a map he traced the route to the Abbey. It began on the south of the Round Pond of Kensington Gardens, ran through Knightsbridge, Constitution-Hill, Birdcage-walk to Westminster Abbey. He felt that after stealing the Stone, the thieves crossed Westminster Bridge, drove through Southwalk, over London Bridge, through Thames Street, over Tower Bridge, Rotherhithe.

He asked the police to drive him to Round Pond in Kensington Gardens. Once there, he went to a particular spot by the pond and said that this was where the raid had been planned.

On Thursday, January 18, the police drove Peter to Lower Thames Street to identify the ruins of the Church of St. Dunston. They explained that when he had mentioned seeing the ruins of a church, they thought possibly he meant this one and that's why they brought him here. What were his impressions? He told them he felt sure that the Stone was in the ruins of a church—but not this one.

Then he asked to be driven to Fashion Street. Once there, he asked them to stop the car, and he began the search on foot. He started down the street, accompanied by the police, and they came to a brick lane. Peter took a few steps and then stopped. He was in front of a store, the equivalent of an American hardware store. This, he told the police, was where the thieves had bought the jemmy. They went into the store, and the police asked the proprietor if he stocked jemmys. The proprietor said he did. The police checked the numbers on the jemmys against the number on the jemmy that was found in Westminster Abbey. They were identical.

Later, back in his hotel room, Peter told the Scotland Yard men that he now felt the Stone of Scone was in Glasgow, Scotland, and that he would like to go there to continue his search. He explained that he felt the Stone had been stolen as a prank by students and that it would be back in Westminster Abbey within about four weeks. His request to go to Scotland to search for the Stone seemed to stir up a great deal of discussion and controversy, so Peter decided that while they discussed the matter, he would go back to Holland and get his car.

When he arrived back in England, he was stopped at the border by customs officers, who detained him for an hour and a half at Dover. They questioned him extensively, searched his car and luggage, and finally permitted him to leave. In London, he continued his efforts to obtain clearance to go to Scotland to search for the Stone.

He had been receiving considerable publicity in the European press. Earlier, he had given a press interview in which he described the thieves, said they were in England but would soon be leaving for Scotland, and predicted, "The Stone will be returned in three weeks."

Besieged by the press, he also issued this statement, which was printed in the *Evening Press:* "I will do my best to find it, [The Stone]. During the war when we were hungry in Holland, Britain dropped us food from the air. Now I would like to help Britain."

His second visit to England was of no avail, so he returned home again. Meanwhile, in Scotland, the Scottish National Congress Committee held a meeting, addressed by Dr. Mary Ramsay of Edinburgh University and Mr. Oliver Brown, a prominent Scottish Nationalist.

Oliver Brown announced that the Coronation Stone was in Scotland "and would remain until Scotland was allowed to control her own destiny."

Dr. Ramsay added, "For many years now it has been the hope of the National party that something of this kind would take place. At almost every meeting plans had been made for the Stone's removal and at last the Scottish National party has seen the result of its efforts."

The recovery of the Stone by Scotland was celebrated at the meeting and Scotland Yard was jeered. "They are trained to track down criminals—not patriots."

A report of this meeting, headlined STONE IN SCOTLAND—NATIONALIST CLAIM, appeared in the London *Daily Telegraph* of January 22, 1951, along with the news that the Scottish National Congress Committee had written to the Dutch Ambassador in London, inviting Peter Hurkos to Scotland so that he could "appreciate the Scottish point of view." He would not, however, be shown the whereabouts of the Stone.

So back to England for the third time. And again he was stopped by the customs officers at Dover. This time they made a two-hour search of his car, deflated the tires, probed into the engine and gas tank, took out the seats—and then gave him clearance to enter England again.

By now it was painfully clear to Peter that he was not wanted to work on the case. Though some of the British press had given him all the credit—instead of Scotland Yard—for turning up clues to the missing Stone, he had also been ridiculed in jokes, editorials, and cartoons, depicting him as a crystal-gazing soothsayer.

On January 24, Scotland Yard issued the following statement: "We are not seeing Mr. Hurkos. We did not ask him to come to London. We have not sought his assistance. He is only one of the many telepathists, clairvoyants and water-diviners, etc., who have offered us information all of which has been tested and sifted."

Although he now had a written invitation from the Scots, he was again stopped from going to Scotland, so he finally decided to give up and let the English worry about their Coronation Stone.

Still, he received so much of the credit that the House of Commons of her Majesty's government felt compelled to deny publicly that his efforts had been helpful.

Just as Peter had predicted, the Stone was found in the ruins of an old church, Arbroath Abbey in Arbroath, Angus, Scotland. And as mysteriously as it had disappeared, it returned—four weeks later, as Peter had predicted.

The students who returned the Stone were later questioned by Scotland Yard but were not arrested. They admitted they took it as a prank, as Peter had also said. Scotland Yard reportedly traced the fugitives to Glasgow and then promised to look away if the Stone was returned intact.

But Peter Hurkos, Scotland Yard insisted, had had nothing to do with finding the Stone—even if he did accurately predict its return.

The moot question, of course, is whether a great police department will acknowledge receiving assistance from a psychic. With his strange gift Peter was being pressured more and more into the role of a psychic detective. It was not something he had asked for or wanted. He would gladly exchange his multiple-mind role for that of plain Peter van der Hurk, whose simple but *single* mind, though uneducated, was also unconfused before his fall. Now . . . what could he do?

But to me it was rather incredible to learn that the two most highly publicized cases of Peter's career—the Stone of Scone and the Boston Strangler—earned him not a penny. He was drawn into both cases against his own protestations, as well as against his better judgment. In both cases he became the target of police and political intrigue aimed at disparaging the work of a psychic, even though he spent his own time and money for expenses, receiving no fee at all.

In the Boston Strangler case there were promises, promises.
. . . But that one was to come later.

After the Stone of Scone fiasco, Peter went into a great
depression.

# · 5 ·

# *Testing, Testing*

Peter spent most of the next five years in Paris, working with the French police. He had earned their respect and had gained recognition throughout Europe for his amazing accuracy in crime cases.

At the same time he was becoming more and more in demand for public performances, benefit lectures, and social gatherings—and he was becoming also more and more ill at ease at these affairs. He did not understand his "gift." He didn't know how to control it. He blurted out whatever he "saw"—including details of death, disaster, and extramarital affairs. As a result, he was not a great social success. Like Edgar Cayce, he was at his brooding best as a loner, working on cases that appealed to him and with problems whose answers came to him spontaneously. Like Edgar Cayce with his strange power, he had decided, "You cannot explain it. You feel it."

Neither could he explain why it worried him so much to have to use his "gift" for entertainment purposes in order to pay bills. He generally received no fee for his police work, although this was the area in which he excelled.

For a while Peter was engaged as a psychic consultant to a medical doctor in Paris who was working on a new polio serum. Several children had died after polio shots from a serum that was too old, and the doctor had risked his reputation by employing a psychic to help him in his research. Why did the children die from the old serum? How could the new serum be improved?

Although Peter had no background in medicine, he apparently performed remarkably well as a medical researcher. At least the physician thought so. A story on Peter's work with the French medical doctor appeared in *Paris Match* magazine. Dr. Andrija Puharich saw it, and soon Peter was on his way to America.

Dr. Puharich, an American of Yugoslav descent, received his medical degree from Northwestern University, where he specialized in physiology and internal medicine. He is also a neurologist and for many years has concentrated on the scientific examination (biological, physiological, and psychological) of the workings of the human mind and such mind phenomena as telepathy, hallucinations, and so-called extrasensory perception.

He is the author of two of the most fascinating and well-documented books in the whole huge realm of psychic literature, *The Sacred Mushroom* and *Beyond Telepathy,* and is one of America's leading medical authorities and explorers in that strange, little-known, intriguing world of the mind.

In 1948, Dr. Puharich founded a research laboratory, called the Round Table Foundation, in Glen Cove, Maine, as a center for his experiments in mind phenomena. It was here that he invited Peter to come for six months of experiments to explore the many facets of his psychic power.

This would mean a big change for Peter. Should he leave Europe now, just at a time when he could earn a great deal from his private readings, and go to America to be a guinea pig? He had commitments in Europe. He was on a yearly retainer with several large industrial firms. Would they think he was running away from his responsibilities? The invitation was for only six months, but six months can be a long time in a man's life. For Peter it would mean leaving his family and friends and work, and going to a country where he did not even know the language. Yes, it would definitely mean a big change in his life.

But beneath the façade of fame and success Peter was a man still driven to find answers to the questions he had been asking ever since he had received his "gift." Perhaps in America he would find them. . . .

That six months stretched into nearly two and a half years of working with the Round Table Foundation. In fact, Dr. Puharich was to spend a great deal of his time over the next seven years collecting laboratory and field material about Peter. He probably has the most complete file in existence on Peter Hurkos. The amazing results of his tests have been reported at length in Dr. Puharich's books, but in a nutshell Peter did as well in the laboratory, under controlled conditions, as he had done in his crime work and spontaneous readings.

Puharich admitted that it took him two months to become convinced of Peter's special ability in psychometry, but he could not deny the evidence. Four times out of five, when researchers handed Peter a concealed object—a butterfly, a safety pin, a button, sometimes even a blank sheet of paper—in a sealed envelope, he was able to tell what was inside by merely touching the envelope.

In spite of all the comprehensive testing by Dr. Puharich, through the years there has been one objection that keeps popping up: Has Peter Hurkos ever submitted himself to the ESP tests at Duke University? And if not, why not?

The inference is clear: Peter's psychic powers will never get the Good Housekeeping Seal of Approval until they pass those ESP card and dice tests at Duke. To most laymen the word "psychic" means ESP, and ESP is synonymous with Dr. Joseph Banks Rhine, formerly of Duke University and coiner of the term "extrasensory perception."

Peter first met Dr. Rhine in Miami. Word had spread among the academic parapsychologists (physical researchers) of Peter's astonishing success in Dr. Puharich's laboratory experiments in Maine, and some of his interested sponsors had arranged the meeting with Dr. Rhine in hopes that Rhine would invite him to Duke.

Peter says that Dr. Rhine asked him if he would first be willing to take a lie detector test. And even with Peter's limited knowledge of English, he took this as an insult.

"In front of everybody he said it, would I take a lie detector test," Peter recalled. "And I say, 'What you think I am—a criminal?' So I say to hell with him and I go back with Dr. Puharich."

I personally brought Peter and Dr. Rhine together again at a meeting in Milwaukee, but nothing was accomplished, and I know others who have tried to persuade Dr. Rhine to accept Peter for laboratory experiments, and who have even offered to subsidize the experiments, but for reasons known only to himself, Rhine has refused to accept Peter as a subject for his ESP experiments. In discussing the matter with him once, Dr. Rhine told me that "people like Hurkos have no place in any scientific investigations of ESP."

I sensed that he felt it would be somewhat beneath his academic dignity to permit such a highly publicized psychic—and one smacking of commercialism—to enter his sacred portals. And yet I wondered: Why was it so wrong for a psychic to use his "gift" to earn a living? And why wouldn't a man of Dr. Rhine's reputation and stature seize the opportunity to test this big, bumbling Dutchman—and prove him a phony?

Let's again turn back the clock to Edgar Cayce. Cayce's psychic powers didn't get Rhine's Seal of Approval either. Cayce had no patience with the professor's highfalutin experiments. He considered them trivia. But in 1935, Dr. Rhine wanted Cayce to prove himself by Rhine standards, and a test was arranged— for Cayce to describe the contents of a package in a filing case in New York.

Cayce didn't approve of the test, noting in a trance, "Unless such experiences create such in the lives of individuals that interest or apply themselves in the study of such lives, then it is indeed of little thought, nor has it any place in man's experience, and is not worthy of consideration of any sort."

But his son Hugh Lynn urged him to cooperate for the recognition it would bring. Among other things, Cayce was asked to read Rhine's three-year-old daughter, who was ill. Rhine said Cayce's diagnosis was inaccurate—because it didn't conform with the medical diagnosis. Thereafter he frequently blasted Cayce and the Cayce movement, as he has frequently blasted Peter. However, a number of knowledgeable critics, including John Scarne, the noted card and dice expert, have also blasted the ESP tests as worthless, and in view of all the controversy surrounding them, it is questionable whether they could have proved anything about the psychic powers of Peter Hurkos or Edgar Cayce.

Dr. Puharich's approach to the investigation of psychic phenomena has embraced a great deal more than ESP card tests. In working with Peter, he made a study of his brain cell function during ESP cognition from EEG readings, gave him the so-called sacred mushrooms, which produced various stages of trance and hallucinations, and subjected him to experiments with the Faraday-cage method and apparatus for inducing states of consciousness in an individual with particular application to telepathy.

Peter's first day in the research laboratory was a frightening experience. The laboratory was filled with mysterious cables, machines, and brainwave equipment. And he was terrified of that strange, walled-off cubicle called a Faraday cage.

The Faraday cage is a copper enclosure whose walls prevent electromagnetic waves and electrostatic effects from passing through to the inside. If a radio is taken inside the Faraday cage it will continue to play as long as the door of the cage is open. But as soon as the door of the cage is closed, and providing there is no electric wire passing through the walls, the radio will be completely cut off from the broadcasting station. The radio waves are stopped by the copper wall and cannot penetrate to the interior of the cage.

Also, if an electric charge is placed on the walls of the Faraday cage, a person inside will feel no electricity—even if he touches the inside walls of the cage.

The Faraday cage is an isolated and insulated cubicle, covered by fine copper mesh through which a generator pours twenty-five thousand volts of electric current. As Dr. Puharich explains it, the purpose is to set up an electrical field, through which no electrical waves can pass. The purpose of the Faraday cage is to try to isolate a psychic—or a "sensitive," as Dr. Puharich usually calls him—as much as is humanly possible, to test his powers without either interference or help from outside sources. Thus a person's telepathic ability could be measured by rigidly statistical standards, even by such simple tests as tossing a coin in the air and calling out whether it will land heads or tails. Or the Match-

ing Abacus Test, MAT for short, which consists of two matching
sets of ten different pictures. Each set of pictures is placed in a
row. Both rows of pictures are shuffled, and the trial matching
of the pictures is called a run. The pictures are placed under an
opaque screen so that the sensitive (the receiver in telepathy)
can handle them but cannot see them. The receiver is also blind-
folded so that he cannot see the sender. The pictures are placed
in clear plastic boxes so that the receiver cannot touch the picture side of the card, but the sender can clearly see each one.

The receiver places his left hand on one picture in the row
closer to him. The sender now knows the picture that the receiver will seek in the other row. The receiver then passes his
right hand over the other row of pictures and attempts to find
the mate to the picture under his left hand.

For all readers who may wish a closer scrutiny of the tests
Peter was put through by Dr. Puharich, I recommend reading
both his books, named earlier in this chapter. Obviously they
cannot be condensed into this one.

But a few incidents are relevant here. One evening while Peter
and Dr. Puharich were relaxing in the kitchen with their after-
dinner coffee, Peter turned to Puharich in great excitement and
said, "I see it. I see it, just like a film. I see a hand in front of my
eyes. It's hanging, the wrist is cut, and there is blood coming
from it."

Dr. Puharich by this time had become used to Peter's spontaneous bursts of ideas, visions, and telepathic messages. He
assumed that in this instance the vision had some special significance for Peter.

"Peter," he said, "what are you talking about?"

"It's a hand! I saw a hand in front of my eyes, and the wrist
is cut, and it's nothing in this room; it's in my mind that I see it."

Dr. Puharich knew that the vision could either be a literal telepathic impression or one that could have a symbolic meaning.
When he pressed Peter further, he mentioned that it had to do
with suicide.

"Whose suicide?"

It developed that Peter had foreseen the suicide attempt of a
man living in Albuquerque, New Mexico, who had a business

relationship with Puharich. Although the man's friends had sensed that something was wrong with him, they could not take seriously Peter's vision of a cut wrist and a suicide threat. But it happened just like that. The man was hospitalized and placed under maximum security, but as soon as the attendant turned his back he smashed his reading glasses on the floor, picked up one of the larger pieces of glass, and slashed both wrists. Fortunately, he was given immediate medical attention and recovered completely. The date on which this suicide attempt occurred was December 23, 1957.

In May, 1959, two businessmen, C. V. Wood (the man who later bought London Bridge for Lake Havasu in Arizona) and Tom Slick, wanted to test Peter's ability to get intelligence from an object sealed in a package. The object in this particular instance was a metal dog chain and some brown dog hairs, and the dog was a brown poodle named Cocoa, who had been sick for several weeks. Peter diagnosed its ailment and told how it would be cured.

Puharich was impressed with Peter's accuracy in medical matters and anatomical details. He recounts one case in which Peter described in great anatomical detail a disease that a person had, and made a drawing to illustrate what he was trying to describe, since he did not have the command of medical language with which to verbalize what he saw. He drew an outline of the uterus and Fallopian tubes of the woman and precisely outlined the anatomical abnormalities present. Furthermore, he said that the disease process was such that it would require an operation in order to clear it up. At the time of the reading, Puharich had no way to check the accuracy of Peter's vision. But seven months later the person whom he was describing became acutely ill, entered the Mayo Clinic for observation, and was operated on for the disease that Peter had described.

According to Puharich, the picture that Peter had seen in his mind of the disease process in the Fallopian tubes was confirmed exactly by the pathological findings during surgery.

As I mentioned in an earlier chapter, even Hugh Lynn Cayce was astonished at Peter's accuracy in medical matters. And although he has never claimed to be a psychic diagnostician or healer, his gift seems to lend itself in that direction. Who knows but that in a different era, or under different circumstances (before the AMA powerhouse), Peter Hurkos might have been as successful as Edgar Cayce as a psychic healer—if he had put his mind to it.

In June 1960, Peter Hurkos burst upon the scene of a sensational Virginia murder probe in a bright blaze of publicity. It was the famous Carroll Jackson case—and more of that in its place. Peter was brought in on the case by Dr. F. Regis Riesenman, a well-known Washington, D.C., psychiatrist and criminologist, who got a surprise bonus by engaging a psychic on the case.

Peter was visiting Dr. and Mrs. Riesenman in their home, and he seemed drawn to their daughter, little Mary Alice, then about two and a half years old and the youngest of the seven Riesenman children. She had been ill almost from birth and could not walk or toddle. The doctors had said that she suffered from cerebral palsy and would never walk.

Peter put his hand on her back and said, "She'll walk on her birthday, December 21, for the first time, and then four days later, on Christmas, she'll walk to the tree and pick up her presents and will continue to walk."

This was on June 11, 1960. And it happened exactly as Peter had forecast. On December 21 she miraculously took her first few tentative steps.

She fell down, but she got up and started over again. And on Christmas Day, exactly as Peter had forecast, she toddled triumphantly over to the Christmas tree and stood there smiling, and she has walked ever since.

Peter had told me this story, and I had also read about it in Jess Stearn's *The Door to the Future*. I knew Jess Stearn and his reputation as a journalist, and I had no reason to doubt a word of this story, but my natural skepticism impelled me to double-check personally with Dr. Riesenman.

Was the account accurate?

"Very accurate," he replied promptly. "And then some."

What did he mean by that?

"Peter also said that our daughter would have some metabolic disturbances," he told me. "This has come to pass only recently. We put her on a special medicine just last week."

"Is your daughter still walking all right?" I asked him.

"Yes, she is walking very well now," he replied.

I asked him how he would compare Peter Hurkos with Edgar Cayce, and he replied without hesitation, "Edgar Cayce was the greatest psychic who ever lived. He was able to transcend time and space and communicate with a universal subconscious mind to treat the ill and predict the future. . . . Peter Hurkos, on the other hand, is the greatest psychic who ever lived with the gift of retrocognition. That means regressing, seeing into the past, going back in time for his psychic knowledge. Yes, he also has the gift of precognition, foretelling the future, but not to the extent that Edgar Cayce had it.

"Peter's real gift is retrocognition, going backward in time for spontaneous readings on people, and his best work is done on criminal cases. I say he's the greatest psychic who ever lived in this field—reading people both spontaneously and on demand in criminal cases, especially murders and missing people."

Did he think that Peter had healing powers, like Edgar Cayce?

"Who can say? He has never consciously practiced healing, as Cayce did. But the power may be latent. I can only accept the evidence. He predicted that my daughter would walk after five doctors had said otherwise, and he predicted the exact date. To me that is evidence of precognition, though I can't say it is evidence of his own healing powers. But he does seem to have some psychic knowledge of medical matters," Dr. Riesenman said.

Once, when Peter was shaking hands with a woman he had never seen before, he said abruptly, "You have arthritis."

"Yes, since I was twenty-four," she replied.

Peter asked her to write something for him on a slip of paper. He rubbed his fingers across it and said, "Your mother is ill . . . through here . . . she is having trouble in this area." He drew his hands down to his pelvic area.

The woman, amazed, admitted that her mother had fractured her hip and was now convalescing.

Peter once shook up one of my guests at a party by telling her about a miscarriage.

"You have two little children, haven't you?" he asked. That was true.

"You would have had three, but you lost one, last August. A miscarriage. And then you became pregnant again right away." Also true.

I barely knew the lady, and certainly knew nothing about her personal life—until I found her, dazed and trembling and white as a sheet, cowering alone in my kitchen after her impromptu reading from Peter.

"Even my husband didn't know about my miscarriage. How could *he* know?" she asked.

He had mentioned other intimate details about her marriage which she assured me were true. And to top it all, he pointed a finger at her mouth and said, "You need a filling in this tooth. This one. Right here." Sure enough, she did.

Peter once told Hollywood writer Joe Hyams, who is married to actress Elke Sommer, "There are times when your arms are so heavy you can hardly raise them. Go to a chiropractor. Have him work on your spine, and you will be well. Also, your son has a tendency to ear trouble, doesn't he?"

Hyams, once a skeptic, admitted that Peter was right on both counts. He did go to a chiropractor—"who straightened me out." And his son did have ear trouble.

Curiously, most of Edgar Cayce's medical readings, though given while asleep or in trance, have revealed a subconscious knowledge of terms or treatments used by chiropractors and osteopaths. Over and over again he has found spinal lesions of one sort or another as the cause of an ailment and prescribed spinal manipulation for its cure.

If Peter Hurkos could heal nobody else, at least apparently he could heal himself. Even Henry Belk, though no longer friend or believer, still swears by this incident. It happened on the evening of May 17, 1958, in Belk's New York apartment. A group of Belk's friends and business associates had gathered there for a sociable evening. Peter was there, too. At some point during the evening, Peter tripped over something and fell, twisting his leg so badly that, according to Belk, "One of the bones broke clear out of his skin. There was blood all over the place."

While Peter cried out in pain, some of the men lifted him onto a bed. As Belk tells the story, Peter bowed his head as though in prayer, "And before our very eyes, the bone went back into place and the torn skin healed and became smooth. I was there. I actually saw the bone stick out and go in." Belk himself told me. Those are his words verbatim from my notes. He also told essentially the same story to Jess Stearn (*The Door to the Future*) and played him a taped recording of that memorable night, with testimonials from the other eyewitnesses. Jess Stearn still couldn't believe it. And neither could I.

But when I asked Peter about it, as usual he couldn't be budged, and his sincerity couldn't be questioned, although his story is a slight variation from Belk's.

"I did not fall," he said. "My foot was under the bed. I had my scrapbooks on the bed, and I turned around to show the people my scrapbooks. It was a low bed, and I didn't want to walk around it. So I leaned over to pick up my scrapbooks, and my foot was under the bed, and I twisted it and broke my ankle between the bed and the floor. I remember the bleeding because I was embarrassed. It was a brand-new carpet.

"There were nine people who saw it. I remember the pain was tremendous and my foot was swelling up and my ankle was hanging there. They put me on the bed and took my shoe off, and I pulled the bone back with my hands. I said to the people, 'Let me rest, leave me alone.' It was such tremendous pain, and I kept thinking, 'What am I gonna do now? I gotta work. I don't want to go in the hospital.' I don't know what I did, but in about an hour I was walking. Still some pain, but I was walking, and next day I didn't have the pain. There's still the scar on my foot. Anyone can see."

It's true, there is the scar for anyone to see, just as there is the scar on the back of his head from his accident, and let those who doubt disprove it.

I asked Peter whether he had used self-hypnosis in healing himself.

"I don't know what I did," he said. "Concentration, that's all . . . I'm thinking, 'What am I gonna do now? I don't want to be in a hospital.' I think it's what you call mind over matter."

"Do you consider yourself a healer?" I asked.

"No. Absolutely not. I never have healed anybody. It isn't true if they say I am a healer." He was most emphatic about it.

Although it was Dr. Puharich who invited Peter to come to America and be tested at his Round Table Foundation laboratories, actually it was Henry Belk who financed most of the project. Belk, too, had read about Peter's work in Europe. He had his own psychical research foundation, and his own reasons for wanting Peter to come to this country.

As he told me, "I had read about Hurkos. So I got to thinking we could use someone like him to help us operate our stores. We had some trouble with shoplifting and dishonesty among employees, but we couldn't put our fingers on it, and I thought someone like Hurkos would be the answer to the problem. . . . So I put Puharich and Hurkos together on a farm to experiment on Hurkos. It cost me fifty thousand dollars—the cost of maintaining Hurkos, the experiments, and the money I lost because of Hurkos. . . . I wouldn't trust any psychic. No man should ever trust a psychic for business purposes. . . ."

Belk's disenchantment with Peter Hurkos apparently stems from one extraordinary confidence he placed in him—in both business and personal affairs. For one thing, he became disgruntled when the stores he opened in Miami and Atlanta were not as successful financially as Peter had predicted—although some observers have noted that the stores later did well under different auspices.

But it was a family tragedy that really soured Belk on Peter, and to this day the memory of it is still almost as painful to Peter as it must be to Henry Belk.

In June of 1957, Belk's ten-year-old daughter disappeared from their home in North Carolina while playing. Police combed the grounds and the area surrounding for hours. Then the distraught father telephoned Peter at his home in Miami in the hope that he could help locate the child. Peter thought for a while, silently, but drew a blank. He told Belk that he would concentrate and then call him back.

"I got the call late at night," Peter recalled, with a shudder. "I never forget it. Belk [he always pronounces it Bellek] said,

'Peter, my daughter is missing in the woods, I couldn't find her.' And I said, 'Oh, don't worry. She will be back.' But I didn't see anything. Nothing comes to me then. I tell him I gonna concentrate and call him back.

"Then, soon as I hang up the phone, I saw a clear picture that his daughter was drowned by the boathouse, in six-foot-deep water. I don't know how to tell him this, but I call him back and I tell him she is drowned, and that is too much for him. I tell him to look by the boathouse and go the last pole on the left side of the river and there he will find his daughter in six-foot-deep water."

Belk went directly to that spot on the edge of the river, and there he found his daughter's body exactly in the position where Peter said it would be.

Belk was inconsolable at the loss of his only daughter, and very bitter at Peter. "If he could see ahead, why couldn't he have told me what was going to happen in time to save my child?" he asked.

"He has never forgiven me," says Peter. "He kept asking, why didn't I tell him that his daughter was going to drown? He says I spend whole days with him, and I give him readings about his stores and his business and salesmen and advertising. Why couldn't I tell him about his daughter?

"But I didn't see it. I can tell only what I see. I was never in Belk's home. How could I know that his daughter was going to drown? But then when he calls me and says she is gone, soon as he hangs up the phone, I see the whole picture and I call him back. But he said, 'You could have saved my daughter. You should have said this to me sooner and saved her.' So he fired me. And he has never forgiven me. But how could I tell him I saw her if I didn't see her until after she is already drowned in six-foot-deep water?"

As Peter talked, he became more and more agitated at the memory of the tragedy. It seemed as fresh in his mind as though it had only then happened, and he was grieving for Belk. "It was his only daughter," he said. "A beautiful child." He seemed to be blaming himself for the tragedy. And then suddenly, bitterly, he asked the same question that the grief-stricken father had asked:

"If my gift bring me the picture after, why can't it bring it sooner so I could save his daughter? Why? Why? I'm sorry, but I can tell only what I see."

It was Henry Belk who subsequently labeled Peter a zombie, who concluded, along with Peter's father that the real Peter had died the day he fell on his head and that he was now possessed of some other spirit.

There were times when this theory seemed almost credible, and times when the heavy burden of Peter's strange "gift" was painful to behold.

# · 6 ·

# *Odic Force*

In this country, Peter's reputation as a psychic detective spread rapidly, and he soon became a regular crime consultant. He had moved to Miami while working for Henry Belk, and the Miami police began calling on him for help in solving their cases.

He is perhaps best known there for his work on the Smith case, which involved a double murder on the same day in October 1958. A navy commander was shot to death in his Key Largo apartment, and a few hours later, a cab driver was shot and killed in downtown Miami. Both men were shot by bullets from a .22 automatic, and police theorized they might have been killed by the same person. But weeks dragged on, and they uncovered no clues. They called in Peter on the case and without telling him of the two killings, asked him to sit in the cab driver's car and tell them what impressions he got, if any. They were amazed when he began describing not one murder but two, and he said the same man was responsible for both murders. He described the man as tall and thin, with a tattoo on his right arm and a slow, ambling gait—"like a sailor."

And he did something that even the best of psychics rarely do: he even named him. "He is a man well known in Havana and Detroit," said Peter, "and his name is Smitty."

That was close enough. The man's name, it developed, was Charles Smith, a merchant seaman who had shipped to Cuba.

Peter also said that he had been in trouble before, and as it turned out, he had served time in Michigan.

Miami police obtained a rogues' gallery picture of Smitty from Michigan authorities, and a Miami waitress identified the man as a customer whom she had overheard boasting one night of killing two men. Her description of the man also tallied with Peter's—tall, thin, and with a "rolling walk like a sailor." Miami police circulated flyers with his picture and description to other police departments around the country, and less than a month later he was picked up in New Orleans after pulling a stickup there. He was returned to Miami for trial, found guilty of the cab driver's murder, and was sent to prison for life.

The man who directed the investigation was Lieutenant Tom Lipe, head of the Miami homicide squad at the time. Shortly after my first encounter with Peter Hurkos in Miami, when I went there to expose him as a fraud and failed, I had talked with Tom Lipe about him. And I could scarcely believe my ears. I had more than a nodding acquaintance with the police in my work as a newspaper reporter. I had covered a few murder trials myself, as well as a good many other things on police beats. And to tell the truth, a veteran hardheaded police officer was the last guy in the world I would suspect of being a patsy for a psychic.

Lieutenant Lipe told me that some of his colleagues disapproved of any publicity connecting them with a psychic and that was why in some published reports of the case Peter didn't rate even a mention. But his personal praise of Peter's work was certainly an impressive testimonial, and all the more so since it came from a chief of police detectives who had worked with him on the spot and on a number of other cases.

"I suppose some people would think we're lunatics for accepting the help of a psychic in solving our crimes. In fact, some of the other officers here don't approve of it and won't admit that Peter Hurkos has been of any help to us," he explained. "So far as we know there isn't even any scientific proof of this whatever-it-is that he has. I don't understand it. I don't know how Hurkos does it. I can only tell you what I have seen from working with him. And it is astounding—not only to me but to everyone else who has worked with him, if they would admit it.

"In my job I think I know how to spot a phony. Hurkos is a humble and honest man. I can't say with positive proof that he alone has solved any of our cases. Maybe we could have solved them eventually without him. But he has come up with some amazing things that have helped us in my opinion."

Lieutenant Lipe reminded me of a technical point—that information gained through so-called psychic powers is not admissible as legal evidence. "But neither are lie detector tests," he pointed out. "And a few years ago even fingerprints were not accepted. Who knows, maybe what Hurkos is doing will be accepted as commonplace twenty or thirty years from now. I don't know what it is he has, but whatever it is, it's enough to shake people up and give them something to think about."

Lipe admitted he was particularly impressed with Peter's work on the Smith case, but he admitted also that he was completely baffled about how he did it. He hastened to add, however, that he felt that Peter was completely trustworthy, that he didn't use tricks or gimmicks, didn't ask leading questions, and didn't seem as much concerned with what the police told him as with what he was able to "see" himself.

"If anyone breaks in on him when he's talking, he tells them not to interrupt. He doesn't seem to be interested in knowing what the police know. He just wants to be let alone to concentrate and see what impression he comes up with himself," he said.

I can verify from my own experience with him that this is indeed a very accurate description of the way Peter actually works. As he says, "All I want the police to do is take me to the scene and leave me alone." Then, as he concentrates on the crime, he "sees" pictures, like flashes of newsreels unfolding before his eyes. "It's like a film being played only for me," he says. "I can see all these things, like pictures they come boom, boom, boom. And I can only tell what I see."

On Lieutenant Lipe's recommendation, Peter was also consulted in the famous case of missing Florida Judge Curtis Chillingworth and his wife. Long before the case was finally cracked, Peter had told authorities that the judge and his wife were abducted and their bodies tossed in the ocean. He said that Mrs. Chillingworth was killed only because she was a witness, that both were put into a rowboat, then beaten with the oars, and dumped overboard to the sharks. Their bodies were never found. He also accurately described the instigator of the crimes, former Judge Joseph Peel of West Palm Beach, who is now serving time for masterminding the murders.

One of Peter's most highly publicized cases in this country, second only to the Boston Strangler case, was the Carroll Jackson murder case in Falls Church, Virginia, in June of 1960. Personally, I am inclined to agree with Dr. Riesenman that this was one of Peter's most fantastically successful cases—even though the Washington newspapers ridiculed him as a flop.

To me, it is an intriguing case of psychic double identity, or crisscrossed vibrations, but what I really loved about it was Peter's utterly enchanting candor when I asked what went wrong on this one.

"Oh, I picked the wrong man," he said. "I found the right house, the one the murderer lived in, but he had moved, and now his friend, the trashman, lived there. He was a friend of the piano player. I was not sure which one did it, the trashman or the piano player, but it was one of the two, and I picked the trashman. This was my mistake. It was the piano player who was the murderer. But the trashman confessed, and anyway I found the right house."

This is a rather good nutshell summary of the case, which was already eighteen months old when Peter was brought into it by Dr. Riesenman, the Washington psychiatrist and criminologist I have mentioned earlier. Police had already picked up and questioned more than fifteen hundred suspects in the quadruple slaying of the Falls Church family, Carroll Jackson, his wife, and their two small daughters. The authorities had one hundred and sixty-five suspects under consideration, including two of Riesenman's private patients. He was concerned with clearing these two, since he felt they were innocent. Also, like many concerned citizens, he was anxious to have the Jackson murders solved. The case had dragged on long enough.

Because of his professional interest in mental phenomena and his professional curiosity about Peter Hurkos, whom he had never met, he was willing at his own expense to bring him east to work on the case, providing, of course, the police were willing to cooperate and accept the services of a psychic. They agreed.

The police, understandably, were not anxious to have it broadcast that they were working with a psychic, and Peter also had specified that newspapermen not be present during the time he was working on the case. But a good newshound can smell out a story miles away. And Peter's arrival in Falls Church was greeted with a blare of publicity.

On the day of his arrival, he predicted on a television show that the murderer would be arrested within fourteen days and that he would eventually be indicted for nine murders. Then he proceeded to draw a picture of the murderer's home, saying, "You find this house, you get your man." Peter frequently draws pictures of his psychic impressions, which are generally much more explicit and helpful than his chopped-up, broken-English, chaotically confused verbal descriptions.

He remembered the house well when he described it to me nine years later. "It had a broken chair here on the porch and a carton of old books, and it was out in the woods on about a half an acre. I go with the police and we find the house, and I know it is the murderer's home, but I did not know the murderer has moved and it is the trashman who lives here now.

Also what Peter did not know was that both the trashman and the man who had previously lived in the house were among the hottest suspects on the police list. When Peter led the police to the house, they were amazed to find that its occupant was indeed the thirty-four-year-old trash collector from Falls Church who was one of their prime suspects. They were even more amazed when Peter led them to an abandoned shack in the woods only fifty feet from where one of the murders was committed, and said, "The killer has been here. If we look, we will find something." Poking around in the sand outside the shack, they found the trash collector's silver ID bracelet.

Convinced they had their man, they picked him up for questioning—and he confessed the crimes! And the newspapers had a field day crediting a psychic with cracking the case after only three days on the scene.

But ten days later the Hurkos bubble burst when the FBI arrested another man in Arkansas, thirty-one-year-old Melvin Davis Rees, a jazz musician from Hyattsville, Maryland. Rees was also implicated in the murder of another woman, Mrs. Margaret Harold, whose body was found not far from where the bodies of Mrs. Jackson and her daughter were later exhumed.

With the arrest of Rees, the Washington newspapers did an about-face, lashed out against "crystal-ball justice," and strongly denounced Peter as well as the Virginia police who had cooperated with him. Rees was later tried and convicted of the crimes.

Why did Peter miss on this one? Why did he pick the trashman instead of Rees?

According to Dr. Riesenman, who has stood staunchly by Peter in this case despite all the adverse publicity, Peter actually described both men—the trash collector and Rees. Both, as mentioned—and it should be emphasized—had been hot suspects in the case. If a psychic can sense things through "vibration"—telepathic or otherwise—it should not be surprising that he would "see" both suspects.

It is possible, too, that he could get their "vibrations" mixed up. The difficulty in this case, Dr. Riesenman told me, was that Peter got one through telepathy and the other through psychometry. That is, he read the minds of the police officers who thought the trash collector was guilty, and he got Rees through his contact with the dead people's belongings—or what Dr. Riesenman calls the "odic force."

Peter was taken to the churchyard where the Jacksons were buried. He handled some of their clothing and personal possessions and amazed police with his psychic impressions. He described the positions in which the bodies lay when they were found, told how each one had been killed, and in what order, and said that Mrs. Jackson had been sexually assaulted—a fact that only the police knew then.

He also described both suspects, Dr. Riesenman said.

Then why did the newspapers say he flopped on this one?

"You're a newspaperwoman, you ought to know," Dr. Riesenman chided me. "It just happened that he came up with the trashman first because of the house. The papers leaped on it and blew it up all out of proportion. They thought they were on to a sensational story—Psychic Nabs Murderer.

"Then when the FBI nabbed Rees, that killed their big story, and it didn't make them look too good. So to cover their own tracks, they had to blame Hurkos. You see, the papers went so overboard on the trash collector, they didn't even know that Hurkos had also described Rees to the police. And he was quite specific, down to the last detail. He got his height correctly—slightly over six feet—said he was left-handed with a tattoo on his arm and that he walked like a duck and stood like an ape. That description fitted Rees to a T."

Why didn't the Virginia police—instead of the FBI—pick Rees up?

They were going to, Dr. Riesenman said. In fact, they did send two men to Arkansas to pick him up, but the FBI got there first. As Peter admitted, "While I was working on this one, the FBI grabbed the piano player." The press apparently lost interest in Peter's role in the case after the first couple of days—or when they learned that he had picked the wrong man as the killer. It wasn't important that he picked the right house, the one occupied by both the murderer and his pal, the trashman, though at separate times.

Reporters apparently did not know that Peter had described Rees as well as the trash collector. Neither did they know that police had taken him to the Harold murder scene and that he had found the victim's skirt on a bush where it had hung unnoticed for three years. He told police that Mrs. Harold and the Jacksons had been killed by the same man.

How did he get these impressions?

"Odic force," says Dr. Riesenman. It is his theory that the murderer leaves a trail of emotion—anger, fear, resentment, appendages of the crime—that the psychic can latch onto years after the incident. Similarly, a psychic can enter a room where diplomats have sat and penetrate their plans better than any spy. "Give Peter Hurkos a scrap of clothing or a wisp of his hair," he said, "and he might be able to tell you everything a man has done or is planning to do."

Part of the answer lies in the word "psychic" itself, which is derived from the Greek word *psychikos,* meaning "of the soul or life, spiritual." It also means: sensitive to nonphysical forces. Thus, the interchangeability of the terms, "psychic" and "sensitive," and thus the ability to pierce the past through a kind of aura, as some call it, or odic force, as Dr. Riesenman calls it, that supposedly clings to a person's clothing or other personal possessions. This explains too why a man as sensitive as Peter to nonphysical forces can become an expert at what Dr. Riesenman calls "retrocognition." "That's why he is so fantastically great on criminal cases. He can pick up all these impressions through the odic force," Dr. Riesenman said.

When I asked Peter whether he knew about the odic force, he gave me a blank look. When I tried to explain it to him, he seemed childishly amused. "That Dr. Riesenman," he laughed, "is a very fine man. Good education—up here." He pointed his forefinger to his head.

I explained to him Dr. Riesenman's theory of the murderer mix-up, that he felt Peter got the trash collector through telepathy and the piano player through psychometry. "Whatever Dr. Reisenman says must be right," he said. "I only know what I see. I see the murderer's house, but the murderer doesn't live there anymore. That's why I got the wrong man."

To him it was as simple as that.

"Why did the trashman confess?" I asked.

He shrugged. "Lots of people like to confess to murders," he said. "Makes them feel big. Look at the Boston Strangler—he confessed all those murders but he wasn't the real strangler. . . .

"Maybe the trashman saw the killing. He wasn't at home the night of the murder, he was at the empty shack where the police find his bracelet, fifty feet away from the last killing. That's why the people think he's the murderer. The two men knew each other. Maybe one was inside peeping and the other outside killing. Who knows?"

Inspector Jack Hall of the Virginia State Police, who handled the investigation, confirmed both Dr. Riesenman's and Peter's side of the story, adding that the two suspects "had a lot in common."

"They even lived in the same house for a while," he said,

"though not at the same time, and Hurkos might have confused the pair there. But that man could pick up the strangest things. He even told us that Mrs. Jackson had only thirty-one teeth, and when we checked the autopsy report, we found out he was right."

But one of the strangest things Peter told Inspector Hall had nothing to do with the Jackson case. When he shook hands with the inspector, he suddenly blurted out, "You haven't had any children in eighteen years, and you don't expect any more, but you're going to have another child, a girl, and she will be born on June 24, 1961, just about a year from today."

The officer laughed at him and said it wasn't possible. But three months later his wife was pregnant, and a baby girl was born one year and five weeks later, on June 24, 1961, on the very day Peter had predicted.

One final word on the Jackson case. On Peter's arrival in Falls Church, he had predicted that the murderer would be arrested within fourteen days and that he would eventually be indicted for nine murders. The trashman wasn't actually arrested but only picked up for questioning and committed for observation at his wife's request. The piano player, Rees, was arrested two weeks after Peter's prediction, was officially tied to five murders including the Jackson family's and Mrs. Harold's and Inspector Hall confirmed that police eventually uncovered clues linking him to four more, totaling nine.

Dr. Riesenman, who personally footed the bill for bringing Peter in on the case, said the total cost for expenses and a modest fee for Peter—which he did not want to take—came close to three thousand dollars. "But it was worth every cent of it," he said, "in more ways than one."

He was alluding mainly, of course, to Peter's prediction that the Riesenmans' child, Mary Alice, crippled by cerebral palsy, would walk again by Christmas. But there were some other remarkable incidents, too.

For example, when Riesenman met Peter at the airport, he recognized him from his pictures—they had never met before—but when the doctor reached into his wallet for an identifying card, the picture of an elderly man fell out. Peter picked it up and handed it back to Riesenman, saying, "That man is eighty-two years old. He has had four accidents in the last two years, and his condition is going to gradually deteriorate, with the blood vessels shrinking in his head. He will live from six to twelve months."

The picture was of Riesenman's father, who lived in Meadville, Pennsylvania, with a son, Joseph. Peter's prediction was accurate. "Though I didn't think so at the time," Dr. Riesenman told me. "The doctors had said that my father was improving and that he would live another five to ten years. Peter said he would live from six to twelve months. He died eight months later from a blood clot in the brain."

Peter is not 100 per cent accurate and has never claimed to be. If he were, then I would know that he's a phony, or at best that he is using the tricks of a professional stage telepathist or medium. And they do have a bag of tricks. Their infallibility is the tip-off. They can't afford to make mistakes in front of their audiences.

Though Peter is sometimes pooh-poohed because of his mistakes—as in the Jackson case—to me at least it is this very fallibility that gives him the ring of genuineness. I must admit that sometimes his fallibility goes a little far for someone who is supposed to be a true psychic. I have seen him draw a complete blank. For example, I once gave him a box containing jewelry and trinkets that had belonged to a teen-age girl who was murdered in Chicago. Her grieving father had implored me to take them to Peter in the hope that he could help find the murderer. His score on this one was zero. He couldn't even tell me what was in the box, much less anything about the murderer. But at least he admitted it instead of making up something. "I'm sorry," he said. "I don't see anything. I don't feel anything. Nothing. I don't know why. But I can't tell you what I don't see."

And when he doesn't "see" or "feel" anything, there is no point in pressing him. He can also become very irritable when asked to read something if he's tired or if he isn't in the mood—as I found out soon enough in the process of doing this book. A dear friend of mine who had adopted a Vietnamese girl and was sending her to college wanted Peter to give her a reading from the girl's signature, which she enclosed in a letter to me. I started to give him the slip of paper before one of our interviewing sessions one day. He irritably brushed it aside and snapped, "Don't ask me to work now when I don't feel like it." That was the end of that.

On the whole, however, he is as docile as a lamb, and far more patient and cooperative than I had any right to expect him to be in the impromptu "tests" I sometimes sprung on him. And he scored far more hits than misses. But his most amazing and successful performances were the spontaneous ones, those that catapulted out of him unexpectedly, in a sudden, inexplicable burst of psychic insight. During our long and close working relationship in the preparation of this book, I deliberately refrained from asking Peter's advice or impressions about my personal affairs—partly, I suppose, because of my fear of knowing the future and partly because, in spite of my increased trust in him, I still found it difficult to overcome my instinctive skepticism. After all, I really didn't believe in that sort of rot, did I? Well, believe in it or not, there were days when Peter's uncontrollable outbursts of psychic prognostications regarding my personal life and that of others around me left me so shaken that I seriously considered giving up on this book. He really spooked me at times. . . . Most of his spontaneous impressions came when he accidentally touched something of mine—a notebook or a pen or a book on my desk.

And yet when I gave him the murder victim's jewel box, he drew a blank. How does one explain this? I don't. And neither does Peter. Like Edgar Cayce, he says of his "gift," "You cannot explain it. You feel it." And who knows how or why it turns on or off?

Sometimes when Peter seems to be mistaken on certain details, later developments prove that his "second sight" or "sixth sense" wasn't so muddled after all.

A case in point involves an AWOL marine, Corporal James Belyeu, twenty-one, from Houston, Texas.

On September 1, 1968, Dr. and Mrs. Robert Bucklin of Houston consulted Peter concerning their missing marine son, who had disappeared while on R & R (rest and recreation) leave from Vietnam, while serving his second tour of duty in the war area. Peter told them that their son was alive but had a head injury and was wandering around Australia in a confused state of mind—probably near Melbourne. He had been listed as a deserter by the Marine Corps, but the Bucklins were convinced the boy had not "gone bad." They had decided to go and find him even before they consulted Peter.

And when they finally did find him, it seemed at first that Peter had missed on several points. The boy was married to a twenty-two-year-old Australian waitress and living near Sydney —not Melbourne—in hiding from authorities. But as his story unfolded, Peter's predictions began falling into place.

Corporal Belyeu told Dr. Bucklin, who was his stepfather and a county medical examiner, that he had become convinced he would die in battle. "He had seen his friends predict their own deaths down to the hour," Dr. Bucklin later recalled. "Confused and frightened, he saw the rest and recreation leave in Australia as his only chance for life. The boy made up his mind on the last day of his leave, the same day he met the girl," the doctor said. "But he didn't leave the marines for her. She was incidental.

"James had been wounded by shrapnel in the back and legs —which might have been the injury Mr. Hurkos saw—and the two of them wandered around Australia during the last few months, covering about three thousand miles," Dr. Bucklin said. "They were near Melbourne about the time we talked to Mr. Hurkos. So actually the only thing he missed was the location of the wound. He's an amazing man."

After a one-day reunion in Sydney (Corporal Belyeu had been missing since May), the Bucklins persuaded him to turn himself in to the authorities. They returned to Houston, satisfied that their boy had been saved the possibility of spending a lifetime "on the run," and giving Peter full credit for helping them locate him.

In a letter they later wrote to Peter, expressing their gratitude "for the most remarkable thing you have done for us," the Bucklins enumerated twelve major points Peter had told them during the consultation and added their own comment, "Correct" or "Incorrect," beside each one, with elaborations. For example:

"Mentally disturbed. Correct. Dr. Bucklin and I both believe this boy is not himself. He is so emotionally disturbed about returning to Vietnam that he turned his back on all he loved here. . . .

"Wounded on patrol. Correct. . . .

"Best friend killed. Correct. . . .

"You saw him in an isolated area. Correct. . . ."

They marked him "Incorrect" on only one of the twelve points: "Head wound received in Pan Dong," Peter had told them. Actually, he was slightly wounded by shrapnel in the flank and knee, not in the head.

To me one of the most fascinating aspects of Peter's mental phenomena, particularly in his so-called mistakes, is his off-beat timing, like an out-of-sync film. For instance, when he told the Bucklins their son was "wandering around Australia in a confused state of mind—probably near Melbourne," it had already happened.

The Bucklins went to Melbourne because of Peter's suggestion and followed numerous leads given by persons who positively identified their son through his pictures. And though he was finally located not in Melbourne but in Sydney, he had actually been in Melbourne for a period of about two weeks and at about the time Peter was talking with the Bucklins.

In December 1968, I happened to be in Palm Springs, California, at the same time that Peter was there appearing in a night-club act at the Chi Chi Club. On a Sunday morning he received an urgent call from Officer Bert Swift of the Palm Springs Police Department, asking for help in locating a missing plane.

It was a private airplane piloted by Swift's friend, navy chief hospital corpsman Robert Cline of San Diego. In addition to being in the navy, Cline was a private flying instructor, and had been enroute from Phoenix back to Brown Field in San Diego with a copilot, Frank Carpenter, and a student. On December

12, Officer Swift got a call from San Diego that the plane had lost radio contact with San Diego. Swift and another friend, Ken Lester, from nearby Chula Vista, immediately joined in the search for the missing plane. Swift, Lester, and Bob Cline had all been navy pilots and buddies. Search teams, including the Civil Air Patrol, underwater demolition teams, and some twenty vehicles, scoured the area for two days—and finally gave up. They had found no evidence of a plane crash; the possible area in which it could have happened extended as far as New Mexico, much of it mountainous terrain recently ravaged by some of the winter's worst storms; and already another of Bob Cline's pilot friends from San Diego, who had joined the search in his own plane, had crashed and was killed. The search crews reluctantly decided to abandon the search.

But two of Cline's closest friends, Swift and Lester, refused to give up. They had read that Peter Hurkos was in Palm Springs, and they had heard of his reputation as a psychic detective. They were, of course, skeptics, but they were willing to try anything to find their missing buddy—or his body.

Peter agreed to help them if he could, and he told them he could do best if they would bring him an article of clothing belonging to Cline.

Police Chief Robert White and Officer Swift had agreed to let me sit in on the session with Peter. It was late afternoon when the contingent arrived, bringing T-shirts and other articles of clothing dispatched from San Diego, as well as some photographs of Robert Cline.

Officer Swift laid them out on a long table, and Peter began handling them, one by one, concentrating intensely. After what seemed like an interminable time he finally spoke, quietly, without looking up. His first words were, "Both dead. I'm sorry. I hope I'm wrong. But that's what I see. He changed course in the storm. . . . Nine miles off course . . . I see two dead. . . ." He described Cline, then said, "This is not a new plane, it is a secondhand plane, leased. . . . The engine was overhauled not long ago. . . . The trouble is not with the engine but with the tail. There is too much pressure on the tail. . . ."

From the expression on the men's faces I couldn't tell what

they were thinking, and Peter obviously didn't care. He was totally immersed in, apparently, the odic force. He never looked up, never asked leading questions, and got nary a yea or a nay from his listeners. No one spoke a word.

"Now give me the map," Peter said, pushing the articles of clothing aside and spreading out a large map Swift had brought of the total area in which the plane could have crashed. Peter took a pencil and began tracing lines on the map. "This is where they started," marking an X at Phoenix, "and this is where they got off course . . . in these mountains. He planned that course exactly, he is a good pilot, but when the storm comes he changed course. The plane is not in a lake, but I see water, like a creek or a stream. The plane is near a stream, under trees and bushes, hard to find. . . . Here." He marked a big X where the plane had crashed into the mountain. The men stepped closer for a better look at the map.

"That's near Pine Valley," one said.

"I do not know the name, but here is where you find your plane, with two bodies," said Peter, throwing down his pencil as much as to say, "That's it. *Finito.*"

I had been watching his pencil tracing the map—and I watched in absolute disbelief. I stepped up to the table for a better look. I looked again. Then I looked around at the faces, all apparently mesmerized, all staring in stunned silence, incredulous.

I finally broke the silence. "Peter," I said, "do you know you have this map upside down?"

"Of course," he said, "I always work with maps upside down, or maybe back side up."

In this case the map was face up on the table, but the printing was pointed toward us on the other side of the table, and Peter, sitting on the other side of the table opposite us, was looking at it upside down. At other times, he explained, he would simply turn the map over, with the print side down, and "read" it with his fingertips.

"Why do you work with maps upside down?" I asked.

"Because if I see the names on the map, then I get mixed up. I do not know the names. It they are names of streets or towns and I have not been there, then they mean nothing to me. It is better if I do not see them when I am working with maps. Mix me up too much. Better I feel with my fingers."

Well, that's the way he works. If I hadn't seen it, I wouldn't believe it. I had read, of course, that he amazed investigators with his psychic upside-down readings of the city maps of London and Boston when he worked on the Stone of Scone and Boston Strangler cases, but actually seeing him do it was something else again.

And how accurate was the reading? Not 100 per cent exact, but accurate enough to lead a new rescue crew to a specific mountain and to the discovery of the plane and the victims.

Peter had drawn a rectangle, three miles by six miles in area, blocking out part of Mount Laguna. Then he drew an X where he thought the plane had crashed into the mountain. Bert Swift immediately relayed the information to rescue teams in San Diego, and they resumed their search at once, concentrating on the area Peter had pinpointed. Within a few hours they had found the plane. The site of the accident was six miles due east of the X which Peter had marked and three miles outside the rectangle which he drew on the map.

He was accurate in his description of Robert Cline and his small plane. It was a leased plane (a Piper Cherokee), and its engine had been recently overhauled. And Cline apparently had changed course in a storm at about the spot Peter marked on the map.

But he was wrong about the number of persons on the plane. He "saw" only two bodies, not three. But strangely when they were found, two of the bodies were outside the airplane on Mt. Laguna, and the other one was lodged inside the plane, in the fuselage.

Bert Swift and Ken Lester were so impressed with Peter's overall score that they were inclined to attach some psychic significance to the reason he missed on the number of bodies. Maybe he didn't "see" the third one because it was lodged inside, in the fuselage? Even the rescue crew almost missed it. . . .

I talked to both Bert Swift and Ken Lester later, and they seemed to share the same awed puzzlement. Did they really believe that Peter Hurkos had psychic powers? As Officer Swift said, "Well, I have no other choice. He told me too many facts that were correct for me to believe otherwise."

There is an odd postscript to this chapter, which I am adding long after the chapter originally was written. In fact, my entire manuscript was finished and the book was in production when something happened that I feel must be included here. And it happened only last night and today, as I write this, September 25, 1969.

I came back out to Palm Springs for a few days' rest, after working with Peter on the Sharon Tate case (Chapter 12). My husband showed me a story in the local newspaper, *The Desert Sun*, about the discovery of a skeleton—or skeletal remains—in the upper Tahquitz Canyon area, believed to be remains of Stephen Gallagher of Long Beach, who had disappeared in 1967. Gallagher, who had just completed service with the Air Force, was reported last seen, in the nude, near the upper falls, on January 29, 1967. The story, dated September 24, continued:

"Famed clairvoyant Peter Hurkos, who was in Palm Springs last December, expressed belief at that time that Gallagher's remains would be found near the upper falls. The remains recovered . . . were found about 3/4 of a mile from the area indicated by Hurkos where he thought the bones might be found. . . ."

I remembered very well the day Peter had set out climbing up Tahquitz Canyon—against my vehement protests. He had no business risking his neck in those rugged mountains. It was winter; there was snow in the mountains; and Peter had a bad hip. He had just finished volunteering his services on one case, the missing plane, and personally I felt this was enough for the moment. Stephany, his fiancée, and I both begged him not to go. A lot of good it did. We worried all day until he got safely back down the mountain. I was so relieved I didn't even bother to ask him what the case was about. All I knew was that it had something to do with a missing person and that Peter said he told police where they would find the body.

I attached no importance to it and in fact had completely for-

gotten about it until the news story reminded me. I telephoned
Peter in Los Angeles and read the story to him, thinking he would
be pleased to know he had scored again.

"Ya," he said, "that's what I tell them, so they find the body, ya?
But, dear, would you do me a favor and call the police chief and
ask him if he got my painting what I send him."

He seemed far less interested in the news confirming he had
been right again than he was about whether the police chief had
received a painting he had sent him. Because of his language
difficulty Peter doesn't like talking on the telephone, but he explained that he had promised to give Police Chief White one of
his paintings, that he had painted one especially for him, and that
he had sent it to Palm Springs via a friend, but had never heard
whether Chief White had received it.

"Please, dear, would you call him right away and let me know,"
he begged.

How many psychics do you know who not only volunteer their
services to police but also give them paintings?

I called Police Chief Robert B. White. He said he had indeed
received the painting, that it was beautiful, that he had been expecting to see Peter in Palm Springs again. I had not intended to
ask Chief White about the Gallagher case, because my book was
finished. I called only to ask him about the painting Peter had
sent to him. But I got an unexpected bonus when the chief
voluntarily began talking about how amazed he was at Peter's
"revelations" on the case. His mind was obviously more on the
case than on the painting, which was understandable since the
skeleton had been found only a couple of days earlier.

"And in the exact location where Peter told us last December
the body would be found," he said. He seemed not only willing
but anxious to tell me about Peter's work on the case and to give
him full credit for his psychic revelations.

It started when Peter dropped in to meet the police chief personally soon after he had worked with Officer Bert Swift on the
missing plane.

"I had heard a lot about Peter Hurkos," said Chief White. "I
knew of his reputation on the Boston Strangler case, and I was
interested in meeting him. While he was in my office he asked

whether we had any complicated cases we were trying to solve. I told him yes, as a matter of fact we had several. I asked Captain Richard Harries to bring in some of the folders of unsolved cases. He brought in several.

"Peter Hurkos laid his hand on the top folder, which happened to be the Gallagher case, and began verbally telling us almost verbatim what was in the report. Both my captain and I were amazed. We had never seen Peter Hurkos before. He had no way of knowing what was in that folder. The case was a year old, and it hadn't been in the news recently. Yet Peter began telling us about it exactly as though he were seeing through that folder.

"He said it was the case of a missing boy. He named the correct number of persons involved—three. He identified the vehicle they were driving. He told us there had been a little 'party' and there were lots of narcotics involved. This also was correct. The three boys had been off on a little 'trip' on LSD.

"Peter Hurkos also pretty well described the general area where the missing boy was last seen. He said it was a remote area with lots of rocks and boulders and brush. If you know the Tahquitz Canyon area [I do], you know that's what it's like.

"He also said he saw the boy nude, and it is true that he was last seen in the nude, but Peter also said that he had been in uniform, that he had been recently released from the military, though he did not see him in the Navy or Marine Corps. The folder contained a picture of the boy in his Army Air Force uniform.

"Peter said he saw some blood, and then he stopped. He couldn't do any more. My captain and myself and others were all amazed. We all knew there was no way for him to know the contents of that folder."

They then asked Peter whether he would go with them to the area, and he of course agreed to go. Peter had never been in Palm Springs before, much less in Tahquitz Canyon, but he led them up the mountain to the top of the first falls and to the exact location of the boys' camping area.

What amazed police most was that Peter identified a flat stone as the one on which the missing boy's clothing had been found.

"If you know that area, you know it's full of rocks and boulders," the Police Chief repeated. "But Peter went over to a certain flat stone and said he visualized some of the boy's clothing on top of that rock. It wasn't just any rock, it was *the* rock where we had found the missing boy's clothing nearly a year before.

"Peter indicated another area, farther on near the upper falls, where he said the body would be found. He said it would be wedged under a rock and partly in water.

"My captain's first instinct was to try to reach that area, but it would have been too dangerous to attempt it, especially in the winter months. Tahquitz Creek was extremely high, and there was snow in the mountains. It's hard to get into that area even in good weather, so we decided against it."

But that's exactly where the skeletal remains were found, scattered over an area of about fifteen feet just off a place called Lost Trail, north of Tahquitz Creek in the mountains that border Palm Springs. They were found by two young hikers, who told the police, and subsequently a helicopter was flown into the area to collect the remains.

"I don't know what it is Peter Hurkos has," said Chief White, "but I know that his revelations on this case impressed all of us who watched him work. How he could reveal to us the contents of that folder—well, it makes you wonder a little bit. I have been a policeman for twenty-two years, and I've seen all kinds of phenomena but nothing ever like this."

As for that painting, he promised to sit right down and write Peter a thank you note.

## · 7 ·

# The Boston Strangler Case

By far the most sensational criminal case Peter has worked on in this country was the case of the Boston Strangler early in 1964.

He also served briefly—very briefly—as "consultant" on the movie of the same name, starring actor Tony Curtis in the role of Albert DeSalvo, the self-confessed Strangler.

Mr. Richard Fleischer, one of Hollywood's top movie directors, was assigned to direct the picture for Twentieth Century-Fox film studios, and as might be expected, he had some fascinating off-screen experiences in working with Peter.

He told me of some rather amazing things Peter "saw" at a party the Fleischers gave at their home in Brentwood. It was a warm, balmy spring night, Fleischer recalled, and among the invited guests were many who would be working together on *The Boston Strangler* picture, including Producer Robert Fryer . . . and of course Peter Hurkos.

As usually happens, many of the others present were asking Peter a lot of questions, most of them with skepticism. At one point during the evening, he abruptly turned to Fleischer's wife, Mary, who was not asking questions, and said, "Tell me your birthday." She was taken aback and a little amused. "Well," she confessed, "there is some confusion about my birthday, and I really don't know exactly what date it is. It's either July 19 or July

22. My family really didn't know. . . . I'm trying to get my actual birth certificate from Montreal."

Mary was born in Montreal of Catholic parents, and it seems that there was some conflict between the baptismal record and the medical record about her actual date of birth. Such confusion with birth records is not uncommon, but most families settle on one definite date. Mary's family could never decide whether her actual birth date was July 19 or July 22.

"But it was one or the other," she assured Peter.

"You are wrong," Peter informed her. "It was neither one. It was July 24."

In recounting the story to me, Richard Fleischer said, "We all laughed at the time and thought nothing more about it. That party was a little more than a year ago. We finally got a copy of my wife's actual birth certificate from Canada. And Peter was right. The real date of her birth was July 24."

One of the guests at the same party was another Hollywood producer, Milton Sperling, who produced *Battle of the Bulge*. Fleischer told me that Peter suddenly turned to Sperling out of the blue and announced, "You have a round clock that always runs twenty minutes fast. Why do you let it be twenty minutes fast?"

Sperling laughed and went along with the gag. He took out a pen and pad and said, "I'm going to make a note of that so I don't forget to check our clocks when I get home."

The party went on until past midnight. It was nearly 3 A.M. when Richard Fleischer was awakened by the telephone. Milton Sperling came on like gangbusters in the dead of the night:

"Your Peter Hurkos is a liar."

Sleepily, "Why?"

"It's not a clock, it's a watch, and it's only eighteen minutes fast."

It seems that Mr. Sperling had gone prowling for all the timepieces in his house and had indeed found one, a large round watch on a dresser, that was running eighteen minutes fast. Peter had missed by only two minutes.

It might be asked, What good is a psychic gift like Peter's if only to know about such trivia as a watch that runs eighteen minutes fast? It is such trivia that add up to triumph, however, in the solution of many crime cases, as, for example, the case of the Boston Strangler.

I asked Richard Fleischer for his honest opinion of Peter's work on the Strangler case.

"Remarkable," he said. "Absolutely remarkable. The only trouble was he picked the wrong man."

"You know Peter says *you* picked the wrong man," I told him.

"Yes," he laughed. "He told us that several times."

Peter has absolutely, steadfastly refused to budge from his original stand that the man he picked for the Boston Strangler is the Boston Strangler—and Albert DeSalvo is not.

"They spend millions on this picture and they had the wrong guy," he insisted.

This was the reason that Peter's stint as "consultant" on the picture was extremely short-lived.

In no uncertain terms, he repeatedly told Producer Robert Fryer: "You have the wrong guy, sir, and I have the right guy. You gonna hurt yourself with this movie, because you have the wrong guy."

The moviemakers, of course, paid no attention to Peter. They had bought the rights to Gerold Frank's best seller, *The Boston Strangler*, which had been hailed as a superb reportorial account of the stranglings and of Albert DeSalvo's boastful confessions to the crimes. They had already cast Tony Curtis in the DeSalvo role, and they felt certain of a smash hit. They weren't about to back out.

There were many descriptive parallels between DeSalvo and Thomas P. O'Brien (which is not his real name), the man Peter picked as the Strangler. Peter refused to recognize the parallels —or to be convinced that his descriptions of the Strangler could apply to DeSalvo as well as to O'Brien. "No, there is no parallel. My man is the man," he said. When the moviemakers, weaving their story around Albert DeSalvo as the Strangler, offered to change the script and portray Peter as putting his finger on De-Salvo instead of O'Brien—which would have made him look much better in the movie—Peter emphatically said, "No! Definite no!

DeSalvo is not the killer, and nobody can make me say he is."

Thus it was that his role as technical consultant on the film was a brief one.

Long before we got into this chapter I had asked Peter if he had any tape recordings of the case. I didn't expect him to have copies of the official tapes made by the attorney general's office, but did he have others? Yes, he said, he had a summarized transcript of all the tapes made by his bodyguard, Jim Crane, but he had lent it to Tony Curtis to study for his role as the Strangler. I explained to Peter that we would need this transcript and asked him to get it back from Curtis.

Weeks went by and Peter still hadn't produced the transcript. Tony Curtis had just taken a new bride, his third, and was off in Europe on his honeymoon. Neither his secretary nor other members of his staff seemed to know anything about the transcript. Finally, I gave Peter a deadline, with specific instructions. If Tony's staff couldn't come up with the transcript by the end of the week, Peter would have to go to Tony's Bel-Air mansion and find it himself.

"But my gift never works for me," he reminded me. "You know, I told you, I can't even find my own shoes."

"But if you can't find those tapes, especially since it's your own voice on them, then how do you expect people to believe you're psychic?" I needled him.

"O.K., O.K., I go look," he said.

Anyone who has ever seen even the outside of the mammoth Tony Curtis chateau, reposing on five acres of elegantly manicured lawns and hedges bordered by a wooded area of eucalyptus trees and lemon groves, and barricaded from the outside world by high electric-eye iron gates, would assume the impossibility of Peter's mission. It is a baronial place, befitting the grand manner of a Hollywood superstar, and adjoining the equally baronial all-pink palace of the late Hollywood super-sex-star, Jayne Mansfield.

Peter had never been inside Tony's home, and I could sense that he didn't really want to go. But at this point it seemed to be our only chance of retrieving the on-the-spot transcript of his work on the Strangler case. So he went. (We had, of course, called ahead to arrange for him to be admitted through the gates.) And back he came in about an hour with the transcript in hand and a beaming face. He was clearly as surprised as I was that he had found the transcript.

"See, I find it, I find it! I can't even find my own shoes, but I find this!" He waved the brown-covered sheaf of typewritten pages in front of my eyes. On the cover page was a white label with the title:

BOSTON
January–February
1964

I had not seriously expected Peter to find the transcript of tapes in Tony Curtis' house. He said the servants showed him through the house and offered to let him freely search desks and drawers where the transcript might be. But it didn't take him long to find it. He went first to the library, took a fast look around, and said, "Too many books. No, not here. Show me his bedroom." There, like a bloodhound on the scent, he nosed over to a bedside commode, opened the top drawer, and *voilà!* The transcript. Of course, it might be argued that the transcript could have been found easily without the aid of any psychic ability, but after digesting the contents of the transcript, a more relevant question would seem to be, Why argue? . . .

The transcript, which Peter turned over to me, is the most complete account on record of his day-by-day and hour-by-hour role as a psychic detective on the Boston Strangler case. As previously mentioned, it was based on the tapes made by Jim Crane, a West Coast speculator who had appointed himself as Peter's bodyguard on the case.

Peter had once advised Crane against an investment in some bar gold. "It's not real gold; it's gold-plated and copper inside, and that man is a conman," Peter told him. Crane was all set to invest eight hundred thousand dollars in the gold-bar deal but decided to take Peter's advice and later found out that he was right. Since then Crane has assumed the role of a self-appointed guardian angel to Peter when the occasion calls for it. When I telephoned him in San Francisco for permission to use his name and excerpts from his transcript, I could sense his overly protective suspicion. He put me through the third degree, asking all kinds of questions, until I told him that Peter was sitting right beside me.

At that he brightened. "Oh? Let me talk to him." I gave the phone to Peter, who assured him I was O.K., and it was an entirely different Jim Crane who came back on the phone, saying, "Let me know anything I can do to help." Such is the loyalty Peter inspires in his friends.

Thus, this chapter, Peter's own version of the Boston Strangler case, is based on the only complete transcript of his role in the case, which has never been made available to anyone before, and on a fifty-page transcript of my own tape-recorded sessions with him on the Strangler. Some of the facts were included in Gerold Frank's book. The book, of course, realistically chronicles all the repugnant details of the crimes, and of the painstaking search for the Strangler, but this chapter will be concerned only with Peter's role in the case.

I was astonished to learn that Peter hadn't even read *The Boston Strangler*. In double-checking certain facts, I had to read to him the parts that concerned him. Neither is he reading the manuscript of this book. I am reading it to him, chapter by chapter, as we go along. As Peter himself admits, "I cannot read books. My mind will not concentrate."

He worked only six days on the Boston Strangler case but lost fifteen pounds, and it took him months to get over it. "I was a broken wreck," he admitted. It was torture for him to relive the case for me—and the tape recorder. As it was, he didn't quite finish. Near the end of our final session, after wretchedly reenacting for nearly three hours the sickening things seared in his memory, he abruptly stood up and said heavily, "Emotional upset. I go upstairs. Stephy finish."

Stephy is his fiancée and Girl Friday, an attractive and bright little blonde whom he calls "Mother Superior."

He turned and lumbered out of the room. We found him later

sitting upstairs alone with a tall glass of Scotch and water and a bottle of aspirins. He was just sitting and staring dazedly into space.

It is inconceivable that anything could ever match for sheer horror the series of grossly grotesque stranglings by a sexual psychopath who made fiendish assaults on his victims—all women— and then left them in obscene positions, shockingly exposed as though to debase and degrade them.

Peter was brought in on the case after the Strangler had finished with his eleventh victim, and his youngest—nineteen-year-old Mary Sullivan. This was the one that compounded all the horror of the ten previous stranglings and raised such public clamor that the attorney general's office of the Commonwealth of Massachusetts stepped in and took over the investigation of all the stranglings, a step that did not set well with Greater Boston police who had been working on the case, and that was to have far-reaching political implications.

The attorney general at that time was Edward W. Brooke, Jr., the nation's first Negro attorney general and a Republican—who had won a resounding victory in a strongly Democratic state. He created a special Strangler Investigation Bureau and placed Assistant Attorney General John S. Bottomly in charge of the entire operation. Later Brooke and Bottomly were to go their separate ways over a disagreement that they said had nothing to do with the stranglings. Bottomly resigned as assistant attorney general, and Brooke went on to the U. S. Senate, winning the seat relinquished by Senator Leverett Saltonstall when he announced his retirement.

But in their early days of coordinating the Strangler investigations, they concentrated on assembling every clue, every tip, every lead, no matter how farfetched, that might shed some light on the crimes.

Exactly who suggested that Peter Hurkos be brought in on the case has remained a well-guarded secret. Gerold Frank says that the offer came from a well-known Boston industrialist who wished to remain anonymous but who was so convinced of Peter's abilities that he and a group of friends, he said, would pay Peter's fee—"perhaps a thousand dollars or so—and expenses."

Peter's expenses were paid by someone; he doesn't know whom. But contrary to all the reports, he was never paid a fee, a fact that was verified in the numerous documents and correspondence he turned over to me, some of the latter from his lawyers trying to collect the fee.

In any case, Brooke and Bottomly apparently were intrigued with the idea of bringing a psychic in on the case. Why not? What did they have to lose? They might risk criticism, of course, for permitting a psychic, seer, or person of "supernatural powers" to work on the case. It might smack a little of witchcraft . . . shades of the Salem witch trials of the 1690s. Still, it would cost the Commonwealth nothing, and at this point anything was worth a try. Bottomly obtained a copy of Jess Stearn's *The Door to the Future* and read the chapters on Peter Hurkos with both skepticism and amazement. Then he checked with Officer Tom Lipe in Miami, as well as police in various other cities where Peter had worked. All recommended him highly. . . .

Peter was staying with actor Glenn Ford in his Beverly Hills home when the call came. A television documentary ("One Step Beyond") had been made on Peter and his strange gift, and a full-length movie on him was then tentatively being considered, with Glenn Ford portraying Peter. Peter had been more or less commuting between Miami and Hollywood and was in the process of moving permanently to Hollywood. He was also in the process of being divorced by his second wife. His "second sight" has never been exactly conducive to marital bliss. His personal life was in an upheaval; he has never made any bones about admitting that his gift has been no good in helping him manage his personal affairs. With all his problems, and with the lure of a better life beckoning him toward movies and television, he had grave misgivings about leaving Hollywood to work on a murder case at that time.

"I didn't want to take the case," he admitted. "But that man Bottomly keeps calling, please can I come out and help them. He said private people have put up the money, they make all my arrangements. I don't like the idea of going up there to Boston. I know something is wrong on that case. I don't know nothing about it, I don't read nothing about it, I never been in Boston, and I don't know why but I don't like this case. I don't want to go. So I ask my friends should I go, and they all say yes, I should do it for humanity. They say it is my duty to go and help find the killer. That is the opinion of my friends when I ask them. So I tell Mr. Bottomly, I cannot promise anything but I will try.

"So then my friend, Jim Crane, says, 'Peter, I like to go with you there. You never know what is going to happen. I am a big guy, and I have nothing to do anyhow, and I want to go on the trip.' But the attorney general wouldn't pay his plane fare. So Jim Crane have to pay his own plane fare. That's O.K. He wants to come with me.

"So the man, Mr. Bottomly, tells me he wants us to fly another way so we won't land in Boston because they don't want any publicity or any press to know about it."

Peter had one important item to check out before making his final decision. He consulted his good friend Tracy, another psychic. I thought at first he was putting me on. He was dead serious.

"I call Tracy and tell her I have to go on a case, should I do it? She say, 'Yes, it have to do with a cold climate and a lot of killings. You have a bad time, but you be O.K.,' she tell me. I ask if I'm gonna find him, the killer. She say, 'You will have trouble, but you will come out good.' Tracy's a very good psychic."

Incredulous, I asked, "You mean you consult other psychics, Peter? Why?"

"Well, now let me explain," he said. "You know psychics go to other psychics like doctors go to other doctors. And you know I can't tell anything about myself. The reason I ask Tracy is I want to know if I'm going to have it tough. I want to find out if there is going to be danger about it. I always call Tracy if I work on a murder case. She's the best psychic I know—next to Mary Pickford." (More on her later.)

He also explained that Tracy couldn't "see" for anyone else—only for him, and she was usually 100 per cent correct, he added.

"You know, when I went on the Jim Thompson case, she told me I'm going overseas to find a very important man, and I said,

'What area?' and she said, 'Well, it have to do with China.' Jesus Christ, I almost flop out my chair. Anytime I ask Tracy what she thinks if I'm gonna do this or that, she tells me how it will come out, and it always comes out like that. She is a true psychic."

Facetiously, I asked him if Tracy got that way from falling off a ladder on her head. "No," Peter replied seriously, "Tracy's gift is from the gypsies. Somebody in Tracy's family always had the gift and could tell things psychic. They got it from gypsies."

At any rate, with Tracy's blessing, and with his bodyguard, Jim Crane, Peter landed on American Airlines Flight 296 at Providence, Rhode Island, about fifty miles from Boston—per instructions from Bottomly—at 8 P.M., EST, on Wednesday night, January 29, 1964.

They were met by John Bottomly and Detective Sergeant Leo Martin, who drove them to the Battle Green Inn, a motel in Lexington, about fifteen miles from Boston. Arrangements had been made for them to register under false names. Apparently the attorney general's office had gone to a great deal of trouble to camouflage their little conspiracy with a psychic, and rather than have him stay in Boston, where reporters might get wind of his presence, it was thought best to keep him stashed away in the suburbs.

There was no doubt that Bottomly and Martin were impressed with Peter from the moment they met him. They found him to be a very engaging man, completely uninhibited, and from the moment he landed, things started happening in rapid succession. On the way to the motel, he told Sergeant Martin all about his mother's varicose veins, and described to a T the liaison man Bottomly had assigned to work with him, Julian Soshnick. The next morning he met Attorney General Brooke and told him, "I see you as a senator and then maybe further up, in politics." As we know, he is now a senator.

Peter met with various investigators in John Bottomly's private office. But there were three men with him almost constantly, waking or sleeping, throughout every day, every hour, nearly every minute of his eighteen hours a day on the job. These men were Julian Soshnick, Jim Crane, and his longtime friend and mentor, Dr. Andrija Puharich, who was permitted to stay by Peter's side at all times as an observer.

In the afternoon of his first day on the case (Thursday, January 30, 1964), Soshnick and his men arrived at Peter's suite with two large boxes of objects for him to "psychometrize"— nylon stockings and scarves that the Strangler had used on his victims, and nearly three hundred police photographs of the strangling scenes. Each set (on each victim) had been placed in an identical plain manila envelope. Soshnick now removed them from the envelopes and carefully placed them in stacks, face down, on the bed. Peter began fingering through the stacks, suddenly stopped and cried, "Phony baloney! This one not belong!"

He was right. Soshnick admitted that he had included one picture purposely to throw Peter off the track, to test him. It was a picture of a woman in a murder case, but the case had already been solved.

Peter was furious.

"You want to play tricks, ya? I fly all the way here to help you, and you think Peter Hurkos a faker? I show you, sir. You see this?" He ran his fingers over the back of a photograph and said, "This is a dead woman, legs apart, here, I show you." He flopped down on the floor and rolled over on his back, spreading his legs and turning his head, with a slight grimace, precisely simulating the position of the victim whose photograph he had fingertipped on the back side.

This was only the beginning. One by one, to the astonishment of everyone present, he accurately described most of the significant details of each strangling as each set of pictures was presented to him.

Late in the evening a detective arrived and began apologizing for being forty-five minutes late. He said his car had broken down on the way from Boston, and also that the traffic had been very heavy.

Peter had never laid eyes on the man before, but he turned to him abruptly and said rather harshly, "You do not tell the truth. You are not late because your car broke down. You took time and stop by your girl friend's apartment and did a quickie one, huly-buly, hanky-panky. Am I right, sir? And then you come here."

The poor guy turned red as a beet while the other officers guffawed. Peter even described his girl friend's apartment. After recuperating from the shock, the detective finally admitted, "Yes, you're right, it's true—but how did you know?" He shook his head in consternation, and asked the others, "Has he been right here? Was he following me?" He was promptly informed that Peter had not left his suite all day. . . .

Throughout the days and nights of Peter's work on the Strangler case, there were periods when his psychic powers seemed to work better than others, times when he apparently was overly tired and could not concentrate well.

In Jim Crane's hour-by-hour, minute-by-minute, report of his observations, he noted:

"Peter is now going through the suspect photos. He has approximately 100 all separately divided into white envelopes. He seems to be having trouble getting going. Perhaps because he has worked so hard all last night. He also seemed not to be able to work this afternoon. He said he had a headache and he seemed to be slow in his thinking. This afternoon he tried to work but it seemed every time he tried, he turned cold and could not seem to concentrate. The same symptoms are also present now. . . . 12:20 A.M.—Still working hard and seems to be doing a little bit better. . . .

"He went into his own bathroom about three minutes ago and brought out two wash cloths and a bath towel. He placed a wash cloth over each eye, and a bath towel over the wash cloths and had me tie them behind his head. Evidently he is afraid that we think he can see through the envelopes which the suspect pictures are placed in. He now explains that the reason for the towels over his head is to shut out any other vibrations because he says there are too many people in the room and they disturb him.

"Also he says that everybody staring and watching him bothers him and he cannot concentrate. . . . Peter starts going through the numerous suspect photographs and he says that the killer is not in this pile of photographs, he says that there are two rapists and one murderer in the photographs, but he will not discuss them because they do not have anything to do with this case and he does not want it to confuse him now. The local police officers in the room were very upset. They have become interested in Peter's work and believe him and are a little disturbed because they have a murderer and two rapists, and Peter will not stop to show them what the pictures look like. . . ."

(In most cases when either Peter or Jim Crane referred to "police officers," they meant the special detectives assigned to the attorney general's office, or those recruited from the Boston Police Department to join Bottomly's investigative staff and concentrate full time on the Strangler case.)

At one point in his readings, Peter stopped abruptly and said, "I need map. Get me a map. I show you where you find the murderer."

Someone hastily produced a city map for him. "You are all skeptic," he said. "Please put the map upside down, because I do not want to see the streets. If I see the whole city and too many streets, I get confused. Now, bring me object from one of the girls. . . ."

Someone produced a small hair comb of one of the Strangler's victims, and with the teeth of the comb, Peter began tracing the upside-down map of Boston, in the same way that I had watched him trace a map in Palm Springs to locate the missing crashed plane. He moved the comb back and forth, up and down, back and forth, until it finally stopped in the Newton-Boston area, in which are located Boston College, a Jesuit institution, the residence of Cardinal Cushing, and St. John's Seminary, none of which was even remotely familiar to him. He moved his fingertip over the area and began sputtering, in his guttural Dutch accent.

"Here . . . here . . . you find the killer. He looks like priest, dress like priest. . . . see many priests. . . . He gets thrown out by the monks. . . . He speak French, English. I hear French accent. He talk like girl—like this—" Peter's voice became a falsetto. Suddenly his face changed. "Goddamn, this guy, he's no good son of a bitch, he's pervert. . . ." He tossed the map aside and did an imitation of a homosexual. Presently he said, "I stop now. Too tired." He was soaked with perspiration. He slumped into a chair, and Jim Crane produced a big Dutch cigar for him. The detectives had observed his entire performance in stoic silence. They left him alone to rest for a while.

The next morning Soshnick drove Peter and Jim Crane into Boston to confer with Bottomly. While they were waiting for him in his office, Sergeant Leo Martin came in and handed Peter a letter, asking, "What do you make of this?" Instead of reading the letter, Peter crumpled it in his fist, closed his eyes, and concentrated. Perspiration poured down his face. Suddenly he cried, "By God, son of a bitch he do it! This the one—he the murderer! Yes! He the man!"

I have a copy of the letter, along with photographs of the man whom Peter still adamantly insists is the real Boston Strangler. Gerold Frank also reproduced the letter in his book but changed the name of the signer to Thomas P. O'Brien. Peter indignantly objected to the name change, in spite of my attempts to explain the legal necessity for it. The man was never officially charged with the murders, never indicted, tried, or convicted. Neither was DeSalvo, for that matter, but he confessed, thus eliminating Peter's man.

Throughout all our tape-recorded sessions, Peter absolutely refused to refer to his man as O'Brien and even begged that if we couldn't use his real name we should use one that sounded more like the real name. But in order not to complicate further what was already one of the most complicated whodunits in criminal history, I am here using the name Thomas P. O'Brien for Peter's Strangler (over his protests) because it's the one already familiar to readers and moviegoers.

O'Brien and DeSalvo were the two principal suspects in the Boston Strangler case. Peter picked O'Brien—but DeSalvo confessed.

Here is the letter which to this day Peter has never read with his eyes. He has "read" it only through the vibrations of the crumpled paper in his hand. And the detectives in Bottomly's office must have had a real jolt to see the sender's address in the upper right-hand corner. It was in the very area where Peter had moved a victim's hair comb over the map.

It reads:

Boston College School of Nursing
Boston College
Chestnut Hill
Newton 67, Mass.
c/o Nurse Director

Dear Madam:

I have a difficulty (please pardon this pencil script) perhaps you'll smile when you read about it; but I'm coming to you because I think you can help me.

I'm a BC grad, and when I look at the years I've been out of school, "I stroke my longish beard"; I've tried selling, off and on, for quite some time, and now I'm still in the selling field; I even made a do or die try to become a newspaper comic strip artist, only to fail, and before the year is out I hope to have another try at it: drawing comic strip for kids, and such a comic strip that even grown-ups will like it.

My reason for writing now, is to say that I am a bachelor and for some long time I've wanted to meet a good Catholic nurse who might have graduated from nursing school about 1950; even an under-grad about that time would be O.K.; one who is working in or near Boston.

I've even had the idea of doing an article on this class, interviewing as many as possible, to learn their opinions and experiences, in training and in the field since graduation; then offering some nursing publication such an article.

Perhaps while interviewing, I might see a nurse who might like me as much as I'd like her, and if so, we could begin a friendship that might lead to the altar.

Chances maybe, however, that very few nurses of the year 1950 (grads) are eligible, or might even consider me eligible. O.K. If there are such, maybe there is a better way to meet them than the way I have suggested here.

I'd be glad to call at the office to see you about this, if you

wish; at any rate, may I hear from you? If you'd like to, you
could call Dr. Richard H. Wright, of 1190 Beacon St., Brook-
line; he has known me for many years.

    With every best wish,

I am

Sincerely,

_____(s)

Thomas P. O'Brien

(not his real name)

Boston College had turned the letter over to police, who had
sent it to Homicide that very morning. Bottomly immediately
telephoned Dr. Wright, who was, it developed, Cardinal Cushing's own physician. Yes, he had known O'Brien for some time.
He was a man in his fifties, with a history of mental illness. He
had many problems. . . .

From the photographs and various articles of clothing belonging to the Strangler's victims, Peter had described with uncanny
accuracy certain details of the crimes that were known only to
police and medical authorities working on the case. Now he began to come up with a description of the murderer:

"He is not too big, maybe five feet seven, eight . . . high hairline, with a mark or spot on his left arm, something wrong with
his thumb. He has an accent . . . a French accent . . . he has to
do with a hospital . . . he is a homosexual and a woman hater.
He is taking blood and washing his hands in the blood. . . . He
does not do normal work, he is not normal himself. . . . He has
blue-gray eyes, a killer's eyes. . . . His hair is thin, he has a sharp,
pointed, spitzy nose and a big Adam's apple. . . ."

He drew a picture of the murderer for the police, accentuat-
ing the high, receding hairline, the pointed "spitzy" nose, and the
prominent Adam's apple.

He stated that the murderer had the energy of a twenty-six-
or twenty-seven-year-old man but that his actual age was about
fifty-two.

In the file that Peter turned over to me, containing miscellan-
eous documents and material relevant to the Strangler case, are
copies of the official police photographs of the victims (you

need a strong stomach to look at them) and four photos of the man Peter insists is the Boston Strangler. He is a slight man, with a high, receding hairline, a sharp, pointed nose ("spitzy"), and a prominent Adam's apple. On the back of the photographs are the police notations: Name, address; date of birth, 9/10/07, which made his age fifty-seven instead of fifty-two; height, five seven, weight, 123; hair, gray; eyes blue; complexion light; build, slight; remarks: scar on right wrist, scar left forearm.

These photographs, of course, were obtained *after* Peter had pinpointed the man as the Strangler and led the police to him.

Following are additional excerpts from Jim Crane's transcript:

"Peter mentions that the man has a stiff thumb . . . and a scar on his left arm. . . . He has a narrow pointed nose, puffed-up eyes and an Adam's apple that sticks out. He says the murderer often wears glasses but does not need them. [Of the four photographs I have of Peter's Strangler, only one shows him wearing glasses; three show him without.] He says the murderer is or has been an orderly in a hospital, that he is a homosexual and that he washes other men. . . . He has a French accent and is a woman hater and lives in or near a seminary where priests are. He knows that he will be caught and wants to be caught, but also wants to kill again. . . . He has something to do with monks. . . . fat monk with glasses . . . was fired for homosexuality . . . he is a sex pervert. . . .

"Peter also explains that the murderer is a smart intellectual and has had considerable education, that he lives, or has lived in an area where he gets free soup. . . . He loves the Parish . . . but he is dangerous and he loves naked women with open legs. . . . He says this man killed to offer God a sacrifice. He also practices extreme sexual perversion on himself. . . . After he kills, he offers these women to God. He says he offers a clean woman. He did not touch her. He is an angel because he doesn't have intercourse with them—the women he has just killed. . . .

"Peter explains that the murderer washes his hands in the toilet. . . . He sleeps in his clothes, and if there is a bed to sleep on, he takes the mattress off and sleeps on the springs. He wants to torture himself as though there are pins on the springs. . . . He believes that God wants him to do this. He sometimes sleeps naked on pins. Not pointed pins, but on some type of metal which would give pain. This pain is meant to be some type of punishment from God after he has committed a murder. If he does not commit a murder, he sleeps on the mattress on the bed.

"When he kills and goes to bed he takes the mattress off and sleeps on the pins—or springs, like iron. Peter says he sees the killer opening some dresser drawers and he sees shoes in these drawers. Also he sees shoes in a suitcase that is located in a spot in the basement of the building where the murderer lives.

"Peter indicates that these shoes in his room could be his samples which the murderer sells from door to door and also that the shoes in the basement are from the victims which he has killed. He says the reason he has these shoes is because the killer thinks that God cannot accept these victims with shoes on. That since Jesus Christ did not wear shoes that these victims cannot wear shoes either. Therefore, he kills the victims, removes their shoes, and offers them to God as a clean woman. He is mentally sick and he could sell the shoes and deliver the shoes by the nurses. . . ."

I mentioned in an earlier chapter that Peter sometimes talks in his sleep, especially when he is overly tired or under great strain as he was while working on the Boston Strangler case. And just as so many of Edgar Cayce's prophecies and psychic revelations of illness and disease came to him while he was asleep or in trance, so much of what Peter knew about Thomas P. O'Brien was revealed to him in his sleep. Bodyguard Jim Crane, who shared the suite with Peter at the Battle Green Inn and who apparently hovered over him every minute of the day, waking and sleeping, kept his tape recorder going even while Peter was talking in his sleep. Some of it, of course, was incoherent, or incomprehensible. And some was lost in the transcription of the tapes, undoubtedly because of the confusion of voices—Peter's own voice with its heavy and thick Dutch accent, and his "other voice," the high, effeminate voice of the Strangler—and the noises of the flailing around that Peter was also doing while he was sleep talking.

Jim Crane had told Julian Soshnick that Peter sometimes talked in his sleep, and Soshnick and three detectives were present throughout most of one night to witness the amazing dialogue between Peter and the other strange personality that possessed him. I remembered what Peter's father had said, that his real son had died in that fall from the ladder but was reborn and came back with two minds—two minds in one body. I remembered Henry Belk's words, too, that the real Peter died the day of his fall and that he was now a zombie—controlled by some discarnate spirit. Probably at no other time in his career have the two minds in one body, or the discarnate zombie been more in evidence than during Peter's sleep talking on the Strangler case.

From Jim Crane's report:

"At 2:30 A.M. on Monday, February 3rd, 1964, Peter is talking in his sleep. . . . 'Hallo, hallo! Engineer . . . W2DK, W2DK. . . . W-two-D-K, W-two-D-K. . . . Sophia mortica. . . . Sophia mortica. . . . Sophia. . . .'"

(Sophia Clark, a Negro girl, was one of the Strangler's victims. A check with the Berlitz School disclosed that the language Peter was speaking in his sleep was Portuguese. He speaks five languages, but Portuguese isn't one of them. It was later found that Sophia Clark was only half-Negro; her father was Portuguese. And a small ham radio station in New Jersey with the call letters W-2-D-K was owned by a man who turned out to be Sophia Clark's cousin.)

"At 3:24 A.M. February 3, 1964, Peter gets extremely stiff in his horizontal position and says, 'Kill that bastard.' He lifted his fist and doubled it up and strained it to the point where his knuckles turned white. Then he drove his fist into the headboard of the bed to the point where we thought he would damage his hand. . . . The fist is now relaxed. He says: 'You rotten blue eyes. Get out of my mind. I'll kill you.' . . . At 3:45 Peter gets up and goes to the bathroom and when he comes back I ask if he is OK. He says yes, but he asks me once again why he has this power and why he can't get the killer out of his mind. He says that he can't sleep even when he goes to bed and that he dreams peculiar things that he cannot understand. I do the best I can to quiet him down but it isn't seeming to work or do much good so he gets up and walks around the room for five or ten minutes and smokes a couple of cigarettes. He seems extremely tired and

I finally convince him that he should go back to bed and try to sleep. . . . Then while he was asleep his voice changed to that high-pitched effeminate voice and he was carrying on a conversation with the killer. He spoke to the killer in his own voice, and the supposed killer spoke back to him in the killer's voice. For some time both of them talked back and forth. . . ."

Peter's own thick Dutch voice would change to a high, feminine falsetto: "I take the shoes off! Here is the body! I take the shoes off! I undress her! Oh, I go to church, I go to church. I do nothing wrong. I do right: I wash my hands in toilet."

And then back to Peter's own voice, but a voice of anger and disgust. "You call this holy water? For the monks? You're nuts."

Five years after he worked on the case, even the minutest details were still as fresh in Peter's memory as though they had happened only the night before. It was sheer torture for him as he relived them for me, trying to explain exactly how his "gift" worked and how it was possible for him to know about the stranglings and the Strangler.

"Most of it I saw in my sleep," he said. "But I was always working from the clothing and the pictures. I lived through the killings, I lived through the mind from that man. It was so emotional inside. I mean I was living all the cases, so I couldn't sleep. Yes, I was talking in my sleep, but I was overtired. I am working eighteen hours around the clock. The police tell me, 'Peter, why don't you go to bed?' I said, 'I cannot go to bed, I cannot sleep.' And finally overtired, I fell asleep, and I was talking and dreaming.

"The first night I was working with all the pictures. The next night I work also with the pictures, but also with the clothing. I went to bed with clothing from the girls, and this is where I get the key to the murderer. I take a blouse, a nightgown, some clothing from the girls who were killed, and I sleep with it, and that is how I saw the murderer. [Remember, Edgar Cayce slept on his schoolbooks to learn his spelling lessons.] And then I describe the murderer in my sleep, and I hear two voices, my normal voice, and his high voice, and then I was fighting mad. I want to kill him, and the police say I got white and my hand was hurt while I was fighting with the murderer in my sleep."

In his sleep Peter also saw and described the room the killer lived in ("like a junk pile") and the way he slept ("on a cot, on springs, without mattress"), and even more important as a clue, he told police they would find a diary in the man's room which would definitely prove him to be the Strangler.

"When I am sleeping and when I am dreaming, I see the diary and the handwriting. And it's all there in the diary how he gets his satisfaction, how the woman lets him in because she thinks he's a nice man and he is bringing her shoes, and he says let's see if the shoes fit, and then he grab her, most of the time in the back. . . . And then he says to God how strong he is, he doesn't touch her sexually. . . ."

(The police records verified that the Strangler did not have normal sexual relations with his victims but that he satisfied his sexual urge in abnormal ways.)

All of this and more was the picture Peter painted of the Boston Strangler, a kaleidoscope of his psychic impressions from articles of clothing and photographs, from dreams, nightmares, and sleep talking, from a city map of Boston, and from a crumpled lonely-hearts letter to the Boston College School of Nursing from a bachelor named Thomas P. O'Brien.

Further checking by detectives promptly turned up more fascinating facts.

The state police produced a record on O'Brien; as far back as 1962 someone had sent in an anonymous tip on him. A brother had tried to persuade him to commit himself for treatment. O'Brien had briefly been in a monastic order, as Peter had said. He had lived with the Trappist Monks at St. John's Seminary, but the discipline was too much for him. Peter had said, "He was thrown out by the Monks. . . ." It was a French order; many spoke with a French accent, as Peter had said. Its members dressed like priests, they were fed bread and soup. . . . Yes, he had worked as a salesman, a door-to-door salesman of ladies' shoes—more specifically, nurses' shoes.

As one by one all the facts began falling into place exactly as their psychic detective had somehow divined them, the other, nonpsychic, detectives on the case grew more and more tense. They couldn't let a mystic come in and solve their case for them.

It simply couldn't be. What would people think? Yet people were clamoring for the case to be solved—or, more important, for the stranglings to stop. John Bottomly and Julian Soshnick looked at each other in uneasy silence. Then Bottomly assigned his detectives to accompany Peter and call on O'Brien the next day.

Peter had accurately described for them the area, the rooming house, and the tiny "junk pile" room O'Brien lived in. There would be a single cot on the floor, he said, some stacks of dusty books, and a washbasin but no bath. He used the shower and toilet downstairs, Peter told them; and furthermore, he always took his showers with his shoes on.

"Ask the landlady," Peter said. "She tell you."

Peter also assured the detectives that the murderer would not be violent when they went to pick him up. "He knows he will be caught. He wants to be caught. But also he wants to kill again."

The detectives also warned Peter that he was not to touch the man. "Hands off," they said.

"They tell me I am so strong, and they afraid I grab him," he recalled. "They say if he do the murder he be committed, but don't fight, they tell me. I say, what the hell, I would knock the hell out of him, but I promise them I won't do nothing. . . ."

Next morning they set off to find Thomas P. O'Brien. On the way, in the car, Peter kept talking about the killer's eyes. "The killer has funny eyes," he said. "He has killing eyes." They found the address, a dilapidated rooming house, and O'Brien's room was on the third floor. One of the detectives rapped on the door. After a moment the door opened stealthily, only a couple of inches, and the face of a slight, middle-aged, sharp-nosed man with a prominent Adam's apple and pale blue eyes peered out at them.

"Yes?" he queried in a high, effeminate voice.

Peter turned a gray-white in color and started to perspire.

The detective began, "Mr. O'Brien, you wrote a letter to Boston College—"

"I don't want to see anyone," the man said, and slammed the door shut. They could hear him put a chair underneath the knob of the door.

As Peter tells it, "So I go with the police to his room, and when he heard his voice in the door, then the police get scared and say, 'Jesus Christ, that's the voice from you, what you did in your sleep.' And I say, 'Yes, that's him. That's the voice and the killer-blue eyes.' Oh, I want to catch this bastard, but he slammed the door. I tell the police, Jesus Christ, get him out of the room and in a hospital. Then he will confess."

Twenty minutes after they left the rooming house, they were conferring in Bottomly's office on how they could get to O'Brien to question him. There were no criminal charges against him. They couldn't arrest him. But under a state statute, a doctor could commit a person to a mental institution for ten days of observation if circumstances warranted it. Arrangements were made for this.

Meanwhile, Soshnick also obtained a warrant to search O'Brien's room for evidence that might link him with the stranglings.

Back in October 1963, a psychiatric social worker had described O'Brien as a "classic picture of paranoid ideation."

Peter exploded, "Paranoid! What is paranoid? I tell you this man is dangerous. . . ." He couldn't seem to get the man out of his mind. As Jim Crane noted, "The murderer stays with him day and night and he cannot get any sleep. Peter looks very tired and he has dark circles under his eyes."

Peter told Crane, "I can't get it out of my mind. It will drive me crazy. When I finish this case I work no more. No more like this one. I will never work another murder case. It will drive me crazy. I will lose my mind and health."

Crane asked Peter if he thought he might lose control of himself and hit O'Brien if they met again.

"I might, yes," Peter replied. "When I talk to him and see these things that he has done I will hit him. A paranoid doesn't have the guts to go door to door selling shoes. This man is a killer. When he goes to the hospital he will confess. He still wants to be caught."

Early the following morning, Soshnick, accompanied by two detectives and a physician, again went to the rooming house where O'Brien lived. Peter had been instructed to stay behind until they had picked up O'Brien and had him safely out of the house and on his way to the mental hospital. The attorney general's office wasn't taking any chances on Peter's losing his temper and creating a scene—which might result in unfavorable publicity. He was to stay out of sight until given the signal that he could join the search of O'Brien's room. Later, he would be permitted to talk to O'Brien in the hospital—with plenty of guards on hand.

They knocked on O'Brien's door. O'Brien opened it. Soshnick formally introduced himself and the others. "I'm from the attorney general's office. These gentlemen are police officers, and this is a doctor. May we come in?"

"Yes, of course," said O'Brien. Then, in his high-pitched voice, "I'm so glad you came finally." Just as Peter had said. It reminded Soshnick of the notorious lipstick murders in Chicago in the 1940s when the murderer scrawled a message with lipstick on the walls of his victim's apartment: "For heaven's sake catch me before I kill more; I cannot control myself."

Here was the tiny, cluttered room, perhaps eight by ten, as Peter had described it, with cartons and boxes, stacks of books, pamphlets, and paper clippings; and here was the single cot with no mattress—only bedsprings.

Was this the Strangler who stood before them?

He was a small, emaciated-looking man who could not have weighed more than a hundred and thirty pounds, about five feet seven—exactly the height Peter had said. He was in his mid-fifties, effeminate in manner. He stood rather apologetically to one side, nervously rubbing his hands together. It must have been a somewhat nerve-wracking experience for the detectives, too, as they stood looking at the little man and noting that his nose was thin and sharp—"spitzy," as Peter had called it; that on his left arm was a scar—as Peter had said; that the thumb on his right hand was deformed—as Peter had said. Peter had been right in every detail, and as of that moment Boston's hard-bitten criminal investigators had every reason to believe, whether they wanted to or not, that the big dark-eyed Dutch mystic had indeed led them to the real Boston Strangler.

The doctor questioned O'Brien at some length. Yes, he had once tried to get himself committed; he thought he might have blacked out several times. The physician signed the commitment papers on the spot. Minutes later he was on his way to Massachusetts Mental Health Center with O'Brien, while the others were eagerly digging into the piles of clutter in the shoe salesman's room.

As soon as Peter got the signal to join them in the search, he bolted into the room, dropped to his knees, and began crawling about excitedly, snatching papers and pamphlets from the piles of clutter.

Sure enough, they found a penciled diary that dwelt at length on the man's sexual deviations and fetishes; a pamphlet on Yoga with a number of black and white drawings depicting various positions—and with eleven female figures blotted out with India ink (one for each strangling, Peter said); a drawer full of men's scarves and ties tightly knotted, and a note pad with penciled sketches of apartment buildings.

I asked Peter, "By diary, do you mean a regular notebook diary or loose pages?"

"Yes, yes, loose like this. . . . [He picked up a wad of my typing paper and shuffled it.] On white papers all clipped together . . . Handwriting . . . He started from why he's emotional upset. . . . It said in the handwriting, 'Thank you my Lord, that I sleep on a steel mattress and thank you that I have no pain in my foot any more. That I take a shower once in a while with my shoes!"

O'Brien's landlady told the investigators that she knew little about the man except that he never used the mattress and that he took showers with his shoes on, which she thought was a little peculiar.

Entries in the diary corroborated many of Peter's psychic revelations. The entries told how O'Brien had sought to become a Trappist monk nearly twenty years earlier, but had failed. He had tried one job after another but was able to get mainly dishwashing and laundry jobs. Sometimes he sold shoes. "I can't hold a job," he had written. "I have made a shambles of my life."

He also confessed his abnormal impulses in the diary, his struggle to control his "improper acts" and to "master human nature." He admitted in writing that others had called him a "menace," a "disgrace," "a womanish man"; that he had been

At age two with his brother Nico and mother.

A family portrait taken in 1921. From left to right: Peter, Elsa (a German orphan who lived with the family for five years), Allie, Father and Mother.

In front of house where he was born in Dordrecht, Holland. From left to right: brother Nico, Peter, sister Allie, Mother and Father. Picture was taken in 1916 when Peter was five.

In Port Said, 1930. Peter, a ship's
cook at the time, is third from left.

With first wife, Bea, and son
Benny, five months old. Picture
was taken in 1938.

Recent photograph of building in The Hague where Peter was painting when he took his momentous fall in 1941. He fell from the fourth floor as indicated.

In Paris, 1947.

This is the photograph sent out in the publicity kit to the television station for testing Hurkos' psychometric skills. (*Preben*)

With Fabian. Peter helped him find his cat, Silly.
(*Stephany Courtney*)

With Tony Curtis. (*Stephany Courtney*)

With Sheila MacRae. She calls him "a simple man with a complex gift."

With Stephany Courtney. (*Jan Snoids*)

With Norma Lee Browning in Milwaukee, 1963.
(*Russ Ogg*)

With Norma Lee Browning as Nostradamus
and Madame Blavatsky.

*Russ Ogg*

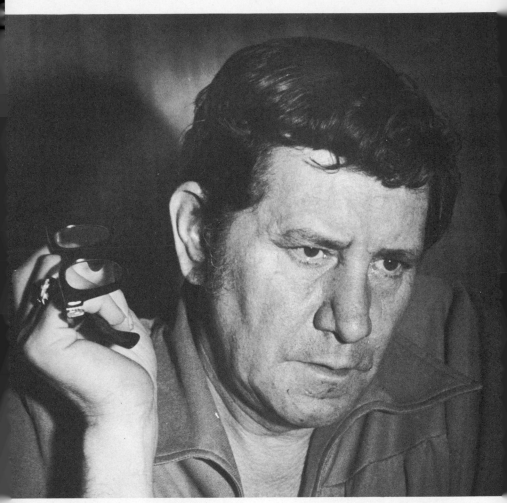

*Stephany Courtney*

*Stephany Courtney*

*Russ Ogg*

advised by a doctor that he needed "nerve treatments," which turned out to be shock therapy, he said. . . .

Before the officers took Peter to the mental hospital to confront O'Brien, they again extracted a promise from him that he would control his temper and not take a punch at his man with the killer-blue eyes. They were frankly worried about Peter's impulsiveness—as well as his strength, which was enormous compared with skinny little O'Brien's. They had seen Peter in action, fighting the murderer in his sleep. Peter could easily kill him. But he told the officers not to worry. They introduced him to O'Brien as another doctor who had come to test him.

"I was very calm, and I put my hand on his shoulder to ask him the questions. And he was very calm," Peter said.

He looked up at Peter and said, "I was waiting for you."

"I know," said Peter. O'Brien apparently recognized him from his accent and from that fast glimpse of his face just before he slammed the door shut on their first visit.

"May I have the file, please?" Peter asked the investigators. They passed him the file, and Peter slowly pulled out photographs of the Strangler's victims, saying, "You have done a very bad thing."

"Yes," O'Brien said, "I must have done a very bad thing, a very bad thing." He seemed in a daze. "But I don't remember it."

"Think," said Peter. "Don't you remember selling shoes to the women, don't you remember that you couldn't see ladies with their legs crossed, and you get panicky, and you want to kill, it was against God."

O'Brien didn't answer. Then Peter said, "You know you cannot lie to us. We have your diary."

At this one of the attorney general's men produced the diary and asked, "Is that your handwriting?"

"Yes, that is my handwriting." There was a tone of relief in O'Brien's voice. He was quizzed about many of the entries in the diary and admitted writing all of them, but when it came to admitting the killings he lapsed into a loss of memory. "Yes, I have done something very wrong, very wrong," he would say when shown the photographs of the victims and pages from his diary. But when questioned specifically regarding the slayings he always came up with the same answer, "I can't remember any more."

He did remember and admit that he had spent an evening with one of the victims, Mary Sullivan, but he insisted that Mary's roommate and another friend were there also. However, he mentioned that Mary's roommate "got tired and went to bed"—and then he became very nervous when this conversation had become a little more detailed and he realized that he had said that he and Mary Sullivan were alone.

When the physician who had questioned him in his room suddenly asked, "Why do you sleep on a steel mattress?," O'Brien asked vaguely, "How do you know that?" Then he said in a womanish whine, "Yes, I have done a wrong thing, very wrong. I was very bad. I think I should stay here. I don't want to go out. I don't want to go back to that place."

Thus ended the official interrogation of Thomas P. O'Brien. Thus did Thomas P. O'Brien, with his "spitzy" nose, his killer-blue eyes, his repugnant fetishes and sexually psychopathic deviations, cleverly eliminate himself from trial on charges of being the Boston Strangler by voluntarily committing himself indefinitely to a mental hospital.

Police apparently found more evidence against him, though no one was telling just what. But when his ten-day commitment expired, doctors recommended thirty-five additional days of observation. And when that ended, O'Brien voluntarily recommitted himself to the institution. He said he needed some rest. He didn't even want to stay with his family or friends (though it was never established that he had any of either). He wanted only to stay in the hospital.

And he is there to this day.

Peter's work was finished. He left Boston and flew to New York. He had worked eighteen hours around the clock without pay.

"Dr. Puharich take me to attorney general's office and ask if I can get my thousand dollars what I have worked for all week, and he said, 'Yes, we send it up.' But I never got the money,"

Peter told me. The newspapers reported that Peter was paid two thousand dollars for his work on the case.

"I think the police were too upset that the attorney general hired me as a psychic. It became a whole political issue. And I am still waiting for that check," said Peter.

There is still absolutely no doubt in his mind that he found the real Boston Strangler. "I have to sleep with myself," he said. "I know DeSalvo is not the guy."

"Did you ever meet DeSalvo?" I asked.

"No, no, never. He was picked up a month later, after I left," Peter said. "But he roommated with O'Brien."

"He what?"

"Oh, yes, they roommated together in the same mental hospital. That is how DeSalvo knows everything to confess."

Why would anyone want to confess to the stranglings? I had asked the same question about the trashman in the Carroll Jackson murders.

In the case of the self-confessed Boston Strangler, Albert De-Salvo once admitted that he enjoyed the publicity from his confessions of the stranglings. Also, there were unconfirmed rumors that he received some of the reward money, which totaled in the neighborhood of $120,000, and used it to send his wife and children back to Germany.

There were numerous suspects in the Boston Strangler case. Thomas P. O'Brien was only one of them. But for a time he seemed to be the most important. Understandably, the attorney general's office and indeed the Commonwealth of Massachusetts were perhaps too anxious and impatient to "get" the Strangler—and possibly therefore too ready to accept the dramatic confessions of Albert DeSalvo. After that they simply lost interest in all previous suspects. All paled by comparison with the boastful and colorful DeSalvo. But four years later the Strangler probe was to be reopened, with statements by public officials that DeSalvo was *not* the Strangler, and in view of this it seems relevant here to take a second and more complete look at Thomas P. O'Brien, whose psychopathic personality, upon close inspection and comparison, fits that of the real Boston Strangler far better than that of the man who claimed credit for the stranglings.

At 3:30 A.M. on February 8, within seventy-two hours after he had left Boston, Peter was roused from sleep in his New York hotel room and arrested on a charge of impersonating an FBI agent.

The incident made headlines across the country and was clearly the work of someone trying to discredit Peter—and/or the attorney general who had brought him in on the case?

According to the published accounts, Peter had allegedly posed as an FBI agent while buying gasoline in a Milwaukee suburb on December 10, 1963—nearly two months previously. He indignantly denied the charge, claiming that it was all a misunderstanding caused by his bad English.

Bottomly and Soshnick, of course, were stunned. They felt that this was really hitting below the belt, that Peter's arrest was inspired either by the Boston police, who had made no secret of what they thought of Peter, or by politics. Some felt that local Democrats had engineered the arrest to embarrass Attorney General Brooke, a Republican, on the eve of his campaign for reelection. Others, according to Gerold Frank, found an even more Machiavellian plot. The Kennedy family, they suggested, might like to see one of their own candidates as Governor of Massachusetts in the near future but would be reluctant to have this come about at the cost of defeating so popular a Negro as Edward Brooke, Jr., if, as appeared possible, Brooke were to be the Republican candidate. It would be far better to trip up Brooke in the attorney general contest now, thus eliminating him as a gubernatorial candidate later. So the theory went.

Charges and countercharges filled the press. One newspaper headlined its story HURKOS FRAMED. Bottomly demanded to know why the FBI hadn't told him they planned to arrest Hurkos; it was a courtesy due the attorney general's office. And why had the arrest taken place at this particular time, on the very heels of Peter's work on the Strangler case—and so long after the alleged offense?

"It took us two hours to find Hurkos in an actor's home in California, yet it took the FBI nearly two months to get their man," Bottomly declared angrily. At the State House rumors flew that the FBI had originally planned an even more spectacular denouement to the Hurkos chapter—to arrest him in the attorney general's office itself—but finally decided this would be going too far. (From Gerold Frank's *The Boston Strangler*.)

And while all the charges and countercharges were going on, Peter was naïvely wondering what all the fuss was about.

"I lose fifteen pounds, and I was a broken wreck. And then I get in jail for no reason," he said. "I never hold anything against the FBI. It was not the FBI's fault. They were just following orders from someone. And when they came to the door, I said, 'Why do you need four guys to arrest me?' They said, 'Peter, you are a tough guy. We don't take any chances.' But they were nice and polite. They didn't put handcuffs on me. And they brought me to jail in a private car. On six o'clock on a Sunday morning. They were very kind. They asked if I would like something to eat, and they explained, 'Peter, we have a note here from Milwaukee that you say you was an FBI man.' I said, 'Oh, no, I never say I am the FBI. I say I am *more* than the FBI.'"

How did it all happen?

"Well, I will tell you exactly the story," he began. "It was the tenth of December. It was snowing at ten o'clock at night, and I went to a gas station. My things were all packed in the trunk of the car—my tape recorders, paintings, and rifles. I collect guns and paintings. I never carry a gun, I don't need to have a gun, I am strong enough to handle myself. But I was just divorced from my wife, and I was cleaning out my house and taking my things to California.

"I have a Lincoln Continental, see, so I stop in a gas station to fill up my tank, and I say to the man, 'It's bad weather,' and he said, 'Yeah, sure is,' and I say I have to go to California and he said, 'Why you going to California?' I tell him I'm gonna live there."

Peter said that when he started to pay the attendant he remembered that his wallet with all his credit cards was in the trunk of the car. He went around and opened the trunk, found his wallet, and gave the station attendant a credit card. The man's eyes popped when he saw the rifles and guns stashed away in the trunk.

"Hey, what are you going to do, hold up a bank?," he asked.

"Don't worry about it, I am working with the police department," Peter said. And he explained to me, "I didn't tell him that I am Peter Hurkos the psychic what works with police on cases, so he got scared from all those guns, and then another smart alec came out and said, 'How can you work with the police department when you have a Lincoln Continental?' And I said, 'That is none of your goddamn business.'"

"Do you have a badge?" the man asked.

Peter has a collection of honorary police badges, many with his name inscribed on them, given to him by police departments of various cities—and countries—where he has worked with the police on crime cases.

There was even more eye-popping when Peter pulled out all his police badges.

"How can you have so many badges? Are you with the FBI?" they asked.

"No. More than the FBI," Peter haughtily replied, and he pulled out of the station without further explanation.

"None of their goddamn business, all my police badges. I work for them, and they are real badges what I got from the police departments," Peter said, still seething over the incident. When he said, "More than the FBI," it was his way of saying he had worked with numerous government officials on various cases, as well as numerous police departments on all governmental levels (city, county, state), and private investigators. In his untutored mind he makes no distinction. I doubt that he even knows what the letters FBI stand for, though he seems sincerely in awe of the Bureau.

In any case, he hadn't endeared himself to the gas station attendants when he told them, "It's none of your goddamn business." Moreover, they obviously believed that his police badges were false, which made them doubly suspicious of his gun collection.

"They think I'm a burglar gonna hold up a bank with all my guns," laughed Peter. "So they report me. But this was two months before they arrest me."

And that is how he wound up in the same New York City

jail where a famous psychic before him, Edgar Cayce, once spent a brief time.

"They tell me this at the police station," he said. "They say Edgar Cayce stay here, very famous psychic. And they give me very good treatment at the jail. They give me cigarettes, let me wear my own clothes. I want you to wrote down that they treat me very nicely."

He spent only nine hours in jail, and was released on bail of twenty-five hundred dollars to Dr. Puharich. Queen Juliana's private attorney, Baron von Haimstrad, also showed up in court next morning, saying he had been asked by the Queen to represent Peter.

Peter declined with thanks. He told the Baron, "No, I am an American citizen now, and I want to be represented by an American attorney, and I did nothing wrong, and I don't have to fear this case, but I thank you and Queen Juliana very much."

The Boston Strangler case, followed so quickly by his highly publicized arrest, had a depressive effect on Peter's health, as well as his reputation. His Hollywood fair-weather friends dropped him like a hot potato when the news of his arrest was blasted from coast to coast. The movie on his life was scuttled. For nearly a year he couldn't work. His wife had divorced him. His friends had deserted him. And to top it all, Albert DeSalvo came forth with his sensational confessions that *he* was the Boston Strangler. Peter began drinking a great deal. He was more tormented than ever with the strange and capricious "gift" that could deceive him so easily. It indeed seemed more a curse than a gift.

He is the first to admit it: "I was no good. I was a broken wreck. It took me many many months to get over that case."

It was during this period that Peter lost a great deal of the respect he had gained in this country for his psychic powers, that some who had believed in him turned against him because of his personal aberrations and his apparent inability to cope with his own problems. It was also during this period that he met Stephy, who helped him back on the right track.

Stephy surprised me with her own little postscript to the Strangler case.

"Do you know that the book *The Boston Strangler* has done more harm than good?" she asked. "Do you know that it is now used as a bible, a blueprint for other crazy people to kill? I know, because when Peter did his last strangling case, the guy had this book in his car and had underlined certain parts of it. . . ."

I didn't know that Peter had worked on other strangling cases —but he had.

Stephy told me of a case in which a man came to Peter for a private consultation and Peter's "gift" told him that the man was a murderer. Instead of letting him know, Peter told him to come back next day for another reading. Then he notified police. Sure enough, the man confessed to strangling two girls. Police found the ropes he had used in the trunk of his car—along with a copy of *The Boston Strangler* with certain sections underlined, especially those pertaining to insanity laws.

"He knew that if he pleaded insanity, he would get out of it. So he kept saying that his subconscious mind did the murders, his conscious mind would never do this," said Stephy. "So they locked him up for six weeks for therapy and then released him. And the doctors feel that now he is over killing people. That is one of the loopholes in our society today—our insanity laws. I mean, it's the biggest cop-out in the world—insanity."

This was Stephy's oversimplified sum-up of what are indeed one of the stickiest flaws in our criminal laws. And nowhere has it been more evident than in the Boston Strangler case.

The two principal suspects in the Boston stranglings, Thomas P. O'Brien and Albert DeSalvo, were obviously mentally ill. It is perhaps significant that O'Brien, in Peter's mind the real Strangler, voluntarily chose to remain in a mental institution, his own inner sanctum immune from the law.

As for DeSalvo, he had been in and out of jails and mental hospitals for years. He had a long history of sexual assaults on women, because of what his own wife described—and he admitted —as an insatiable sexual appetite, but he was not at all the same kind of abnormal sexual deviate as O'Brien.

And therein lies the crucial difference between the two principal suspects in the Boston Strangler case—for anyone who takes the trouble to compare them.

Everything in the actual records of the case indicates that the real Boston Strangler was truly a breed apart. Though he made sexual assaults upon women, they were not the normal kinds of sexual assault. There is no evidence that he had raped any of his victims or had normal sexual relations with them. In each case—and they all followed a pattern—he had obtained his own sexual satisfaction while assaulting them sexually with such objects as bottles and brooms.

Albert DeSalvo's relations with women were admittedly excessive—but normal. That is, if one can consider a dozen rapes a day normal. The important distinction is that DeSalvo preferred having his sex in the normal man-woman way, whereas the real Strangler's sex habits were obviously those of a twisted, bestial, demented mind—and a woman hater, not a woman lover. The real Albert DeSalvo loved women, or at least he loved his sexual conquests of them.

He boasted freely of his sexual escapades to his cellmates in jails and mental hospitals. Once he admitted to his wife, "I've broken into houses, and I've done some very bad things with women, but I never killed anybody." Everyone who knew him knew of his sexual prowess, his problems with the police, and his boasting. At one point he bragged to detectives, "I've committed more than four hundred breaks, all in this area—and there's also a couple of rapes you don't know about."

And typically, when he decided to take credit as the Boston Strangler, he even upped the number of victims. He confessed not only to murdering the eleven women attributed to the Strangler but to killing two more—though he couldn't recall the exact dates or details of them. Significantly, the official records, case histories, and photographs of the Strangler's victims stop with Mary Sullivan, the eleventh victim, and the last one before Peter Hurkos was brought in on the case. It was widely publicized that there were thirteen victims of the Boston Strangler, but this doesn't square with the police records. Were the two extras merely figments of DeSalvo's braggart imagination?

Everyone who knew Albert DeSalvo was amazed when, while awaiting trial on charges of rape and breaking and entering, he suddenly announced that *he* was the Boston Strangler. His wife knew that he could not be the Strangler. When would he have had time to commit all those crimes? He hadn't been out of jail long enough.

But why would he confess to them? Perhaps it was revenge against her because she had left him and would not answer the letters he wrote her from Bridgewater, the state mental hospital where he was awaiting trial. Perhaps it was only that he wanted to be important. She knew that was why he always lied, bragged, and made up stories. (He once corrected police, who said he had sexually assaulted three hundred women. They underestimated him, he said. It was closer to eight hundred or a thousand.)

She also knew there was a tremendous amount of money involved, a huge reward for the Strangler, and Al was always chasing an easy buck. But would he get the reward if he confessed? She was puzzled.

While he was in Bridgewater, DeSalvo had let it be known to anyone who would listen that he had done something "bigger than the Brink's robbery"—that he was the Strangler. His lawyer asked if he had committed all the murders or only some of them. He said all of them and added that he thought his story might bring some money to support his wife and children. "But I don't want to die for it," he said.

It was at this point that F. Lee Bailey came onto the scene. Bailey was the Boston attorney who had become nationally known when he obtained the release from prison of Dr. Sam Sheppard, the Cleveland osteopath convicted of killing his wife ten years before. It was Bailey, who armed with a Dictaphone, obtained DeSalvo's sensational confessions in detail.

Then came the job of either proving or disproving DeSalvo's claims to the multiple murders. The attorney general's officers went to Bridgewater to interrogate him. But because he was a mental patient, his rights were scrupulously protected. He agreed to tell all, but nothing could be used against him in court, a rather curious arrangement. The confessions went on for weeks. Then followed months of legal sparring.

And finally the trial—but on charges that had nothing to do with the stranglings.

It was a brief trial, beginning January 10 and ending on January 18, 1967. The charges against him were breaking and entering, assault and battery, armed burglary, and "unnatural and lascivious acts" against four women in the Boston suburbs.

It was F. Lee Bailey's hope to win a verdict of not guilty by reason of insanity—and as proof of insanity to put into evidence DeSalvo's long confession of the thirteen stranglings. But it didn't work out that way—and it was Bailey's first defeat in a series of sensational court victories. The court refused to allow any evidence relating to the stranglings, or any testimony from Bottomly or others who worked on the Strangler Case.

The judge admonished, "He is not on trial in this court for homicide."

Psychiatrists for the state agreed that DeSalvo was mentally ill and dangerous but contended that he knew right from wrong at the time he committed his crimes.

An all-male jury, after deliberating less than four hours, found DeSalvo guilty as charged. He was sentenced to life imprisonment for armed robbery, to be served after he completed a nine-to-ten-year sentence on the other charges.

DeSalvo was returned to Bridgewater State Hospital pending the result of an appeal, escaped from the hospital five weeks later, but finally turned himself in and was taken back to Bridgewater.

F. Lee Bailey appealed the case to the State Supreme Judicial Court. The appeal was rejected. DeSalvo was transferred to the Walpole State Prison and has been there ever since, in the prison infirmary, apart from the rest of the inmate population at the institution.

## BOSTON STRANGLER: POSTSCRIPT

So far as Peter Hurkos was concerned, the curtain had rung down on the case of the Boston Strangler.

But has it?

On February 16, 1968, four years after Peter's assignment in Boston with its disheartening denouement, the Boston newspapers announced that the new attorney general, Elliott L. Richardson, had reopened the special bureau investigating the so-called Boston stranglings of 1962–64 because of "new information" concerning Albert DeSalvo the self-styled Boston Strangler.

It seemed that DeSalvo, serving his life sentence in the state prison at Walpole on his other charges, was now "ready to talk" further about the stranglings, and might even confess them to a grand jury.

But District Attorney John J. Droney apparently took a dim view of reopening the case.

"It's incredible how this man can dictate to the Commonwealth," he said. "He's now complaining he doesn't like it at Walpole, and he's masterminding another trial. He would hope to be found not guilty by reason of insanity, and then make a quick recovery."

Droney made it clear that he wanted no part in the plan to reopen a probe and that DeSalvo should "be left to vegetate in State Prison where he belongs.

"There is no public clamor to put this man on trial for the strangulation deaths. DeSalvo himself is the producer and the director of his latest episode and he's making all the arrangements —what he will say and when he will say it. . . . Let us not squander any more money on this man who is out of the way for the rest of his life and no longer a menace to the public."

Droney said he was far more interested in getting to the bottom of the "drab performance" of certain state's investigators who were turning over all their information "to the man who wrote the book on the Boston Strangler and to those who are making a movie of it.

"And I'm going to keep on insisting that Lee Bailey explain what he meant when he said after DeSalvo's conviction that the Commonwealth had double-crossed his client," Droney avowed.

"Who promised DeSalvo what? This would be a serious offense challenging the integrity of the Commonwealth. I'm going to keep on insisting what promises were made by whom," he told a reporter for the Boston *Globe* (February 17, 1968).

On February 24 it was announced that all taped recordings of conversations between DeSalvo and former state officials had been taken from a bank vault and turned over to the office of the attorney general, as part of the plan to reopen the probe into the Boston stranglings—in spite of Droney's resistance.

But Droney suddenly changed his mind after newspapers carried a story on February 28 that a convict named George W. Harrison had charged that DeSalvo was not the *bona fide* Boston Strangler, that he had been tutored for the role by an inmate at Bridgewater State Hospital. He said he had overheard some fifteen to twenty conversations between DeSalvo and the inmate, and according to his story, the unidentified inmate presumably was the real strangler. Harrison was one of two inmates who had escaped with DeSalvo from the Bridgewater mental hospital. He claimed that the real strangler was a fellow inmate at Bridgewater who had been considered a suspect "hot as a pistol" in the investigation of the murders. But state officials had dropped their interest in him when DeSalvo "confessed" the murders.

District Attorney Droney had interviewed Harrison in prison and said he placed enough credence in his story to warrant scheduling a lie detector test for him. Harrison said he was willing to take the test to prove his allegation that DeSalvo was not the real Boston Strangler.

Meanwhile, Droney made another public announcement: "We have information from authentic sources that before all the television, the movies and the books came out about the Boston Strangler, DeSalvo said he had never hurt anyone." He said he was convinced that DeSalvo was not the Strangler, and that he was "play acting," an opinion shared by psychiatrists and correctional officers at Bridgewater.

Lie detector tests were scheduled for both George W. Harrison and Albert DeSalvo, who had said he was "ready to talk" and "tell all."

Then suddenly, on April 25, 1968, a surprise announcement from the office of Attorney General Richardson, the man who reopened the Strangler probe, said that the probe was being officially closed—permanently—owing to the inability of psychiatrists to agree whether or not DeSalvo was competent to undergo lie detector tests and interrogation.

It was disclosed that three days before DeSalvo was scheduled to take the lie detector test and be questioned, he "inflicted superficial wounds on his right forearm with a razor blade." As a result, the psychiatrists could not agree that he was mentally competent, and the state was forced to cancel the test and interrogation.

Thus the Strangler probe that had been reopened in February came to an abrupt end two months later, officially closing the book on Albert H. DeSalvo as the alleged Boston Strangler. Presumably this rang down the final curtain on the investigations into DeSalvo's claims that he was the Boston Strangler.

But it left many unanswered questions in the minds of many who had worked on or are familiar with the case.

One of the most important is, Was it only a coincidence that the Boston Strangler probe was reopened and then closed abruptly at precisely the same time (February–April, 1968) movie cameras were rolling in Boston for *The Boston Strangler?*

Why had DeSalvo at first been "ready to talk," to "tell all," and then suddenly changed his mind? Did someone change it for him? Why did he slash his wrists—and especially with only "superficial wounds"? Because he knew this would get him off the hook and he wouldn't have to take the lie detector test? What scared him off? Possibly the charges of convict George Harrison and *his* willingness to take the lie detector test? Possibly the knowledge that indeed he was not what he claimed to be—the Boston Strangler?

There are those who like to remind us, "But there have been no more stranglings in Boston." But is this because DeSalvo is behind prison bars—or because Thomas P. O'Brien is in a mental institution? Both have been stashed away for some time now, and are no longer a menace to the public. And I would be inclined to agree with District Attorney Droney: Why squander any more of the public's money—on either of them?

Still, it is one of the most fascinating whodunits of modern times, and in fairness to all whodunit fans, as well as to all believers in psychic phenomena and most of all to Peter Hurkos, whose chronicler I am, it would be gratifying to see the Boston Strangler case come to a more satisfactory conclusion. I checked with newsmen in Boston who worked on the case. It is their consensus that DeSalvo is not the real Boston Strangler and that the case will one day be reopened.

The case is unique in criminal history. Neither DeSalvo nor O'Brien—nor anyone else for that matter—has ever been formally charged with any of the murders. The only official comment from anyone in authority is that DeSalvo has remained "a suspect." Nothing more. Other than his own boastful confessions, no one was ever able to come up with one shred of evidence that he was the Strangler.

And to anyone who studies the case carefully, with specific attention to the clinical details of the crimes which indicate definite psychosexual abnormalities, the character of Albert De-Salvo simply doesn't fit that of the Strangler. I would say this even if I had never heard of Peter Hurkos or his own hand-picked man, Thomas P. O'Brien. Being a Missouri-born show-me skeptic, I wouldn't presume to say which of the suspects was the Strangler. I'm only a reporter, not a psychic. And having covered a few murders myself, I know how easy it is to be so sure—and then be so wrong!

I have tried to present here an objective and carefully re-searched picture of Peter's role in the Boston Strangler case. Although I cannot say with the same strong certainty as he does that he got the "right guy," I certainly would bet my last sweet bippy that DeSalvo is the "wrong guy." And I must say that of all the other suspects I was introduced to in my research (only on paper, of course), the one known as Thomas P. O'Brien seems to fit the psychopathic character of the actual Boston Strangler better than any of the others. Whether he's the right guy or the wrong guy, only the most muleheaded nonbeliever would deny that Peter's psychic performance on this one was quite remarkable.

Yet in the public's mind Albert DeSalvo *is* the Boston Strangler, an impression even more solidified now with the release of the movie—and in spite of new evidence that he was *not* the Strangler. Remember, the movie cameras were just beginning to roll in Boston in February, 1968, when the Strangler probe was reopened. But with ten million dollars at stake and Tony Curtis as their Strangler, you certainly cannot expect the movie makers to admit they've got the wrong guy, now can you?

# · 8 ·

# The Jim Thompson Case

On Easter Sunday, 1967, a wealthy American, Jim Thompson, known as the Thai Silk King of Bangkok, suddenly vanished, totally and mysteriously, into the Malaysian jungle, leaving behind a tangle of international mystery and intrigue surpassing even that of the celebrated Judge Crater case.

A year later *The New York Times Magazine* published an article, "Is Jim Thompson Alive and Well in Asia?," by William Warren, a teacher at Bangkok University, reporting that there had been no letup of interest in the case and giving credence to some rather remarkable things turned up by Peter Hurkos, including his astonishing pronouncement that Jim Thompson had been abducted and was alive and being held captive in Cambodia.

James H. W. Thompson was a former architect from Wilmington, Delaware, who first went to Thailand during the war as an army colonel in the Office of Strategic Services (OSS), which was a predecessor to the CIA. His postwar military duties took him traveling all over the Thailand frontiers, where he saw dazzling specimens of Siamese silks, then a dying art. He became fascinated by the old and worn samples in Siamese costumes, homes, and temples, and soon began collecting odd bits of Siamese silks as a hobby. His interest at first was purely esthetic, but he decided to try to revive this long-lost art of the Siamese people and suddenly found himself wrapped up in the textile business on an international scale.

Over the years, Jim Thompson had become something of a legend in Southeast Asia. He had become wealthy from his business in Thai silk. His elegant home, with its gardens and its fabulous collection of Asian antiques, was one of the showplaces of Bangkok. He also had gained fame as a host to a wide variety of guests—world-traveling celebrities, politicians, and Thai officials. There had been rumors that he was still involved in army intelligence. After his disappearance, these rumors were revived with an interest livelier than ever before.

His circle of friends encompassed people of varying pursuits and professions. On that Easter weekend in 1967, Jim Thompson and a friend, Mrs. Connie Mangskau, a Thai businesswoman, had come from Bangkok via Penang to be houseguests of Dr. and Mrs. T. G. Ling of Singapore, who owned a summer bungalow in the Cameron Highlands of northern Malaysia. The setting was a picturesque one. The Lings's bungalow was romantically named Moonlight Cottage, and it reposed on a hill above and away from the main part of the Highlands resort. It was from Moonlight Cottage that Jim Thompson mysteriously disappeared on Easter Sunday afternoon, March 26, 1967.

Thompson had planned to go on to Singapore on Monday for a series of business meetings, but he was looking forward to spending a quiet and restful weekend with his friends. They had gone on a picnic on Easter Sunday, and upon returning to the bungalow, the Lings and Mrs. Mangskau decided to take a nap. Thompson said he was going to sit on the terrace in the sun.

It was approximately 3:30 P.M. when Dr. Ling heard footsteps on the veranda and remarked to his wife that Thompson had probably decided to take a walk.

Were the footsteps those of a solitary person?

As far as anyone knows, this was Thompson's last walk.

When he did not return by nightfall, the Lings notified authorities, and the search began. Had be become lost in the jungle? This hardly seemed likely, for he had had expert jungle training while in the army, and he was known to have a good sense of direction. A package of his cigarettes was found on the terrace.

Did he plan to return shortly; or since he was known to be trying to break the habit, did he leave the cigarettes behind deliberately? Had he suddenly become ill and was thus unable to make his way back to Moonlight Cottage? Seemingly he was in perfect health that weekend, so that appeared unlikely.

The case of the vanishing Jim Thompson, the Thai Silk King, touched off one of the largest manhunts in the history of the area. The official search lasted ten days, involved more than three hundred people, attracted headlines around the world, and produced, ultimately, not a single clue to his whereabouts. It was then, as William Warren has pointed out, that the Thompson case entered its bizarre phase and rapidly gained intrigue.

Southeast Asia is a country where *bomohs*, or witch doctors, are still very much a reality and the occult arts have an established and respected place in the lives of the people. The *bomohs* came forward with a variety of theories about the fate that had befallen Jim Thompson. One said he was in the hollow of a big tree. Another said he was being held captive in a hut by a blonde nightclub singer.

In late April the local *bomohs* began getting some stiff competition from Peter Hurkos, who had been hired by James H. Douglas of Chicago to assist in locating the whereabouts of Jim Thompson. Mrs. Douglas was one of Jim Thompson's sisters.

As mentioned earlier in this book, I had met Peter again in Hollywood—after a few years of being out of touch—at a celebrity party, and he had told me then of his latest assignment, that he was leaving soon to work on the Jim Thompson case. At the time, I really didn't take him seriously. We had a happy, hilarious time that night, and I wished him *bon voyage,* chortling privately in my vodka gimlet, wondering who in heaven's name could be so naïve as to hire a Dutch psychic to help find the missing Thai Silk King of Bangkok—and little knowing that I would soon be enmeshed in writing Peter's life story, which of course must include his work on the Jim Thompson case.

I now regard it as a rather eerie coincidence that long before I had ever heard of Peter Hurkos, I knew Jim Thompson, who was to play the leading role in one of the most intriguing espionage-mystery thrillers that Peter would ever work on.

My mind backtracked to the summer of 1955, when my husband and I first visited Bangkok and met Jim Thompson. He was a tall, tropical-tanned man who might pass for an American cowboy. Each morning about eight, he bounced down some rickety steps and into a narrow sampan, crossed a muddy canal on the outskirts of the city, and disappeared into a labyrinth of Siamese shanties clustered along the riverbank. This is the part of Bangkok that looks like Tobacco Road on stilts—or it did then. None would have guessed that from such an unglamorous setting came some of the world's most glamorous and exotic fabrics, those twenty-dollars-and-up-a-yard Thai silks that have draped America's highest-paid fashion models, Broadway and Hollywood actresses, socialites, and anyone else who could afford them.

Ever since the cast of *The King and I* blossomed out on Broadway in Siamese silks, lo so many years ago, the rush has been on. Women's fashions and men's wallets have felt the impact.

And the man responsible for it all was an American bachelor in Bangkok, a former army colonel who once would barely have known the difference between a silkworm and a strapless sheath.

When we met Jim Thompson his business even then seemed to be booming, but it was only the beginning. We spent some time with him at the shop and in his fabulous home, and we went with him as he made the morning rounds of the weavers.

At that time there were no silk factories as such in Bangkok. The Siamese women worked at looms in their own homes. In the canal village that housed the bulk of Bangkok's silk weavers, there once were only two looms operating. When we were there in 1955, there were two hundred and uncountable hundreds more in country provinces throughout Thailand. There were then more than a dozen silk shops in Bangkok supplying the rich and colorful silks to four distributing companies in America—and the business was only in its infancy.

Thompson had fully expected to go back to his work as an architect in New York after the war, but on a trip home a good friend suggested that he show his collection of Siamese silk "souvenirs" to the editors of *Vogue*. Women's fashions were not in his line, but to please his friend, he dropped in at the *Vogue* offices, and the next thing he knew someone was ooh-ing and aah-ing and asking how soon he could start producing this gorgeous stuff by the bolt.

Thompson suddenly found himself in the silk business, without any silks. He went back to Bangkok and began trying to round up weavers. That was in 1948. The Siamese were accustomed to weaving the exotic silks only for their personal use. Persuading them to do it on a commercial scale was no minor chore. Thompson lost his shirt, and made no profit at all the first two years. But he learned a lot. He learned about warps, wefts, dyes, and silkworms. (The silkworms for Thai silks are raised in northern Siam.) He learned about degumming raw silk, and he learned about colors. He became such an expert on color dyes for Thai silks that he was given a year's appointment by the Burmese government as a consulting dye specialist to Burmese weavers, to help boost their export trade.

Thompson would spend his mornings making the rounds, trying to keep his weavers working (they would weave only when there was nothing more interesting to do—one of the reasons for the high price tags on Thai silks), helping them with color charts and dyes, picking up what they had finished, and ordering as much more as they could produce.

Afternoons he spent in his shop on Suriwongse Road taking care of customers, or in conference with the Queen's dressmaker, helping her plan a new royal wardrobe. Meanwhile, he was picking up enough elementary knowledge of fashions to answer simple questions from tourists who began beating a path to his door.

In 1955, Jim Thompson had not yet grown rich. He was one of thirty-two stockholders in his silk company and drew a salary of ten thousand ticals a month, or about five hundred dollars— a pittance compared with what he might have been earning if he had stayed in New York as an architect.

At the time, Thompson told me that he did not expect to spend the rest of his life in Bangkok. But he admitted that he found it difficult to break away from an oriental niche that offered more challenge than money, and more outlet for his artistic talents than architecture.

Soon the company he had founded was doing a business of over $1.5 million a year; approximately 150 other independent companies started operation; and silk became Thailand's major export.

By 1967 Jim Thompson had earned a fortune, a host of friends, and an international reputation as the Thai Silk King. Why should he suddenly vanish without a trace or a clue?

Grasping at straws, Thompson's sister in Chicago, Mrs. Douglas, persuaded her husband to contact Peter. A letter from Douglas to Peter Hurkos, dated April 14, 1967, says in part:

> "Dear Mr. Hurkos:
>
> "In accordance with our conversation, you have undertaken to go to Bangkok and to Cameron Highlands area of Malaysia to search for my brother-in-law, James H. W. Thompson, of Wilmington, Delaware, and Bangkok, and for information and any possible clues as to his disappearance."

(His next paragraph stipulated the financial agreement.)

> "I enclose a brief summary of information on James Thompson's disappearance; also a description of the terrain around Cameron Highlands and a map of the area. As indicated in the summary, the search carried on was one of great intensity. I might say that parties, in addition to covering the area around Cameron Highlands, are understood to have covered streams in the area for some distance.
>
> "I am giving you three letters [to government, military, and U. S. Embassy officials]. . . ."

Armed with these letters of introduction, tape recorders, and cameras, Peter and Stephany, acting as his assistant and secretary, left on April 19, 1967, for Bangkok.

The plane refueled in Tokyo, and they had their reservations changed so that they might stop in Hong Kong, where Peter wanted to "check out" the Red Chinese border for possible clues. They hired a private car and drove to the border. Peter left the car and, holding a photograph of Jim Thompson, paced up and down for half an hour. He felt nothing, although he remarked to Stephy that he did not think Thompson had been either to Hong Kong or to Red China.

They dispatched a note to Brigadier General Black, a friend of Thompson's who had aided in the official search, informing him that they would be arriving on April 21 and would check into the Rama Hotel in Bangkok.

Just as Jim Crane had followed practically every movement and word of Peter's with a tape recorder, capturing the blow-by-blow account of the Boston Strangler case, so Stephy too tagged along like a shadow with her tape recorder and subsequently wrote an eighty-page report, titled "The Thompson Case . . . What Peter Hurkos Saw and Did!," which they submitted to the Douglases.

When Peter arrived at Thompson's house in Bangkok, he first walked about the grounds, then went inside, checking each room. He entered the guest bedroom and said:

"I see that General Black has slept here. Sukarno was also here, and there have been a great number of important people having meetings in here." As he moved into the dining room he said that many important people had also dined there.

"Thompson was playing with hot fire, sometimes associating with the wrong people; he is very well liked and he just didn't realize . . ."

He continued his tour of the house silently.

The following day he met with General Black, who offered assistance in any way Peter might deem necessary. If it was a question of ransom money, he told Peter, he would be able to obtain that, along with any troops that might prove necessary. He suggested, however, that Peter notify him if there were Communist implications, so that the matter could be handled on a higher level. He also gave Peter a list of persons whom he thought should be contacted during Peter's stay in the Cameron Highlands.

On April 24, Peter and Stephy arrived at Moonlight Cottage. Here again, Peter first walked around the grounds; then he toured the bungalow with a photograph of Thompson in his hand. He then gestured toward a chair on the veranda and said, "This is the chair Thompson last sat on!" And as though to confirm his own statement, he felt the chair and said, "Yes, this is the chair." He sat down on the chair a few moments, then took another quick look around the cottage, came back to the veranda, and sat down, still holding Thompson's photograph in one hand and some maps of the area in the other. He seemed to be in a kind of trance, or a state of deep meditation.

Then the words began tumbling out of his mouth. What he "saw," as William Warren put it in his *New York Times Magazine* piece, "was enough to entrance the most jaded espionage-fiction fan."

The following is a verbatim excerpt from Stephy's tape transcript of what Peter said:

". . . Ah, Prebi oogh. . . . Thompson . . . Prebi, Pridi . . . fourteen people . . . fourteen people captured him. . . . Prebe or Bebe . . . ora blunda Bebe? (Speaking to trackers in Malaysian.) He is not in this jungle. . . . I want to follow the route where they picked him up. . . . He was sitting right there . . . this chair (pointing). . . . There was nobody here except him. . . .

"Everyone was upstairs (pointing into the house). . . . There was nobody in the room (pointing to the living room). . . . They were upstairs. . . . He was sitting outside in this chair. . . . Fourteen people . . . one vehicle, like military vehicle, like a truck. . . . I see trucks . . . ah, truck, about from here on the road he walks down the road. . . . He was resting. . . . Somebody wake him up. . . . A friend of his, Bebe or Prebie. Or Pridi? He has his own army . . . nothing to do with bandits. . . . He walks about half a mile with Bebe or Prebie. . . . A truck is on the road, waiting. . . . Fourteen people. . . . Yes, only one person picked Thompson up, and he knows him. He was sitting on the veranda, and the man came in from here (pointing to the driveway which enters from the road). . . .

"Then they went down the road to the truck. . . . Now they get morphine . . . morphine. . . . He sleep in the truck. You can check sixty miles and you won't find any trace of Thompson. . . . No track at all. . . . There is morphine in the truck, and then it is moving away. . . ."

At this point Peter took a break. After a cup of coffee and a brief rest, he continued his revelations, repeating, in essence, that Thompson was sitting alone on the veranda when a man named Bebe or Prebie or Pridi, who was known to him, came up to him, and after shaking hands, they walked down the road together. Peter then got up and began walking down the road, with everyone following in suspenseful silence. He suddenly stopped at a spot and said, "This is it. He was picked up here. . . . And around the corner was the truck. . . ."

Then Peter went over to the side of the road and sat down and drew in the dirt the route he saw that the truck had taken.

The truck took the long way down the hill instead of the short way. . . . This way is longer but less people will notice the truck. . . . I'm not sure but either they doped him up by giving him morphine or they put something over his face which made him go to sleep fast."

Peter insisted that there were fourteen men involved. . . . "One man picked him up. . . . Mr. Thompson walked with this man, Bebe or Prebie. He's a friend of Thompson. Prebie is about seventy-two or seventy-three years old. Thompson knows this person, but there were thirteen left in the truck. He was picked up by fourteen men all total. . . . But he is not in the jungle."

The next question, of course, was where was he?

Peter took another break to try to clear his mind. Then said: "Cambodia . . . There he is . . . I see him in Cambodia. He was not picked up by bandits for ransom. This has only to do with politics. He was put into the truck; I'm not sure if it is a green truck or a black truck, but it looks like an army truck. They took the long way down the hill. . . . They dope Thompson, and from the truck they put him on a plane, and the plane went to Cambodia. . . . Yes, he is alive, but it is not necessary to check in the jungles for Thompson. . . .

"I see Thompson walking down the road with this man, Bebe or Prebie . . . then I see them stopping, and I see the man pulling something out of his pocket like a handkerchief, which he quickly put over Mr. Thompson's face. . . . I then see Mr. Thompson falling back and the other man catching him while motioning to a truck, which quickly pulled up, and a couple of men jumped down from the back of the truck dressed in army uniforms. I see them lifting Thompson up into the truck, and then the truck makes a U-turn and drives off down the hill. . . ."

Peter's revelations caused a small diplomatic uproar. I developed that Jim Thompson did indeed know a man named Pridi, one of his political friends from the past. His name was Pridi Phanamyong, and he had served several times as prime minister of Thailand.

Peter was told that Pridi was the man who helped promote the *coup* ending the absolute monarchy in Thailand. Thompson had become friendly with him while working for the OSS. At that time Pridi was working in the underground and planning the *coup*. It was rumored that he also had something to do with the murder of a high official about that time. Anyway, Pridi did not last long in power. He was exiled in 1949 and fled to China, where he was still, as far as anyone knew. His wife and children had escaped to Paris, where they were still living, Peter was told.

Peter, of course, wanted to go immediately to Cambodia and bring Jim Thompson back alive, and for a while it looked as though arrangements might be made for him to enter as a tourist, although no government officials would be able to go along, as diplomatic relations between the United States and Cambodia were strained, to say the least. Cables flew back and forth between Bangkok and Washington, but in the end the plans were called off—for reasons never explained—and Peter, in bitter disappointment, returned to the States, angrily threatening to take up the matter with President Johnson. He, of course, never did.

But he still feels strongly that Jim Thompson is still alive and still in Cambodia. He still feels that the abduction was a strictly political maneuver, and that if he were allowed to go into Cambodia, he would be able to aid in getting Thompson out.

Strangely, in February of 1969, *Women's Wear Daily* carried an item that Jim Thompson reportedly was still alive and had been seen by someone in Asia; where it wasn't specified. And when I tried personally to check the item out with *WWD*, I got the brush-off. Why?

Some who were close to the case have suggested that Thompson might have been kidnaped as part of a Communist plot to end the American bombing of North Vietnam. The theory is that the enemy, knowing of Thompson's prominence, was trying to force him to denounce the Thai government for allowing American planes to fly bombing missions out of Thailand.

A tragic and puzzling epilogue was the murder of Jim Thompson's eldest sister, Mrs. Katherine Thompson Wood, only a few months after Thompson's mysterious disappearance. Mrs. Wood was found savagely beaten to death in her house near Philadelphia a few days before Labor Day. Mrs. Wood was divorced from the son of Major General Leonard Wood (for whom Fort Leonard Wood was named) and lived alone. It was believed that she, too, knew her murderer, for he had not forced his way into her house, and he apparently had not been attacked by her watchdogs. Nothing was taken from the house. There were no clues, and the case was never solved.

Peter believes, as do many others, that there is a link between the two mysteries.

There is still a great deal of speculation on Jim Thompson's whereabouts. The *bomohs* still send their speculative reports to the Thai Silk Company, as do other well-meaning and some not so well-meaning individuals. No reports yet have been as descriptive or as thorough as the findings of Peter Hurkos. No one else has been able to name places or names. Although no concrete evidence has yet turned up to support his theory, neither has there been any to disprove it. And it must be admitted that his preoccupation with the "Bebe or Prebe or Pridi" names was rather spine-chilling, considering Jim Thompson's onetime acquaintance with the ex-prime minister.

If Peter should be correct about Jim Thompson, some questions arise:

Why wasn't Peter allowed to enter Cambodia? Is Thompson being held against his will, possibly by Communists? Why has the man Pridi, who figures so prominently in the case, been so unavailable? He has never been located for questioning.

If Thompson is alive, the answers might lie with him, and finding him would be the only way of solving the mystery. If he is dead, the answers to these and other questions might have died with him.

Peter worked long and hard on the Jim Thompson case. He

was stopped short of what he thought was his goal. Until he is permitted to finish his mission, in Cambodia, or unless Jim Thompson turns up somewhere else in the meantime, no one can say yet that Peter Hurkos failed in his efforts.

Somewhere there *is* someone who knows exactly what happened when those footsteps were heard on the veranda of Moonlight Cottage on Easter Sunday afternoon of 1967. And if that someone should read this, perhaps someday we'll know whether Peter saw it the way it happened to Jim Thompson.

# · 9 ·

# *Hurkos in Hollywood*

Peter was first lured to Hollywood in the spring of 1960 for an Alcoa TV special, "One Step Beyond," based on his own extraordinary experiences as a psychic. It was produced by Collier Young, and it was the beginning of Peter's reputation as a celebrity's celebrity in a town that needs an occasional offbeat celebrity to impress the film celebrities—because normally actors are awed only by themselves. A man like Peter breaks the monotony of it all.

Marlon Brando was one of the first to be awed, and to use the vernacular, that ain't easy, baby!

Marlon had met Peter at Collier Young's house. A complete skeptic, he asked Peter if he was willing to be tested—by Mr. Himself of course. Peter doesn't mind being tested by anybody. The more the merrier. The next evening Marlon returned with his own carefully concealed test objects reposing in two separate boxes that he had wrapped and rewrapped many times. Brando was not taking any chances. He passed the packages over to Peter and sneered in his best method style. "You think you can tell me what's inside them?"

Peter held the packages, rubbing his hands over them, first one and then the other, and concentrating intensely. Finally he said, "I see a fire or an explosion. On the sea. You, sir, have here a golden spike, a nail from a ship." He paused. "And in this package you have a letter, and I am sorry to tell you, sir, but the spelling is lousy."

He was right. Or almost. In one box was a nail—copper, not golden—from the original H.M.S. *Bounty*. In the other was a letter from a psychiatrist friend of Brando's who clearly wasn't the world's best speller. Brando was then making the movie *Mutiny on the Bounty*. But he had told no one about the nail. He was astounded.

Brando promptly joined the Hurkos cult and became one of Peter's biggest boosters—and clients. Through the years he has consulted him frequently on business and personal matters, including his affairs of the heart.

Peter obviously fills a need in Hollywood, a veritable lotusland for all sorts of gurus. His particular talent runs a broad spectrum uniquely suited to Hollywood. The stars consult him as they would an astrologer, an attorney, a psychoanalyst, a psychotherapist, a tea-leaf reader, the police department, Ann Landers, or the Delphic oracle. Some regard him as a terribly entertaining spook. Others seriously rely on him to pull them through any emotional crisis and to advise them on everything from whether to accept a role in a new movie (most common) to how to find a lost cat. In working with him on this book I've had a grandstand view of some of these crises.

Once when we were scheduled for a working session, Peter came by to tell me he had to cancel it. He had his reason tagging along with him, the reason being a very well-known character actor, male, who was going to have a face-lift the next day and was scared stiff.

In this case Peter was more or less playing the role of a glorified baby-sitter and morale booster to prepare the man for the ordeal. He of course also had to put his psychic seal of approval on the face-lifter before the actor would go ahead with it. The man was approaching middle age and obviously was miserable about it, as most actors are when they see their youth slipping away. It's the Hollywood syndrome. The poor guy sat off in a corner all by himself, barely muttering a word while Peter was talking to me. I also saw him after the face-lift and can't say that it did much for him.

Peter has refused to predict anything as hysterical as when *Hello, Dolly!* would be released, but he certainly did predict with absolute accuracy the return of Fabian's lost cat, Silly (that really was his name). It seems that Peter had met Fabian and his wife at a movie. Peter had never heard of Fabian, and *vice versa*, but Fabian's wife, an ESP buff, recognized Peter immediately from his pictures and television appearances and asked him for his autograph. Fabian was strictly a nonbeliever.

But a few days later their cat disappeared, and Fabian's wife became hysterical.

As Fabian himself retold it to me, "She was crazy about that cat. We were about ready to call in bloodhounds when my wife said, 'Why don't you call Peter Hurkos?' Well, I thought that was pretty silly. I didn't believe in all that psychic stuff. But we had done everything. We had combed the whole area for about ten blocks and found nothing, so finally, to pacify my wife, I called Mr. Hurkos. He told us to bring something over that belonged to the cat, so I took some things from his box. I also took my brother along. He thought I was crazy. So did I.

"But we gave the cat's things to Mr. Hurkos, some toys and a blanket, and he lay down on a couch with them, like he was sleeping with them, and then pretty soon he got up and told us that our cat was in an apartment building only three houses away from our house but he didn't know which direction. He said an old lady had found the cat and locked him up and that he would be gone three days. 'After three days you will get your cat back,' he told us. But he said we should go to the third house away from our house and call for him, and he would come."

That is exactly what Fabian and his wife did, and after they had called Silly several times, the cat came scrambling out from under a porch and into their arms.

"I was shocked. I couldn't believe it," Fabian said. Furthermore, Peter told him his movie option for two more pictures was being picked up. "He knew it before my agent did," he said.

Needless to say, Fabian is no longer a nonbeliever.

Postscript on Fabian: One day Stephany telephoned and reported to me matter-of-factly, "Peter just told Katie she's going to have a baby. She's pregnant."

"Who's Katie?" I asked vaguely. I was very busy and had no time for trivia.

"Fabian's wife," she reminded me.

"Oh. So?"

"Fabian's in Miami. He doesn't know it yet. She's on her way to the doctor now," said Stephy.

"Has the doctor told her she's pregnant?"

"No. But he's going to. Peter says she is."

This was sort of too much. I couldn't be bothered. "Let me know what the doctor says," I said. And she did. She called the next day. "Peter's right. The doctor said Katie is pregnant." So O.K. So what? I promptly forgot about it.

Approximately nine months later, in October of 1969, while I was in Palm Springs, my leg gal Vera telephoned with her daily bundle of goodies for our Hollywood column and ended on this little forget-me-not: "I'm sure this will enthrall you. Stephany called from Fabian's house and said they're expecting the baby any minute now and it's going to be a boy."

*What?????* I had really completely forgotten about it and didn't quite know what she was talking about. We both said, "Forget it."

But the next morning Stephany called and announced: "Well, Fabian and Katie had their baby. Born at one-thirty this morning. And it was a boy. Just like Peter said. It's a good thing too, or Peter's head would have been on the chopping block."

I checked it out. Peter had called the shots again, all the way down the line. Fabian had even invested a small fortune in all the trappings for a male infant wardrobe and nursery. Lucky for Peter it wasn't a girl.

Tony Bennett is one of Peter's staunchest admirers. The famous singer says in his case Peter has been right about 80 per cent of the time.

"For instance, it was wild how he jumped on John Bunch [Tony's musical director] and told him he'd once been in a Nazi concentration camp. John admitted that—and it had never been printed because he doesn't talk about it—and Hurkos said, 'No you're lying. You were in two concentration camps.' And that's the wild part because how could he guess that? Not that many people were in two."

Tony says Peter has told him things about himself that he couldn't possibly have known through any normal channels of communication. His summation: "He's uncanny."

Lucille Ball consulted him for advice on whether to have her two children, Luci, Jr., and Desi, Jr., as regulars on her own *Lucy* TV show. She was concerned with what effect this might have on the children, as well as on the show. Peter advised her that she should bring her children onto the show, that it would be good both for the children and for the show. He predicted that the show would be a success—"because you are a tremendous good businesswoman," he told her (everybody knows that). "But you work too hard. You need a vacation. First you take a vacation, then you bring your children on the show and you wait and see. It will be a big success." He was so right that before long show-biz folks were razzing Lucy about how her children were stealing the show from her.

Actor Glenn Ford was once so enamored of Peter's psychic powers that he wanted to star in a movie based on his life. In fact, as mentioned earlier, Peter was living in Glenn Ford's home when he was called east to work on the Boston Strangler case. "He's a real spook," says Ford. "He told me I was going to have trouble with my air conditioning, and I did. He told me the Dodgers would win the pennant when they were in ninth place, and they did. How he does it I don't know."

One night screenwriter Ernest Lehman and director Willie Wyler were invited to a party at Glenn Ford's house. Lehman had just signed to write the screenplay for *The Sound of Music* —the movie that was later to put Twentieth Century-Fox back in business after a costly little fiasco named *Cleopatra* had set the studio back thirty-one million dollars.

Lehman was trying to persuade Wyler to direct *The Sound of Music*, but Wyler argued that it was "too schmaltzy." Lehman kept twisting Wyler's arm until, at Glenn Ford's party, Willie sought a consultation with Peter and asked, "Tell me if I should do *The Sound of Music.*"

Peter, as is his custom, asked to hold the screenplay in his hands. Willie told him the screenplay wasn't written yet but quipped, "Why don't you hold *me* in your hands instead?"

Peter grasped his hands, held them tightly, and blurted out enthusiastically, "Yes, yes, you should do this. I do not like this particular kind of film, but it will have big success, make big money."

Everyone knows what happened to *The Sound of Music*. It became the biggest moneymaking movie of all time.

Ironically, though, Wyler disregarded Peter's advice and turned down *The Sound of Music* to direct *The Collector,* for which, again ironically, he received an Academy Award nomination that pitted him against Director Robert Wise and *The Sound of Music*. Wyler lost.

Another who failed to take Peter's advice was Mickey Rooney. Peter told Mickey he shouldn't marry again—after five wives. "But if you do marry again," he said, "I tell you the next time it won't last three months." Mickey married Margaret Lane in Las Vegas on September 10, 1966—and walked out on December 20. Peter missed by only a few days, if indeed he missed at all. There are some who say this marriage didn't really make it through three months, though for the record the couple lived together 101 days. Mickey has since married again for the seventh time, though by the time this is in print, that one may also be *fini.*

Connie Francis, once a skeptic, became a convert to the Hurkos cult when she was riding in a Las Vegas taxicab with Peter and he suddenly snapped at the cab driver, "You are driving without a license, sir, aren't you?" The poor cabbie was scared stiff. "How do you know?" he quaked. "I'm psychic—up here," Peter said, pointing a forefinger to his forehead. The driver was even more confused. He deposited his passengers at their destination, and when Peter started to pay him, he said, "No, thanks, keep it, but please, mister, don't turn me in, O.K.?" "O.K.," said Peter, and thanked him for the free ride.

Trini Lopez credits Peter with possibly saving his life. They met casually at a party and shook hands. Peter blurted out, "If you don't sell that car you will be dead." Trini looked surprised— and skeptical. "It's a brand new car," he informed Peter.

"I don't care," Peter replied. "I tell you only what I see. I see accident and brakes giving out."

It happened exactly like that. The accident was only minor, but the brakes did give out while Trini was driving. It shook him up enough that he then followed Peter's advice and turned the car in for another.

The much touted Barbra Streisand movie musical *On a Clear Day You Can See Forever*—which deals with the subjects of psychic powers and reincarnation—was at least indirectly inspired by a reading Peter gave lyricist Alan Jay Lerner at dancer Ann Miller's Beverly Hills home. I first heard about it at Paramount's so-called Reincarnation Ball, a fancy costume ball that was dreamed up as a promotional stunt for the Streisand movie. Everyone was to come dressed as the person he would most rather have been in some previous life. I invited Peter to be my escort at this shindig. He went as Nostradamus and I as Madame Blavatsky. It was great fun.

Ann Miller was there as a beautiful Madame Butterfly, and she and Peter laughed as they recalled the party at her home and how shaken Alan Jay Lerner was at some of the things Peter told him at the time.

Ann is probably one of the most avid fans in the Hollywood Hurkos cult. And no wonder! Even as we sat there talking above the din of the Reincarnation Ball and watching the eye-boggling parade of costumed "reincarnated" souls sweep by—including a goodly portion of starlet Eves in their fig leaves—Peter suddenly remarked to Annie, "You know I see you auditioning for something big, very big. Like on Broadway." That was in January. By June, Ann Miller was Broadway's newest *Mame*.

Lerner, of course, was also at the Reincarnation Ball, dressed in western garb and cowboy hat, a reincarnated Tom Mix. He told me that he had been interested in psychic phenomena long before he ever met Peter Hurkos but that Peter had indeed amazed him with some of the things he "saw" for Lerner.

"He has a true gift," he said. "I have been very impressed with his powers of predicting. I think he's a terribly nice but very sad man because he has these powers and doesn't know how to cope with them."

Lerner explained that he already had the idea for *On a Clear Day You Can See Forever* before he met Peter but that he went to see Peter to discuss the play with him because of their mutual interest in the subject of psychic phenomena—and because he had a genuine desire to become acquainted with Peter.

"I didn't want him to give me a reading," he said, "but he insisted, and I must admit he told me some rather astonishing things. He described a robbery that had taken place in our house thirty-one years ago. He also told me about a tragedy that was going to happen to me, and it did. And he told me that my mother was going to have an operation in three weeks. She did—exactly three weeks to the day."

On Art Linkletter's television show Peter once told a man in the audience (selected by Art) the name of the disease which had been fatal to the man's father. Then he came within two hours of telling the time of death. This is but one of thousands of spontaneous readings that add up to his extraordinarily high record of accuracy in matters pertaining to personal health or disease. Again, the comparison with Edgar Cayce is inevitable.

There are many who feel that as a psychic Sherlock Holmes, Peter has no peer. Among those who swear by him are Hollywood actress Kathryn Grayson, who has been a friend of Peter's ever since he helped her locate forty thousand dollars' worth of jewels stolen from her suite at the Palmer House in Chicago.

Multimillionaire C. V. Wood, Jr., president of McCulloch Oil Corporation and master planner of the Havasu Lake development in Arizona, is so sold on Peter that he consults him regularly on business affairs. Peter once forwarned him, "You're going to be hit with a big lawsuit. But don't worry about it, you're going to win."

"The next morning at eleven o'clock I was smacked with a $3.5 million lawsuit from a company I'd never heard of, claiming I had a monopoly on land sales in the state of Arizona," Woody told me. Of course he won the case.

On another occasion, as he was about to drive home after a drink or two, Peter said to him, "You'd better use some mouthwash. I see the cops gonna stop you." They did, Woody said. It was one of those routine checks, not a traffic violation, but nevertheless Woody was glad he had taken Peter's advice and used the mouthwash.

Both Woody and his very attractive ex-wife, Edie Hollingsworth of Beverly Hills and Palm Springs, told me a rather incredible story of how Peter solved a burglary in Edie's apartment. I heard the story from Woody and Edie on two separate occasions —from Woody at his Beverly Hills mansion and from Edie in Palm Springs, and months apart. But my notes made at each time indicate that their stories are identical. I wasn't there, but I'm willing to take their word for it.

Edie was in Honolulu when her maid called Woody and told him that someone had broken into Edie's Beverly Hills apartment. She said the back door was open and there were some paintings missing; she didn't know what else. Woody said he would come right over. (Woody and Edie have remained good friends. As he says, "She's my ex-wife but still kinda my wife. We've been married and divorced a couple of times." As this chapter is being written they have just returned from a round-the-world cruise and their friends expect them to remarry again.)

Woody called Peter even before he called the police and asked Peter to meet him at the apartment. Peter had never been there before, but the minute he walked in, says Woody, he seemed to know exactly what had happened.

He curled his big fist over a doorknob and said, "It's a woman. . . . A man, too, but I see a woman, someone your wife knows. . . . They come up in the alley in a big blue car. The guy comes in first, then the woman. They're only here maybe five, ten minutes. They know the place. They know what they want. . . . They take two suitcases and five furs. . . . It happened about ten-thirty last night."

Woody and the maid checked Edie's closet, did a bit of collective calculating, and then told Peter he was wrong.

There were only two furs missing, they said, and no suitcases. The maid had helped Edie pack and knew which pieces of luggage and furs she had taken to Honolulu. Three of her furs were in storage, they insisted, and only two were missing.

Peter corrected them. "No, you are wrong. I see five furs and two suitcases."

Two weeks later police called Woody to come down to the station and identify his wife's furs and luggage. Sure enough, there were five furs stuffed in two suitcases. One was a bag he and Edie had bought in Turkey, which Woody had forgotten about. The other was one he had never seen; Edie apparently had bought it herself. The furs were immediately identifiable from Edie's initials, which the thieves hadn't yet bothered to remove.

"The maid and I both would have sworn that three of them were in storage," Woody said.

As for the other details, police established that the burglary took place between 10:30 and 11 P.M., that the car was a big blue 1963 Oldsmobile, that there were two persons involved in the theft—a man and a woman. And when Edie returned from Honolulu, she confirmed the final fascinating filament in Peter's remarkable psychic web of Sherlockian deduction—that the lady burglar was indeed (and alas!) a personal acquaintance of hers.

Sheila MacRae's thumbnail description of Peter, I think, is one of the best: "He's a simple man with a complex gift." Sheila first became acquainted with Peter's "gift" via long-distance telephone from Miami when Jackie Gleason challenged him, "Come on, pal. Describe to me who's this here standing beside me." He didn't specify male, female, or neuter gender.

"He told me absolutely everything," says Sheila, "all about the black cloud hanging over us and how my mother's house had to be sold. . . . And then I saw him at the Diplomat and gave him this locket and he said, 'This isn't yours,' and it wasn't. . . . And he told me many fantastic things. . . ."

Sheila felt compelled to call on Peter again, this time in rather unusual circumstances. She was appearing at the Lake Geneva

(Wisconsin) Playboy Club near Chicago when thieves looted her suite while she was on stage and made off with thirty thousand dollars in furs and jewelry.

The furs had been in storage, and for some obscure reason they were not insured, Sheila told me in recounting the events. She had reported the theft to the police, of course, and after a couple of days when she felt that nothing was being accomplished, she suddenly decided to call Peter Hurkos.

"I don't know exactly why I decided to do this," she recalled. "It had been over a year since I met this man. But I was so stunned by the loss of my jewelry and furs, and then I woke up one morning very troubled and I had this strange feeling that maybe he could help me, so I just said, 'I'm going to call Peter Hurkos,' and I did. But I couldn't reach him. . . ."

In one of those stranger-than-fiction twists of fate, Peter happened to be in Miami trying to contact Sheila MacRae at that moment.

He had flown to Miami on another consultation case and while there he had a psychic hunch about Sheila. "I just felt something wrong. I felt I must talk to her," he explained. When he called her house, her son answered, and Peter asked, "Is everything all right with your mother?" At that time her son did not know of the burglary. He told Peter his mother was fine and playing at the Playboy Club at Lake Geneva. Peter still sensed that something was wrong, and when he arrived back at Los Angeles International Airport, there was the message waiting for him to call Sheila MacRae in Lake Geneva.

He took the next plane out to join the manhunt.

Peter can take no credit officially for helping solve this case. In fact, as this is written it has not been solved, and chances are it never will be. It's one of those sticky situations involving a well-known local character whom Peter pinpointed for the police, but, as Sheila says, "You just can't go around accusing people without evidence." She is convinced, however, that Peter has the right guy and that someday truth will out—even if she doesn't get back her jewelry and furs. In fact, Sheila is so sold on Peter that she flew to Toronto on short notice and subbed for him in his nightclub act when he was felled by the flu bug.

This brings up another facet of Peter's personality that has provoked skeptics to scorn and caused genuine concern among his friends. He has used his gift for material gain, and most especially—horror of horrors!—via the entertainment medium, on television, the stage, and more recently the nightclub circuit. Purists are always quick to tell you that when a psychic uses his gift for material gain he also loses it. Edgar Cayce's wife, Gertrude, continually reminded him of the high purpose of his calling, that he was meant to dedicate himself to the service of others and should not misuse the gift that God had granted him. When he concentrated on making money, instead of using his gift for good, something always went wrong—a blinding headache, an upset stomach, loss of voice. . . .

Peter has been severely criticized by so-called parapsychologists for his "deviation from the scientifically straight and narrow paths of modern psychical research" and for his "multifarious American contacts"—meaning, of course, his involvement with show business personalities and the entertainment world.

But it should be remembered that he gave up a lucrative career in Europe and originally came to this country strictly as a research guinea pig for Dr. Puharich at the Round Table Foundation laboratories, and he spent most of his first years in this country as a research subject, not as an entertainer. It should be noted too that from time to time there were other so-called research groups, pseudo-scientific "foundations," and assorted psychic exploiters who had themselves a field day exploiting their "big dumb Dutchman" in the name of ESP "research" and lining their own pockets at his expense. I knew some of them. I knew some of the deals they made with Peter and the puny financial arrangements offered him. He was new to this country, and he didn't know the wily ways of our fast-buck artists. One phony "foundation," for example, was raking in thousands of dollars from Peter's psychic readings for their "research files"—while paying him the munificent salary of $125 per week.

As for the legitimate psychic research centers (there are several; Puharich's laboratory for example), most are financed by private contributions and are simply not set up to subsidize a research guinea pig indefinitely, even one as intriguing as Peter Hurkos. And as he was soon to learn, the cost of living in America was quite a switch from his peasant background in Holland.

"I would like to give my whole life to scientific research if I could find out about my gift, why I am like this," he says. "But I have to live too. Who will pay my bills, feed my family, take care of my father? I can't live on research."

He probably would have been better off to stay in Holland and set himself up in business as a psychic healer like that other Dutch clairvoyant crime-solver, Gerard Croiset. To the masses of sick and ailing who adore him, he's known as Dr. Croiset. He calls himself a "Spiritual, or Paranormal, Healer . . . endowed with a special extrasensory perception." I attended one of his "spiritual healing" seances in Utrecht once, and it was indeed an eye-opener. I arrived just in time for "ladies' hour." He has so many patients he treats them in groups and categories—children's hour, ladies' hour, men's night, mixed couples, business groups, and so on.

Croiset's treatment room was spacious and barren except for fifty straight-backed wooden chairs lining the walls (and all occupied by women on the evening I was there), and the examining throne in the center of the floor. This was a large, dark green leather chair and foot rest that appeared to be for examining patients.

The examination was cursory and quick, a sort of head-to-toe massage with his fingertips, as though Croiset were tickling a piano keyboard. This little crescendo lasted about two minutes per patient, after which he would wave his arms in an arc and snap his fingers for the next patient. Unacquainted as I am with the Dutch language, I'm not sure of all the diseases Doc was treating, but the lady next to me spoke enough English to clue me in here and there. When a plumpish, pale-faced woman waddled up and squeezed into the chair, my interpreter leaned over and whispered, "Polio. Very bad. She's much better now."

With his eyes closed and his head tilted upward, as though in prayer, Croiset began massaging the woman's temples, then her neck and shoulders, then her hips and thighs, and on down to her ankles.

Lady interpreter leaned over again and whispered, "It's all in his hands. He has electromagnetic waves in them. . . ."

I asked what her trouble was.

"Nerves," she said. "I was a nervous wreck and I had pains in my face. Now I feel fine."

"Then why are you still coming for treatments?"

"I know I'd get worse if I didn't," she said. "He's such a wonderful doctor."

Yet few people in America know Gerard Croiset as a doctor.

He had only a few moments to spare with me before his next group came in for spiritual healing. But he was willing to answer a few questions. When I asked him about his work on solving crime cases, he pointed to his telephone and tape recorder and said, "That's for police work. But I don't do much of it anymore. There's no pay for police work." He gave me a big wink and added, "It's mostly all healing now."

From his crowded docket it would appear that he earns many thousands of guilders a year for his "spiritual healing" work, which so far as I could figure out was neither very spiritual nor very healing.

Nevertheless, Croiset has fared quite well with the psychic intelligentsia because of his collaboration with one Professor W. H. C. Tenhaeff, who is highly esteemed in serious psi circles for having once been director of the Parapsychology Laboratory at the University of Utrecht. (Meaning he's the Dutch counterpart of Dr. J. B. Rhine.) At the time of my visit I could find no office or laboratory listed for Professor Tenhaeff. I finally located his quarters in an office building several blocks from the campus and was granted an audience with his eminence, who turned out to be a rotund and dapper little man with monocle and goatee who greeted me with the warmth of an iceberg, including all of that seven-eighths below water.

He told me that he had "discovered" Croiset and developed his ESP abilities, which, he explained were now concentrated more and more on "healing."

With a little sleuthing I learned that Professor Tenhaeff was not a professor at the University of Utrecht, that he was teaching no classes in parapsychology (or anything else), and that his salary was paid neither by the university nor by the Netherlands government, but by a "sponsor"—the Dutch Society of Spiritual Healers, headed, of course, by Doc Croiset.

As I say, Peter probably would have done better to stay in Holland and set up shop as a psychic healer.

But he didn't. And he has had to bumble along as best he can without the Tenhaeff-Rhine Seal of Approval. Thus he charges fees for his consultations, the same as a lawyer, a psychiatrist, or a plumber charges fees for his services (though Peter's fees aren't as high); and he accepts television, theater, and nightclub engagements because, as he puts it simply, "I have to eat. I have only my gift. What else can I do?"

In Holland, Gerard Croiset has found that "there's no pay for police work," and so he earns his living from "spiritual healing." In America, Peter has found that neither his police work nor psychical research brings in sufficient income to pay the bills, so he earns his living via the entertainment medium, which in my own opinion is at least more honest than his Dutch counterpart's so-called "spiritual healing."

If at this point I seem to be jumping to Peter's defense, you read right. I am. Don't forget, though, that I started out as the complete skeptic, but in the nearly two years that this book has been in preparation I have been rather closely associated with Peter, many times day after day and weeks on end.

I have doggedly double-checked him on thousands of points and found him to be if not always accurate at least always honest. I have watched him at work on the stage, in personal consultations, and on crime cases. I have never known him to use trickery, and I personally feel it is very much to his credit that he hasn't hopped aboard the ESP bandwagon or the astrology boom. He has never claimed to be an "ESP expert" (as some have mistakenly called him); he knows little about so-called "extrasensory perception" (and is probably just as well off). He doesn't operate under the cloak of religious mysticism, or so-called spiritualism. He doesn't boast of having "supernatural" powers, nor does he claim that his gift is a gift from God. He doesn't know where it came from. Though he is personally a God-fearing man and by no means irreverent, he is not the same devoutly religious man Edgar Cayce was, nor does he pretend to be. Nor does he proclaim any "divine" flashes of prophecy, precognition, retrocognition, or any other parapsychological gifts. He doesn't go in for faith healing, psychokinetics, or occultism. He doesn't read horoscopes or write astrology columns, which seems to be the trend for some self-styled psychics these days.

He does not claim to be an astrologer and doesn't know one zodiacal sign from another. He doesn't blindfold himself and go off in a dramatic trance à la Arthur Ford, and he takes a dim view of hypnosis.

"Too much fakery and tricks," he says. "If you have the gift, you don't need tricks."

As I watched offstage as he worked, however, there were times he was concentrating so intensely that he seemed to me to be in a state of self-hypnotic trance—or at least what most observers would describe as such—although any time I mentioned this to him or asked him about it, he vigorously brushed the idea aside, I think because in his simple, unschooled mind he associates the words "hypnosis" and "trance" with trickery.

The paradox is that he has been so vehemently castigated by friend and foe alike for "misusing" his gift, that is, "commercializing" on it to make money, to earn a living. The noted Washington crystal gazer, Jeane Dixon, is a very religious woman who claims that her "gift of prophecy" comes straight from God, and she never charges a cent for her psychic prognostications. Well, why should she? Her husband is a wealthy real estate tycoon, and besides, Miss Dixon undoubtedly does just dandy with her syndicated astrology column.

The famous British psychic Maurice Woodruff is using his "gift" for an entertaining "His" and "Hers" astrology column and TV show.

I haven't heard a single voice of dissent against either of these popular psychics-turned-astrologer for "misusing" their "gift." But then perhaps it is because not so many regard their "gift" as genuine as Peter's.

When I talked to Hugh Lynn Cayce, for example, he seemed

genuinely saddened that a man of Peter's ability had to use his "gift" to earn a living instead of devoting himself to long-range research projects. And as I mentioned earlier, although Dr. J. B. Rhine would not tell me why he refused to accept Peter as a subject for his ESP experiments at Duke University—other than his comment "People like Hurkos have no place in any scientific investigation of ESP"—my own impression was that Dr. Rhine did not approve of anyone who used psychic talents for commercial purposes.

Even author Jess Stearn, friend, critic, and chronicler of psychics, and a true admirer of both Edgar Cayce and Peter Hurkos, said to me in comparing the two one day, "Yes, in many ways they were very much alike. But don't forget—there was one vast difference. Edgar Cayce used his gift to help others, not to profit by it himself."

This is not precisely accurate. It is true that for many years Cayce worked at photography to earn a living for his family, while giving his psychic diagnostic readings at no cost to all who needed them.

But he later gave up photography, set up shop as a psychic diagnostician, and gave daily readings—for a fee. For a while he had a flourishing business as a professional psychic. In addition to the patients who came to him personally, he also had a thriving mail-order business. Sacks of mail arrived daily, asking for readings and enclosing various sums of money. However, both Cayce and his wife apparently had a genuine fear of using his God-given gift for money (both were deeply religious, and Cayce's readings were always sprinkled with quotes from the Scriptures), and Cayce continued to give many readings without charging a fee. He also spent a great deal of his time and money in establishing a research center and hospital, which ran into financial difficulties. And then came the Depression years. Edgar Cayce died a poor man, but his work is still carried on, at his request, by his son Hugh Lynn Cayce and his Association for Research and Enlightenment, which the Cayces formed in 1931 at Virginia Beach.

It is interesting to speculate what the picture might have been if Edgar Cayce and Peter Hurkos had switched places—and eras. The first important notice of Edgar Cayce was a full-page display from the Sunday magazine section of *The New York Times* of October 9, 1910, according to Cayce's biographer, Thomas Sugrue (*There Is a River*). The headline said, ILLITERATE MAN BECOMES A DOCTOR WHEN HYPNOTIZED—STRANGE POWER SHOWN BY EDGAR CAYCE PUZZLES PHYSICIANS,

The first paragraph read:

"The medical fraternity of the country is taking a lively interest in the strange power said to be possessed by Edgar Cayce of Hopkinsville, Ky., to diagnose difficult diseases while in a semiconscious state, though he has not the slightest knowledge of medicine when not in this condition."

What if Edgar Cayce and his strange power had been sprung full-blown on the American public in 1956 instead of 1910? Would he now be doing psychic diagnosing and healing (practicing medicine without a license), performing as a stage hypnotist, or reading horoscopes?

What if Pieter van der Hurk had fallen off that ladder in Hopkinsville, Kentucky, instead of Dordrecht, Holland? Could he have succeeded as a psychic diagnostician as well as Edgar Cayce?

One thing is certain: Hopkinsville, Kentucky, in 1910 and the twenties is not New York, Miami, and Hollywood, in the 1960s. Should a man be censured for using whatever honest talents he has, psychic or otherwise, to meet the high cost of living today?

As for losing his "gift" by misusing it, no one is more concerned about this than Peter himself. He has been told this so often that he believes it. He has asked me repeatedly if I thought he was going to lose his "gift" by using it to make money. How do I know? I can only tell him that if he hasn't lost it after all these years of earning his livelihood with it, then he probably won't.

As for using his psychic talent as an entertainer, he doesn't regard his stage act as entertainment but as a demonstration. And though he cringes at the thought of having to demonstrate his "gift" for nightclub audiences, he regards it as a necessity if he is to eat and keep up his mortgage payments, not to mention taxes. His crime work hasn't paid off financially. He rarely charges fees when he works on police cases. And even though his reputation has been built mostly on his role as a psychic detective, the truth is that he really doesn't like this work.

"These cases make me sick, they are too hard on me, take too much out of me," he said to me. "I am a human being too, you know, even if I do have the gift. I am not a zombie. I feel things, same as you or anybody. And how you think I like it when they bring me clothing with blood, or part of a leg from a dead person? How you think I like it when I see all these terrible things, what the Boston Strangler did to those women, and when a plane crashes with all those broken bodies? No, I don't like working on cases like this. Sometimes they make me too sick to my stomach."

Still, he continues to work on such cases, frequently as a personal favor to the local police department in a city where he is performing, as in the Robert Cline case of the missing plane which he worked on in Palm Springs while appearing at the Chi Chi Club (Chapter 6).

And as I write this chapter, Peter is laid up with a fractured hip sustained while working—without fee—on another missing persons case near Lake Tahoe, Nevada. He was playing an engagement at the Hotel Sahara-Tahoe over Memorial Day weekend, when he was asked to aid the local police department and county sheriff's office in their search for a thirty-nine-year-old mortician, Douglas Grensted, from Grover City, California, who had left home alone to go on a hunting trip, and was never seen again. Grensted's car had been found on a logging road in the Tahoe Paradise area.

The incident had occurred some months earlier, in late September. Grensted had left home on the hunting trip with very little money, some credit cards, a custom-made rifle, and a general destination of Alpine County. He left a wife and two children behind. He was to have been home on October 3. His car was found on October 5. Search posses were formed after Grensted's father, Kenneth, reported his son overdue. A ten-mile area was covered, but the search was abandoned when winter snows began to fall, then resumed again in the spring.

Peter started working on the case first in the Sahara-Tahoe Hotel, in an executive suite where police and sheriff's officers assembled, with Kenneth Grensted, who had brought a picture of his son and an article of his clothing, as Peter had requested. In this case it was a poncho.

"He is not a person to run away from home," Peter began. "There was an accident—not amnesia. It happened in the dark . . . he was looking for a trail. It is night. Not yet a full moon . . . about nine thirty. . . . I see him fight to hold on, he has slipped, he is falling . . ."

His fingers touched the picture of the missing man, and he said, "I feel English. . . . I feel England. . . ."

Grensted's father swallowed hard, and he said, "Yes, his mother was from England."

Peter continued, "I see him two miles from the highway. . . . He slows down. I see him with a rifle in his car. . . . But he does not use the rifle. . . . He is a very quiet man, not much of a talker. . . . He does not carry much money with him. . . ." He paused, then said suddenly, "You will find him in an area off the highway two miles. He falls down, you don't find him up. Bring me piece of paper."

He drew a map of the area he saw. After several minutes of free-hand sketching he asked the officers to look at the map. They verified that the map was generally correct, though Peter had never seen a map of the area or been to the site. They also told him that the campsite where they had found Grensted's sleeping bag, a candy wrapper, and a teabag was less than ten miles away from where he was sitting.

He blinked and said, "Come, we go there."

It was the officers' turn to blink. The camp was located at a 7,400–7,500-foot level atop an area known ironically as Lost Lane and Apache Avenue behind Tahoe College, and it was known as one of the most rugged areas in the Sierras, challenging even the fittest of men on foot. But Peter insisted. And next day, Memorial Day, a four-car caravan headed for the Lost Lane and Apache area—as far as they could go. From there it was on foot, with Peter leading the way up a tortuous, twisting trail. The air became thinner and the going tougher. Great patches of winter snow remained, making the trek slippery and dangerous.

Peter looked toward the summit of the snow mountain and

said, "I see him buried under snow. . . . He fall between the rocks—something like a cave down below—between the rocks. That's where you will find the body." He described how the man had lost his balance, clawing at the rocks in an attempt to keep his balance and finally falling into a cave-covered area, a crevasse.

One of the officers admitted there were numerous caves in the area. "But right now it would be like looking for a needle in a haystack," he said. As this is written, the body still has not been found, and it may never be if it has fallen into a crevasse as Peter described. But even the most skeptical of the officers in the search party later said he had decided that if the body were ever found, it would be "exactly where he said it would be."

It was on the treacherous trail back down that Peter slipped and fractured his hip. He had to be flown back to Los Angeles and hospitalized. And even as this is written, while still in a cast, he's working again on what he dislikes most—another multiple murder case. For psychic-detective sensationalism this one might even outstrip the Boston Strangler. It's the case of the Ypsilanti-Ann Arbor coed murders—but that's another story.

Meanwhile, ironically, Peter is almost as big a hit in his nightclub act as he is as a crime solver. He has had splendid reviews. The one from the Sahara-Tahoe is typical. Susan Tracey, the Tahoe reviewer for *The Hollywood Reporter*, trade-paper and show-biz bible, wrote of Peter's "first professional trek to Tahoe":

"It was obviously an experimental three-day venture at which Peter hoped to prove he not only was gifted with a unique power, but also had the ability to draw capacity audiences.

"Both were proved most amply as witness the fact that the 450-seat Aspen Grove Theatre was packed for every performance.

"The show was a forum completely constructed on audience participation. A 'hot seat' was placed center stage while skeptics, the curious, and those who 'almost believed' but wanted proof, came forth one at a time to test the psychic ability of the Dutchman. Pacing back and forth across the stage, Hurkos, time and time again came up with remarkably pertinent information about participants.

"Hundreds of people flocked to this Tahoe nitery over the weekend, in many cases to prove something to themselves. His show was fascinating from beginning to end. He not only made believers out of many skeptics but perhaps more importantly provided his point that this unique type of entertainment can be a popular draw in a Nevada hotel-casino operation."

Yet a few days after this fine review came out, Peter told me he wasn't doing any more nightclub engagements! From now on, he declared, he would do only concert dates, private clubs, and private consultations. But there is always next week, next month, and next year for him to change his mind again. . . .

The trouble with Peter, I think, is that he doesn't understand his strange, unpredictable "gift," he is basically frightened by it, and can't cope with it—or perhaps doesn't want to. He is bugged by the tensions and pressures that go with it, and the uneasy situations he finds himself in.

For example, gambling. He hates gambling. He refuses to gamble or to give anyone tips on gambling, and he doesn't really like playing the Las Vegas casinos, because he says it makes him nervous. "It's all the wrong vibrations," he says. "No good, no good way to use my gift."

In this respect he is as thoroughly God-fearing as Edgar Cayce about the misuse of his gift. He is absolutely certain that if he used it to win at the racetrack or casinos, that would be the end of his gift.

And he becomes greatly annoyed at the skeptics who insist on jeering: If he's so clairvoyant, why isn't he cleaning up in the stock market, or the casinos?

The truth is, his psychic powers are so strong and his face so well known that he is not particularly welcome in the gambling rooms. The Sahara-Tahoe even put a clause in his contract forbidding him to gamble, though this was entirely unnecessary.

Once at a Las Vegas casino, his little blonde Stephany Courtney blew three hundred dollars at the crap table, then insisted that Peter help her recoup her loss. He did so by sending her to the roulette table and picking the numbers for her. She got her money back on two consecutive spins of the wheel. But there were some unexpected repercussions. Some of the players at the roulette table recognized Peter, bet the same numbers, and the house lost about ten thousand dollars. Peter was invited into the front office and informed that he was welcome to stay there at any time, but please, sir, stay away from the gambling tables, O.K.?

Once when he was working at the Diplomat Hotel in Miami, the owners, who were racing fans, took him out to Hialeah. They had a box in the Turf Club and so were able to go into the saddling area before each race, where Peter could touch the horses. He touched their mouths, where the numbers are held and picked the winners in eight of the nine races. He missed the fifth race. That was the only one in which he didn't go down and touch the horses.

He likes to emphasize that on this occasion he only *picked* the horses, he didn't play them. He doesn't believe in gambling. He normally never goes to the races, and horses just don't interest him.

He requires a great deal of sleep and rest when he works, and he always works on an empty stomach. "If I have to give a performance, I don't eat the whole day. I see better, work better and have more energy when my stomach is empty. It's like all the blood goes to the brain," he explains.

He drinks very little, and never when he is working—though sometimes after a long and exhausting session, he will take a good belt of Scotch to relax him. He has a nagging fear about drink too —that if he drinks too much it will cause him to lose his gift. This of course is the opposite theory from that of some psychical research experts who claim that certain amounts of alcohol sharpen one's psychic senses. According to Peter, Dr. Puharich once tried the test on him, on an empty stomach. He drank half a quart of Scotch, six bottles of Heinekens beer, and two ounces of cognac.

"He was trying to find out whether my gift improved when I was drunk," Peter explained. "But my score was the same. We never did it again."

One of the questions most frequently asked of Peter, as it was of Edgar Cayce, is, If he can see for others, why not for himself?

The question doesn't annoy Peter. He is the first to admit with utmost candor, "I cannot even find my own shoes."

He also doesn't mind admitting that he consults other psychics. The best psychic he has ever met, he says, is Mary Pickford, who predicted the breakup of his second marriage.

He sees nothing peculiar in not being able to apply his "gift" to himself. "After all," he explains, "a doctor sometimes cannot make a diagnosis on himself, or his wife or children. He does not operate on himself or his wife or children. That is the normal way in the medical world. Maybe it is normal for a psychic not to know about himself.

"Sometimes I feel danger about myself, yes. But I'm very happy that I don't know anything about myself. I know it sounds funny, but yes, yes, I am so happy that I cannot know about myself."

He paused, then burst out suddenly in a fit of anguish, "Jesus Christ, you think I want to know when I'm gonna die? No! I don't want to know when I'm gonna die. You think I like to know all these things? You get this gift and it will make you nuts. I would rather be normal. If I didn't have this gift, I would be more happy. If I could switch this off, I would be the most happy man in the world.

"If I could just make money, just making a living, maybe I could sell my paintings or be a cook in a restaurant, but then all these things bother me because of what I see. . . . I go into a restaurant and sit down at a table, and the waitress comes over, and there I am telling her she'd better go to a doctor and have a checkup. . . . People think I am nuts. I am more happy when I am alone and can paint. . . . But soon as I stick my nose out and see people, then I know all these things about them, I see everything. And I am always under tension, under pressure. That is no life. But if I lose my gift, then what am I gonna do?

"If I could only make a living with my paintings or be a cook in a restaurant, even if I made only eight hundred or nine hundred dollars a month, I would be the most happy man in the world, boy! If I only didn't have the gift. All these things that bother me. . . . I'm the most unhappy man in my life."

Here was the simple, true confession of a tormented and mixed-up man whose agents bill him—and audiences adulate him —as "The Foremost Psychic of the Century."

Peter Hurkos is a man trapped by one of the strangest of all "gifts," as was Edgar Cayce at another time, another place. Neither asked for it, understood it, wanted it, profited by it.

In my own opinion these two men are unique, each in his own way, but their "gift" is not, for it has manifested itself in varying degrees in others—religious mystics, primitive peoples, the blind and mentally ill who are withdrawn from sensory contact with reality. In both animals and men, there are senses beyond those well-known physical five senses that most of us use daily. And if one day, after we conquer the moon and Mars, of course, scientists could spare the time to take a closer look at these mental mysteries, then the unhappiness that their psychic "gift" brought to Edgar Cayce and Peter Hurkos might not have been in vain.

# · 10 ·

# Strictly Personal

If anyone had told me a year ago I would be writing what I am now about to write, I would have said he was insane.

Never in my wildest imagination did I think I would ever need to admit that a seer could "see" anything for *me*. Not even Peter Hurkos. Researching and reporting the story of his psychic feats for others is one thing. Becoming personally involved is another. As I have said, I purposely avoided asking Peter for advice or consultation on personal matters. But it was difficult to avoid listening when on several occasions he abruptly started talking about some rather amazing details regarding my private life and certain events and circumstances that he could not have known through any of the normal senses and cannot be explained by simple intuition, logic, psychology—or by hocus-pocus.

I'll begin with the house. My husband and I had listed our Bel-Air home for sale, though as yet the "For Sale" sign wasn't up, and we of course had not discussed the matter with Peter. In fact, he had been in the house only once before, at the Christmas holiday party I mentioned earlier, when he spooked my guests. The next time I saw him was early in February, when he came over with Stephany to ask me to write his book for him.

We were sitting on a black leather sofa in our bar room, when Peter glanced around curiously and suddenly blurted out—in the middle of a conversation about his book—"I feel bad vibrations about this house. You gonna have trouble selling it. You won't sell it until August."

I played it cool. "What's wrong with it?" I asked. As he rambled off all the things wrong with it, I shrugged. He repeated, "You gonna have trouble selling it. Also, I'm sorry to tell you this, but you gonna lose money."

Cheery thought.

"What makes you think we want to sell it?" I asked.

"It's no good for you. Too big, too far . . ." These things of course, he could deduce, and I suppose that anyone, psychic or not, might have guessed that we would not have been averse to selling the place, but Peter seemed to know for certain that we already had it up for sale and that we were going to have trouble selling it. It had been up for sale since September, with practically no lookers. We had only recently changed realtors.

"When did you say we're going to sell it?" I asked.

"August," Peter repeated. "You sell this house in August—wait and see."

I then admitted to Peter that he was right about one thing: the house was for sale. But I laughed at him on his timing.

"You've got to be wrong. We have to sell the house before August." I didn't tell him that we would indeed lose money on it if we had to wait until August to sell it.

"I'm sorry," he said stubbornly. "You do not sell till August. And you lose money on it."

Well, that was a blow. But I didn't believe him. This was only February. Next week the "For Sale" sign went up in the yard; a beautiful brunette real estate lady began bringing other realtors up to look at it; and we eagerly awaited a buyer. A month went by. Another month. Not even a bite. My husband and I brooded in silence for a while, each knowing what the other was thinking, and then finally almost at the same moment, we asked ourselves the painful question, "Was it possible that Peter was right? Were we not going to sell the house until August?" We *had* to sell it before then. We couldn't hold out that long.

Without going into many personal details, it should be clarified that we had invested in the house as a combination home and business, and the business venture hadn't worked out. Unless we could sell reasonably soon, it would mean a financial disaster for us. Naturally, we had not discussed this—or any other of our personal affairs—with Peter. Furthermore, up to this point, my husband was as skeptical of Peter's psychic ability as I was.

Still the house did not sell. Peter never brought the subject up again himself, but I did.

One day at the end of our working session I asked him, "Peter, when did you say we're going to sell this house?"

"August," he said.

"You're positive?"

"Positive."

"Well, we're going to have to hurry. [By then it was late June.] We haven't even had any serious lookers," I told him.

"They come in August," he said. "I tell you something else. You gonna have someone else live with you in this house. I don't mean just some friend overnight or for the weekend. I mean someone is gonna move in with you before you move out."

That wouldn't have been too unusual, as there always seemed to be someone moving in with us for various periods of time. But Peter insisted that this upcoming tenant was different, not a friend of ours, no one we knew, and I sensed that he meant the move-in would be under rather esoteric circumstances, although he couldn't be any more specific than that.

July came—and went. With us counting the days with heavy heart and a diminishing exchequer; and by now hoping—oh, *how* we were hoping!—that Peter was right, and we would sell the house in August.

It was almost too pat to believe, but if you can figure out any way that Peter could have *caused* it to happen like this, let me know.

On the very first Sunday in August, 1968, things started happening. Our house was a beehive of activity, compared with all the previous months. We had about a dozen lookers, compared with a maximum of five or six on any one given weekend day in previous months. At least a couple of them impressed us as being somewhat seriously interested in the house, and said they wanted to come back again. For the first time since we had put the house up for sale, we felt encouraged that it *would* sell—eventually.

But these things take time. Realistically, it was too much to hope that a buyer could see the house, make up his mind, put up the front money, and get the papers through escrow—all in one month.

On the following Wednesday, the first week in August, I spent the day making my rounds of the movie studios for my Hollywood column. I returned home about six o'clock, and my husband, who is an incurable optimist, greeted me with, "How soon can you be packed to move out? We have a buyer for the house. They're coming over at eight o'clock."

I did not greet this news with joy. In fact, I was a little irritated by his optimism, which I took to be exaggeration. I was tired and in no mood for jokes. And he was annoyed by my scornful attitude. We might have had a little domestic crisis on our hands if the phone had not rung at that point. I answered, and our Beautiful Brunette Real Estate Lady asked if we would be at home that evening, she had a buyer for the house and wanted to come over at eight o'clock with the papers for us to sign.

At eight o'clock they arrived, our B.B.R.E.L. and another realtor—with a batch of papers *and* a sizable check for a down payment on the house.

The prospective buyers, who shall be known here as Mr. and Mrs. John Smith, were not with them.

I was frankly flabbergasted. "But who are these people? I've never even seen them looking at the house."

The realtors explained that they were from the East and had indeed looked at the house several times during the past few months—apparently when I was out, although they thought that I had once met Mr. Smith and didn't remember him. He looked at the house first and liked it but had to wait for his wife to come out from the East to see if she approved. She did.

They were making us a firm offer—on one condition: that they could have all the legal property technicalities (geological surveys, etc.) cleared up and the papers through escrow by August 25, which had to be their deadline because of tax purposes. It was all too complicated for me, but it seems that our buyers were also selling a substantial amount of property in the East and for tax reasons had to have all their buying and selling projects concluded by August 25. They wanted also to take occupancy of the house by September 15.

After having our house for sale for nearly a year, I should have been overjoyed finally to have not only a nibble but a firm offer, with check attached. But instead, for some inexplicable reason, I had the sudden overwhelming sensation that I was being pushed—or would the word be conned?—into something against my will.

To the utter astonishment of my husband and the realtors who had finally come up with a buyer, I squawked, "But this is too fast. I'm not signing any papers until I have time to think about it."

My husband reminded me that I was leaving next morning for Chicago, to be gone at least a week, and the realtors said they couldn't wait that long for our signatures, if we were to meet the August 25 deadline.

I felt absolutely panicked—don't ask me why. Perhaps it was an instinctive distrust of signing something hurriedly, or being caught off guard with such a sudden offer when I knew that generally house sales were not made in this manner. Still, I was risking losing our prospective buyers by my indecision. We couldn't afford to lose them. I had to make up my mind.

In a sudden split second of total irrationality which really isn't typical of me, I abruptly got up from the table where the four of us had been sitting in conference over the papers and said, "Excuse me a minute. I'm going to call Peter." It was as though I'd had a sudden inspirational seizure.

My husband explained to our startled guests that Peter Hurkos was a psychic. They obviously thought me quite mad.

I telephoned Peter, explaining the situation to him, and asked whether we should accept the offer. "Definitely," he said. "You lose money now, you lose more if you wait." Correct.

I went back to the table with a feeling of calm and relief.

"Peter says it's O.K.," I heard myself saying, and I saw the two realtors cross funny glances with raised eyebrows. We signed the first papers that evening. And on our way to the airport the next morning we stopped by the escrow office to sign another batch of papers. That was Thursday, August 5. I went to Chicago,

my husband went house hunting, and the escrow sale details
went smoothly—*until!*

On August 20, Mr. John Smith called and said that he and his
wife wished to come over and discuss something with us—with
both of us. My heart sank. They were backing out of the deal,
I was sure. A problem had come up, Mr. Smith said, and he
thought it best if the four of us could discuss it together.

They arrived at the appointed hour. They were a very attractive couple, obviously affluent, well bred, and bright (not the
typical Bel-Air featherbrains).

Mr. Smith began, "We've made a mistake in our calculations.
Our lawyers have advised us that August 25 is not only our escrow deadline but that this is the date when we must take occupancy of the house in order to avoid some very serious tax
problems because of the property we are selling in New York."

He said that he had checked it out completely with his lawyers,
and there was no way to get around it. If they were to consum-
mate the purchase of our house, they must have occupancy by
August 25. Five days. Ours was a two-story house and well
jammed with an accumulation of furniture, antique music boxes,
paintings and treasures from our world travels—plus a complete
photographic studio (my husband's) and an electronics laboratory. We couldn't possibly get packed up and move in five days.

Mr. Smith said he had been advised that taking occupancy
of a place legally meant moving in—in person and with suitcases.
He couldn't merely "take occupancy" on paper. It wasn't necessary to have furniture moved in on the legal "occupancy" date,
but it was necessary to move yourself in with bag and baggage,
he said.

"And so we're begging you on bended knee," Mrs. Smith implored, "would you permit us to move into your maid's room?"

On August 23, two days before their deadline, Mr. and Mrs.
Smith moved into our maid's room (we had no live-in maid),
with bag and baggage and their cocker spaniel—much to the
consternation of our French poodle, Gogi.

We moved up our move-out date two weeks to September 1
and spent the rest of August in a mess of packing crates and moving vans, as the Smiths moved in and we moved out. It was a

cluttered confusion but harmonious arrangement with the four of us sharing the same house and moving vans, as well as a few drinks at the bar. We became good friends.

It was exactly as Peter had told me in February—that we would not sell our house until August. Not only that, but the entire deal was completed within one month, which was rather unusual. We did lose money, as he had predicted, although we knew we would if we had to wait until August—but as he had said, we would lose more if we waited longer.

His strangest prediction, though, was the one that involved our buyers. He had said, "You gonna have someone else live with you in this house. I don't mean just some friend overnight or for the weekend. I mean someone is gonna move in with you before you move out."

He couldn't have been more specific—or more accurate. How did he know? But I'm telling it exactly as it was.

One of the most puzzling and shattering experiences I had with Peter during the months we worked together involved his reading for a friend of mine, which at first I thought was a complete flop, 100 per cent inaccurate.

My longtime friend was the late novelist and political writer, Rose Wilder Lane, whom I had known many years. She had been my literary idol and mentor since my college days, and through the years we had carried on a voluminous correspondence. She knew that I had begun Peter's book, and she was fascinated by him, though they had never met.

In one of Mrs. Lane's letters she had said that she would like to have a reading from Peter. I asked her to write out her full name on a card or slip of paper (instead of her initials, with which she always signed her letters to me). In July 1968, I received a sad card from Mrs. Lane telling me that her Maltese dog, Pepe, whom she adored, had died after a long illness. I had known of his illness and in fact had called Mrs. Lane a few times in recent weeks to cheer her up as best I could on the telephone. She was then living in Harlingen, Texas, although she still had her home in Danbury, Connecticut.

She was eighty-two years old, long ago divorced and childless (although she had an assortment of officially and unofficially adopted children and grandchildren scattered hither and yon), and for many years her sun rose and set on her two little Maltese pets, Pepe and Brother.

Her card telling of Pepe's death was brief and filled with grief. "You, I hope, will never know how I feel—not like writing letters. Please don't write me about it. Otherwise I am O.K. Going abroad—Europe, Asia, etc.—indefinitely. With love and name for [Peter's] reading which I want and thank you for. Rose Wilder Lane."

I was startled by the news that she was going abroad—indefinitely. At her age? She had made no mention of any such notions in her recent letters or in our telephone conversations. I was sure she would change her mind when she recovered from her grief over Pepe.

I didn't even tell Peter that this person was a friend of mine. I asked him only to tell me what he could about the person (I was careful not to specify male or female) from the signature on the card. He asked me to put the card in an envelope, and as he rubbed his fingertips across it, he began:

"This is a person I would not like to have against me. [*Certainly true, but so what?* The same could be said of many persons.] A person who does not forget easy. [She had a memory like an elephant.] This person lives far away from here. [In Harlingen.] I see three people in that family. [*Counting the dogs?*] This person is very active, and is an older person, maybe seventy, eighty, but looks in forties. Wait. I see this person far overseas, traveling. Not alone, and not a vacation, and not Hawaii, but way far overseas. [For a moment I'll admit I was a little shook up. Was he reading my mind or Mrs. Lane's about her going abroad, or was he reading through the envelope with his fingertips?]

"Oh, I see an accident. In the wintertime where there is snow and he will have trouble with slippery roads, and the car slips on the highway and comes into a barn. But he is a good driver, nobody hurt. It's a new car, wintertime, lots of snow, and the car goes on its side. Don't worry. He is a very good driver."

I knew that Peter had to be wrong. In all the years I had known her, Mrs. Lane had never even owned a car, preferring always to be chauffeured in a big black cab or limousine. And besides, Peter had identified her as a "he." I was disappointed. Even I, skeptic, had expected him to do better than that. And there was more to come.

"I am sorry to say this, but this person is tight in money," he said. "And very close to someone named Joe," he added. "Do you know who this Joe is?"

Almost everyone knows a guy named Joe, and at that moment a guy named Peter certainly hadn't done much to raise his stock in my opinion and I told him so.

"You didn't do so well on that one, luv," I scolded him. "This person is a friend of mine, and it's a 'she,' not a 'he.' A woman. She lives in southern Texas, where it doesn't snow, and she doesn't even own a car."

This made not one iota of a dent on Peter. He can be as stubborn as a mule. He didn't budge, he didn't back down, he didn't change his story. "I tell you only what I see," he said.

I also told him that my friend was most generous, and certainly not tight with her money. "I am sorry," he said. "I see money, money fingers, like budget. Maybe not so much to spend."

Mrs. Lane received handsome royalties on her books, I knew. He had to be wrong.

As for the three members of her family, I told him she didn't have any children. He said he didn't care whether she had children, he still saw three in her family. Perhaps his psychic impression really was of Mrs. Lane and her two Maltese pups, who comprised her only family for so many years. Or could he have known something that only a few longtime close friends knew— that Mrs. Lane did indeed have three adopted children, two of whom (brothers) caused her a great deal of heartache?

In any case, I couldn't mark down much more than a zero for Peter on that reading, and I promptly got off an apologetic letter to Mrs. Lane telling her he had not read her so well, especially since he was so far off base about the car, the snow, and her financial affairs.

I also always made a point of telling my bright little assistant and Girl Friday, Vera Servi, all Peter's predictions, impressions, and assorted psychic celebrations that occurred during our working relationship, just in case anyone should feel the urge to double-check. I must say Vera didn't much like having a psychic around the house. She liked Peter personally, but he frightened her. She treated him gingerly, much in the manner of a timid doe hopscotching around a disembodied spirit. For the most part, whenever he was around, she preferred keeping her distance from him, locking herself in her study and emerging most reluctantly and only at my urgent insistence.

When I told Vera that Peter had missed completely on Mrs. Lane, I detected a sneaky look of utter delight on her face. She wasn't disappointed. She was relieved. These spooky things upset her. Much better he not know what ordinary earthlings are not supposed to know.

I mentioned to Vera the specific errors Peter had made, particularly about the car and driving in the snow and Mrs. Lane's being "tight in money," as Peter had put it.

A couple of days later Mrs. Lane's letter arrived. Our letters had crossed in the mail. She had not yet received mine, and so she did not know of Peter's reading. Her letter, dated July 29, reads in part:

"Dear Norma Lee,

"I am sailing on the Bremen, November 9, from New York to Southampton. A neighbor's youngster, luckily 4F (if that is still the designation for invalided out of conscription) is to be my courier and chauffeur, Don Giffin, 22 years old, M.A. University of Texas, a fairly, most-rarely dependable youngster.

"Between here and there, we'll be motoring—Florida and north to New England. I shall wander around the British Isles for a while in a hired car and see something of Scotland and Ireland. Have bought a Volvo sedan and will take delivery at factory in Goteborg, Sweden. After Sweden, I'd like to drive up the Rhine and down the Danube, with sidetrips through France to the Riviera and back through Luxembourg and Switzerland, and on the way somewhere detour through Etruscan Italy. And I want to see Greece and the Greek Islands again, and Cairo and Istanbul and the Fertile Crescent; and this time if possible I'd like to see the diggings in Iraq and go through Iran—which I didn't before.

"The only problem (aside from Iron Curtains) is prices. Roger (her adopted grandson) says that with prudence he estimates I could live 100 days in Europe for about $8,000—i.e. $80 a day. But when, he asks, was I ever prudent about money? Double the estimate to include Don [her young chauffeur]—$160 per diem? O god. I couldn't begin to do it. But if it be possible that abroad two can contrive to live (prudently) as cheaply as one (imprudently) in these USA, then there's no reason why I can't see the whole world's land and seascape, or anyway be doing it as long as I live."

How's that for a spooky letter considering Peter's prophetic reading from a brief postcard? And I had given him a sound tongue-lashing for being so wrong! Not only was Mrs. Lane going to be motoring around abroad but she would be tooling around the northern countries in wintry weather. Utter madness! It gave credence to Peter's prediction of an auto accident in the snow, though he had also assured me that *"he's* a good driver" (italics mine) and no one would be seriously hurt. Still I was concerned.

Mrs. Lane's next letter, dated August 4, and written as soon as she had received mine, indicated her amazement at Peter's reading:

"Dear Norma Lee,

"Your Peter is certainly a wonder. Or, like Bayer's Aspirin, he 'works WONDERS.'

"Now, I wonder how much of what he said, you would have said; i.e., how much was what we (old-fashioned) would have called 'mind reading.' I don't remember when I wrote you; did you know that I am going abroad, buying a car in Sweden ['in the winter in snow'] and so on? [We corresponded so frequently that she had forgotten what she told me and when. My first and only knowledge of her going abroad came on the brief postcard telling me of Pepe's death, but on this all she said was, 'Going abroad—Europe, Asia, etc.—indefinitely.' I knew nothing of her plans, including her intentions of buying a car and taking along a young chauffeur, until her letter came after Peter's reading. So if it was 'mind reading' it couldn't have been my mind he was reading.]"

Her letter continued: "Old and brisk, educated, intelligent, remarkable memory . . . etc. *Your* views????? Your Peter sees me as brisker than I am, which is one thing that inclines me to think it may be mind reading. . . .

"If you didn't know I am buying a car in Sweden, the prediction of an accident is remarkable. And if you were not remembering Joe Kamp at the time, Peter's 'Who's Joe?' is astounding. Because while dashing off a card to you I was mentally writing to Joe a card that I was in a hurry to write, to catch the postman. . . ."

Not until that very second when I was reading that line in her letter did I remember Joe Kamp. He and his wife, Mildred, were living in Mrs. Lane's house in Danbury, Connecticut, and I knew this very well, as I also knew them very well. But I somehow hadn't thought of them when Peter asked, "Who's Joe?" because, I suppose, I now identified Mrs. Lane with Harlingen, Texas, instead of Danbury, and because I thought it was a little silly for Peter to ask such a question. Everybody knows a Joe Somebody! I brushed it off like a speck of dust, completely forgetting that Joe Kamp had been one of Mrs. Lane's closest friends for years, and so far as I can recall now, the only one named Joe whom she knew during the years that I knew her.

It was indeed remarkable that at the very same time Mrs. Lane was dashing off her card to me, she was mentally writing one to Joe.

And I was also convinced that what Peter meant when he described Mrs. Lane as being "tight in money" was her present concern about her funds to finance the trip for herself and her young driver, particularly since she wanted to travel indefinitely.

In the end I had to give Peter a 99 per cent score on his reading. He missed only on one major point, which I shall come to presently.

I flew down to see Mrs. Lane in early October before she left on her trip. She had written other letters in the meantime and told me more of her plans, and I had a premonition that this might be our last time together. She seemed as hale and hearty as ever and bubbling over with excitement at what I'm sure she knew would be her last big adventure in a long and colorful life crammed with adventure.

She was properly puzzled at Peter's psychic "vision" of her automobile accident in wintertime. And she promised to be careful. But she clearly had no intentions of backing out of her plans for the trip.

Mrs. Lane herself was something of a mystic. Despite a monumentally analytical mind in most matters, she believed in ghosts, ouija boards, table tapping, and poltergeists, and possibly even in reincarnation—I could never be sure. But she did have one of the most fantastic *déjà vu* dream experiences that I have encountered in my years of psychical researching. She began dreaming the strange dream while still a child in De Smet, South Dakota, when she was only two years old, and kept on dreaming the same dream for thirty years. She dreamed that she was floating along the top of slopes covered with pine trees and palms (Dakota was treeless plains), and beyond was the shining blue sea (she didn't know what a sea was), and always at the end of her floating she arrived in a double-walled city with cobbled streets and colorful people. Often in the dream there was a big yellow cat curled up in a chair, a cat four times as large as the largest cat she had ever seen.

In 1921 while Mrs. Lane was working abroad as a foreign correspondent, she took a little Jugoslav boat across the Adriatic to the port of Ragusa (now Dubrovnik)—and there it was, just as she had dreamed it. "I was frozen cold when I recognized it all. Ragusa was exactly as I had dreamed it." Even the huge yellow cat sleeping in a café chair!

The dream raises certain questions that may also be relevant to the dream experiences of other mystics such as Edgar Cayce and Peter.

As Mrs. Lane said, "The thing is inexplicable to me. The cat leaves no hypothesis other than that I dreamed (for *years*) a future experience. But I do not at all believe that the future is predictable. To admit that is to deny the existence of liberty, of individual control of choice and action."

Can her dream be explained by reincarnation? Or genetic memory?

Mrs. Lane must have had a psychic kinship with the "sleeping prophet"—Cayce. For during her high school years—or at least during that time when she was being fervently courted by a beau in a rubber-tired phaeton—she always worked out all her problems in math and in Latin while she slept, and always got the correct solutions!

My last visit with Mrs. Lane, which lasted until dawn, was spent talking about many things but primarily about Peter Hurkos and Edgar Cayce and the enigma of their strange mental feats. Feats? Telepathy? Clairvoyance? Precognition? Retrocognition? What do the words mean, really?

Can the future be foreknown and predicted? If so, how?

There was a man, J. W. Dunne, who some years ago wrote a book that provoked a great deal of controversy. It was called *Experiment in Time*, and its thesis, based on systematic records of his dreams over long periods of time, was that all events that ever have been, are now, or will be, are eternally in existence and that we as individuals move among these events. This is the predestined, deterministic view of events, and although Dunne was a very careful and systematic observer of his dreams, his theory and philosophy are not generally acceptable to most thinking.

I don't consider myself a "thinker," and though I do believe in "precognitive" dreams, I can't believe in Dunne's philosophy that the future is fixed and unalterable, that future events are *already in existence*. If they were, the problem of precognition would be concerned only with the *means* by which these events could be known or "seen" in advance. Dunne's view was that this could be achieved in certain states of consciousness, but particularly in the state of sleep in which a person as an observer could observe these predestined events, both past and future.

If we wanted to, we could accept this as an explanation of Peter's ability to see into both the past and the future while asleep—though I don't think this view would be acceptable to many because it assumes the theory that future events are already in existence. I'm willing to leave this to the para-psychologists and philosophers.

More to the point is, How was Peter able to know of Mrs. Lane's plans to go motoring abroad merely by touching a post-card she had written to me?

This brings us to the subject of object reading, or psychom-etry, which is Peter's forte. Psychometry is nothing new. The name was given the phenomenon by an anthropologist named Buchanan. Unfortunately, the word has been misused and abused by phony and fringe "psychics," but a great deal of experimental work (notably by Dr. J. Hettinger and Dr. Eugene Osty) has established the phenomenon of psychometry with a very high degree of probability, and also revealed some of the conditions under which it takes place. Basically, psychometry means that there are some sensitives—or psychics—who, when handed an object, are able to offer information about the person or persons who have previously touched the object. Raynor C. Johnson's fascinating book, *The Imprisoned Splendour,* is one of the most scientifically illuminating on the subject.

As Johnson points out, one of the most interesting and signifi-cant aspects of psychometry is that it is not essential for the sen-sitive to handle the object (which may be in a sealed envelope). It is sufficient for the sensitive to establish some kind of mental rapport with or relationship to it. In other words, it is sufficient for the sensitive only to "concentrate," on the object—though the state of concentration is no greater than that favorable to telepathy.

Dr. Osty, a French physician with a deep interest in, and a scientific approach to, the problems of psychical research, be-came director of the Institut Metapsychique International in Paris and for many years made investigations of a group of tal-ented French sensitives. His contributions to the study of psy-chometry are among the most important in psychic literature. He tested some sensitives while they were under hypnosis, others in the waking state, always using an object that had been in contact with a person.

It was his conclusion that the so-called "paranormal" knowl-edge of the sensitive was derived from the subject, *i.e.,* the person who had once touched the object. Some of his subjects, he revealed, were able to establish rapport on a deeper or "transcendental plane" and at times appeared to have foreknowledge of the future. On this subject Osty's views are in direct opposition to Dunne's. Osty is certain that foreknowledge of the future does not imply determinism, or fixed and unalterable events already in existence.

On the contrary, he says that "foreknowledge . . . is evolutionary and living. . . ." and that the sensitive is able to be most accurate and detailed when dealing with matters *in actual course of realization—although unknowable by inference as to the outcome.*

"Prediction is less detailed where the conclusions are distant in time, just as a traveller moving through new country sees on the far horizon only vague general masses of color, while in the middle distance he can distinguish villages and woods, and close at hand trees, houses, and people."

It is possible that this quasi-scientific explanation of psychometry and how a sensitive gets his "paranormal" knowledge may offer a clue to Peter's psychic talents. There is the further important hypothesis that all objects have a kind of lingering aura called a "psychic ether"—apparently akin to what Dr. Riesenman, as noted in an earlier chapter, calls the Odic force. This psychic ether, so the experts say, is responsible for the phenomenon of retrocognition—knowledge acquired of some past event. Though precognition—foretelling the future—has always attracted far more attention than retrocognition—seeing into the past—the backward view in time is no less mysterious and intriguing than the forward one, when we take into account the psychic ether associated with a place or a person. It is through this psychic ether, again according to the experts, that psychometry is possible—or "object reading," if you prefer.

It has been suggested by some that there is even a kind of persistent memory in the psychic ether associated with a place, to which in a certain receptive state of mind a sensitive person may tune in. It has also been noted that certain recorded cases of retrocognition appear to have been stimulated by the "memory records" of a particular locality or historic building.

Do inanimate objects possess a cognizable memory-record? Absurd.

Rocks of course cannot remember—a function of the instrument known as the mind. But there are those who contend that rocks (for example) may hold a memory in their associated psychic ether, which the mind of man under favorable circumstances can perceive.

In any case, the hypothesis of a psychic ether as an aid to psychometry is regarded by some as the complex bridge between mind and brain—as well as a partial explanation of the strange divining powers of Peter Hurkos.

Well, we can speculate. Was it perhaps a combination of psychic ether (Mrs. Lane's) and long-distance telepathy that gave Peter the knowledge of Mrs. Lane's motor trip in winter via her postcard to me?

Certainly she was the one—not I—who was thinking, planning, and concentrating on her forthcoming trip, and who had made arrangements to buy a car and pick it up in Sweden.

All Peter had to do to know this was merely to pick her brain via telepathy. Thus the only part that was prediction was her accident. And that is where he missed. . . .

We had talked until dawn, and the sun was bursting forth in Mrs. Lane's magnificent walled-in gardens when we finally said good night to catch a few winks of sleep. Next day I straggled aboard a Trans-Texas plane, loaded down with an armful of Mexican paper flowers and a gaudy clown painting that we had bought on a little junket down to Ensenada, across the border in Mexico. . . . She had stood in the hot sun waving while the plane eased down the runway. Though I don't claim to be psychic, I somehow knew that that would be my last sight of her. And it was. But not for reasons Peter had foreseen. Or at least the accident. . . .

Mrs. Lane left Harlingen with her young driver, and I had cards from her along the way—from New Orleans, the Florida Keys, Williamsburg, and Washington D.C. She was having a ball seeing the United States all over again—at eighty-two. Her last card came not from Europe but from Frederick, Maryland, and she was on her way to Danbury.

The call came a few days later. Rose Wilder Lane had died in her sleep, apparently of a heart attack, only two days after she had arrived in Danbury and was en route to New York with her young driver. She didn't make it to Europe, or to Sweden to pick up the little Volvo she had bought. She did not go motoring, as she had planned, through the north countries in winter on slippery roads. . . .

What did Peter make of this?

I told him of her sudden death in Connecticut and that she didn't even get abroad.

He made no explanation or apology. "I tell only what I see," he said. "I did not see death."

Still, what he did see was remarkable, considering that most of it was Mrs. Lane's plans in the making. As Dr. Osty says, the sensitive is more accurate and detailed when dealing with matters *in actual course of realization—"although unknowable by inference as to the outcome. Prediction is less detailed where the conclusions are distant in time. . . ."*

I believe that Peter's special talents must lie in the area of seeing events that are already past or are in the actual course of realization, in the *process of becoming*—as with Mrs. Lane, and with the selling of our house. As Dr. Osty believes, the prediction is less detailed where the conclusions are distant in time. In this regard, Peter scored 100 per cent on the (distant in time) scale of our house—but missed completely on the demise of Mrs. Lane. . . .

There is a curious footnote to all of this which I had completely forgotten until I found some shorthand notes made while I was in Peter's apartment one evening to pick up some files. It was just a very quick social-business call; we weren't working. But Peter insisted on giving me a bit of unsolicited psychic news. He gave me a big bear hug, pushed me into a chair, and said, "Now I want to tell you, before it is February you will get some money what you don't expect from a person who is going to pass away.

You are not in a will, but somebody is going to leave you a little
—not very much but you will be amazed by it."

Those were my notes verbatim, dated August 14. I took the
notes simply as a matter of record—wondering who was going
to die and leave me money. I had no immediate prospects. But
Mrs. Lane died in October, and in January ("before it is February") I had a letter telling me of her wishes regarding a small
financial legacy. No, I wasn't in her will (Peter had said, "You
are not in a will"), but Roger, her grandson and executor, wrote
me about her verbal wishes—which he carried out.

On the same day that Peter gave this good news he also told
me some interesting news about my husband. I didn't ask him.
He just gave it. He said, "Your husband is going to get a job in
about three and a half months which has to do with motion pictures." That was August 14. Sure enough, he had an unexpected
call for a photographic assignment—one involving a kind of documentary film—to start during the Thanksgiving week, almost
three and a half months to the day after Peter predicted it.

Added very personal item: During the writing of this book
my husband has had three major eye surgeries. Peter knew nothing about them except that he was having problems. He abruptly
informed me one day, "Your husband have problem with left
eye. No good." At that time surgery was scheduled for a certain
date—on his left eye. And I'm sure Peter didn't know left from
right so far as my husband's eye problems were concerned. (He
was in Palm Springs and Peter in Los Angeles.) But sure enough
—with the left-eye surgery there were complications. Everything
came out O.K., and details are unnecessary here. But once again
Peter called it right—causing me a great deal of concern at the
time.

One Saturday afternoon Peter and Stephany arrived for a photo
session with my husband. They needed some formal portraits
for publicity and promotion. I didn't even know they had arrived
until Stephy came bounding into my study and asked me to go
out and talk to Peter while he was being photographed.

"He hates being photographed," she said. "Just sit there and talk to him and help him relax. He gets this horrible fixed stare on his face when he's taking a posed picture. He's never able to pose for a picture. It has to be a working picture. He has to be doing something."

Peter was perched on a stool, looking exceedingly handsome in his tuxedo and makeup. Stephy told him to take his shoe off to use for a working prop—by rubbing or feeling it. She explained, "He always works with shoes or clothing when he's working on cases primarily. . . . Shoes or clothing . . . anything that has sweat or perspiration from the body. . . . He seems to be able to get the vibrations better." (Psychic ether or Odic force?)

Personally, I thought he looked awkward holding the shoe in a formal photo. "He wouldn't be working with a shoe while wearing a tux, would he?" I asked. (Since then I have learned better; he does!) My husband, looking into the lens, agreed the shoe wasn't right.

"Here, use this," I said, offering Peter my oversized mod wristwatch, which I had bought for ten dollars in the London airport. I should have known better.

"That should give you plenty of vibrations," I said, trying to be funny.

He fingered the watch, fixed his eyes in that semitrance-like stare of his, and said, "I see you with fee-nancy-owl trouble." That's Peter's pronunciation of "financial"—with accent on the owl. Financial problems.

*Sure, doesn't everybody have them?*

"Hmmmmmm," I said. "Relax, Peter. Smile. Don't be so serious." My job at the moment was to get him to relax for the camera. I hadn't asked him for a reading. And furthermore, I didn't even want one. But he forged ahead.

"I see you getting more money from Doubleday before our book is finished," he said.

"No, Peter, we do not get any more money from Doubleday until we finish our book and give them the manuscript," I told him.

Peter was not familiar with publisher-author contracts and procedures, which include in most cases the payment of half the publisher's advance to the author upon signing the contract for a book and the other half when the manuscript is satisfactorily completed.

This was our arrangement with my editor at Doubleday after I had agreed to do the book for Peter.

Now, when he said I was going to get more money from Doubleday before our book was finished, I was trying to explain to him. . . .

"No, no, no," he said. "This have nothing to do with *our* book. It is something else . . . completely different. . . ."

"Oh. Then you must mean from another publisher?"

"No, no, no. Doubleday," he insisted. "But this have nothing to do with our book."

"Oh, well. O.K., O.K., but you're wrong, Peter. It's impossible." I said it like—so what else is new? His eyes showed hurt and anger.

"I tell you only what I see. Why you think I make lies? I say you gonna get more money from Doubleday, and it have nothing to do with our book," he insisted. "You wait and see."

Having settled that, he raced on to suddenly far-spookier matters. He said that my husband and I were going to get involved in a new "business," and he specified that we would be "working with a magazine." He poured forth a rather startling number of specifics such as that there would be five persons involved, it was a "high-class, high-intellect" magazine, and it needed financing. *Et cetera, et cetera.*

When I started this book, I had not anticipated any necessity for divulging details of my personal and business affairs, but in fairness to readers, as well as to Peter, I feel obliged to include some incidents such as this one, but with certain details omitted for obvious reasons. I hope my readers will understand.

The important and relevant fact here is that only the day before our photo session, on Friday evening and far into the night, my husband and I had been listening to a former magazine editor from New York outline his plans for resuming publication of the magazine—and in a way that would very much involve us. In fact, the three of us had spent a great deal of time together in our home during that preceding week discussing and debating

202 · *The Psychic World of Peter Hurkos*

the proposed project. And Peter, psychometrizing my mod watch, and apparently tuning in to my psychic ether, picked up the details of our discussions with such uncanny accuracy that he could have been eavesdropping.

Yet he couldn't possibly have known about it. That was one week when we were not working on the book, and the magazine project, in fact, had come as a complete surprise to my husband and me. We didn't know the New York editor, had never met him until that week, and had never considered being involved in any publishing business, for that matter. And even if we had, we never discussed our personal affairs with Peter.

As Peter talked, my husband, of course, was shooting pictures of him—from his perch on a ladder. At one point he was so shaken by Peter's remarks that he almost fell off. We were both shooting pointed glances at each other, though silently trying to keep our composures as Peter rambled on, scoring again and again. I knew what my husband was thinking, and I was wondering the same about him.

As soon as the opportunity presented itself, my husband took me aside and whispered, "Have you been talking to him?"

"No, have you?"

We both knew we hadn't, of course. . . .

On Monday morning when my gal Vera came to work, I told her what had happened with Peter over the weekend. Having worked with me for some time, Vera of course knew a great deal more about my personal and business affairs than Peter did, and in fact had been very much involved in the magazine project discussions of the previous week. As it eventually turned out, we decided against going into the project, and so as a sample of "precognition," or foreknowledge of future events, we would have to say that Peter missed. But again he had picked up with uncanny accuracy a set of circumstances that were *in the process* of becoming, or at least being. This was similar to his "seeing" or tuning in to Mrs. Lane's plans in the making. The fact that her plans or ours with the magazine venture didn't materialize certainly should not detract from Peter's high scores on knowing those plans, either through telepathy, clairvoyance, or some other psychic means, at the time that they existed in the minds of others.

Again, as Dr. Osty observed, a sensitive is more accurate and detailed when dealing with matters in the actual course of realization, or in the process of becoming—and less accurate in predictions where the conclusions are distant in time.

Vera and I both agreed that, as far as we could figure out, Peter was 99 per cent accurate on Saturday afternoon's impromptu and unsolicited psychic reading.

There was only one point he had missed on—the money from Doubleday.

"Of course he's wrong on that," I said. "But, oh well, he doesn't claim to be right all the time."

I shrugged it off, and we both settled down to work.

Shortly after noon, as is her daily routine, Vera went upstairs to bring in the mail.

She returned, quietly opened the door to my study, and stood there loaded down with the usual bundles of papers, magazines, books, press releases, and other mail.

There was a stricken expression on her face. Her black eyes looked as though they were about to pop out of her head. She dumped the heavy bundles on the couch and brought the letter-size mail over to my desk. I knew from her petrified, speechless look that something was wrong with the mail—and I knew what it had to be. I also had a sudden sixth sense myself that I was about to lose an able assistant because of my seances with a psychic.

She quickly shuffled the letters and pointed an accusing finger at an envelope, as though it were alive. I recognized the Doubleday envelope from the blue and red stripes running across it.

Now, of course, letters from publisher to author are not all that unusual, but why did one have to arrive on precisely this day, especially when it had been several months since I had received a letter from Doubleday, and also since we had had no problems regarding the book and no occasion for more frequent communication.

"It can't be money, it just can't be," she said, utterly shaken with terror.

"Of course not," I assured her as I tore open the envelope. "See," I said, shaking its contents at her. "No check."

"Thank God!" she cried with relief.

But as I read the pages I held in my hand, it was my turn to be shook up.

The communication indeed had nothing to do with my book on Peter Hurkos. It was a letter from my editor at Doubleday with a legal document releasing movie and television rights on another book I had ghosted for someone. The book had been a disappointment. (And we'll let it go at that.) I had completely forgotten about it. I never expected to hear more about it.

But the person for whom I ghosted it had somehow persuaded Doubleday to have the movie and television rights reverted to us —which does indeed mean money if the book should happen to bring forth a movie sale.

Of course, such deals are all very iffy.

Nevertheless, how could Peter come so uncannily close?

He had insisted the "money from Doubleday" would have nothing to do with his book. And it didn't.

And even though his prediction didn't come *tout fait accompli* with a check, the legal reversion of certain rights certainly might be considered the next best thing. Anyway, it's good enough for me until the real thing comes along. Peter still says it means money, and in effect it *is* money—if the book sells to the movies. And it may yet. We'll see. Peter didn't even know I had written the book.

In the aftermath of all of this, a friend said to me, "You're losing your reporter's skepticism. Don't you know that what you have just experienced is precisely what would have happened if you had been dealing with a fraud or a charlatan? You would expect, for example, to receive such a communication from Doubleday. You would expect him to know about your meetings with the magazine editor. What you should do rather than succumb and be taken in by these small coincidences is to react like a reporter, investigate and check them out, find out *how* he could have known. . . ."

I appreciated being reminded that I was a reporter and tried to react like one. But finding out *how* he could have known—as a charlatan—was easier said than done.

Could he have been bugging the post office? Hardly. A quick check with Doubleday revealed that they were as puzzled as I was.

And when I asked the former New York magazine editor if he knew Peter Hurkos, he replied, "No, I don't. Why? Should I? Is he a writer?"

"He's the famous Dutch psychic," I explained.

"Oh," he said dubiously. Then, "Well, I must say my meeting you had a strange and eerie quality."

"In what way?"

"Well, I hadn't planned to call you here. I didn't know you. But I saw your name in the telephone directory when I was looking up another number. I had a flashback of memory. I used to live in Illinois and I read the Chicago *Tribune* religiously. When I saw your name I suddenly remembered, 'Hmmmm, that's the girl reporter who used to do all those quack exposés in the *Tribune*. . . . So I called you. Somehow I had the feeling that I was being led to you. Hmmm, there is something very strange about it, isn't there?'"

I said, Hmmmmm, yes, indeed, it was all very strange to me, and I didn't want to be mixed up in any psychic mishmashes. At this point I was beginning to think the editor was a little fey.

He looked at me curiously and asked, "Did you say he's that famous Dutch psychic?"

"Yes, Peter Hurkos."

"Didn't you do an exposé of him once? In the *Tribune?*"

"Not exactly. I tried to. It didn't work."

"You don't really believe in all that rot, do you?"

"No, I guess not. Not really . . ."

But then I remembered the words of a believer, "There are people who say God is dead, too. . . ." And I remembered something that Hugh Lynn Cayce had said to me about his father. "He was a seer in a seerless culture."

# · 11 ·

# *Of Death and Disaster*

In August 1969, Peter made a guest appearance on *The David Frost Show* in New York with another guest, columnist Leonard Lyons. I did not see the show, but many TV viewers who did see it have told me that Peter gave one of his most remarkable performances, particularly in his reading of a sealed box that was presented to him to test his psychic insight.

It was a cardboard box about a foot and a half square. The only person who knew what was in it was Leonard Lyons. Not even David Frost knew.

Peter began rubbing his hands over the box. His reading, as many will remember, went something like this:

"I see wires, yes . . . wires and hooks . . . steel hooks shaped like this [moving his arm in an arc]. . . . Oh, my God, terrible. What this man did to this world, it is too terrible. He's a genius but a bad man for what he did to the world. Yes, wires and hooks . . . Wait, I see now. It's a telephone. I see a telephone. We must pray for this man's soul."

When the box was opened, there it was—a telephone. Not the kind of telephone familiar to most of us, to be sure, but nonetheless a telephone and a very special one.

It was Hitler's telephone, the one he had had in his mountain villa at Berchtesgaden. How Leonard Lyons came by it I'm not quite sure; probably it was a memento picked up on one of his assignments abroad.

But again Peter had scored with stunning impact while millions of TV viewers watched.

For those of you who have heard rumors that Peter has "plants" in his audience, either for his TV appearances or stage demonstrations, I can tell you right now—forget it! As I have mentioned before, Peter has a terrible temper, but I have never seen him more violently riled than when a certain booking agent suggested to him not long ago that he have a "plant" in the audience during his engagement at a certain theater in Los Angeles to "beef up" the show and give him a higher percentage of accuracy.

Peter exploded. "That's dishonest! It's for crooks!" he shouted. Needless to say, he speedily detached himself from that certain agent. . . .

Many have tried to pull tricks on Peter, such as sneaking in a picture that has nothing to do with the case he is working on, as happened while he was working on the Boston Strangler case. Usually Peter can tune into these tricks, which invariably make him violently angry.

But one television interviewer sneaked in a picture that brought forth a most unusual reading from Peter. This person, he said, was tall, dark, and wearing a dark suit. "He is a nice fellow, but he has a terrible temper. Sometimes he blows up and shouts when he's excited, but he doesn't mean it. It doesn't last. Two minutes and he's over it. He likes parties, likes to have people around, likes a good joke. He is a very generous man, a very unusual man. . . ."

He was very upset when the interviewer showed him the picture. It was a photograph of Peter himself—a picture that had been sent out in his publicity kit. And Peter had described himself to a T. It had never happened before. It was the first time Peter had ever been able to "see" anything about himself, and he was very upset by it. He was both amazed at himself and infuriated at the TV interviewer. It is the only time he has ever given a reading on himself (and so accurately!), and yet with all his psychic insight he did not know that the picture he was fingering was Peter Hurkos! He was also depressed after this incident. Generally he never knows whether what he sees is past, present, or future, but he definitely does not relish the idea of seeing anything for himself as he sees things for others.

In July of 1968 while Peter was appearing at the Three Rivers Inn in Syracuse, New York, a local radio station arranged with him for a series of demonstrations involving readings of personalities in the news. Photographs of the persons were placed in heavy manila envelopes, and the envelopes were not marked, so Peter had no knowledge of their contents.

The newscaster pushed an envelope toward him and Peter began:

"This is a person what should be under doctor's control every day. Absolutely quiet. No working. He should be resting. I see him in a small room . . . and a piano there on that side of the room. . . . I see beams in the house. . . . Beams . . . yes, and also an easel there in the corner. And paints. He paints. That is his hobby. . . . But if this was my brother I would take him out of circulation. He should have nothing to do with politics anymore. He should have complete rest, and there will be again for him a hospital, yes, there will be again a hospital. . . . I hope that he will have a long life. Let's pray for this man. He is a fine person. But I am sorry to say I do not see a long life for him. And he needs medical care every day if possible."

"Do you mean that he is nearing the end of his life?" asked the newscaster.

"That's what I see, I can't help what I see," Peter replied.

The newscaster then held up the photograph for the audience —and Peter—to see, and said quietly, "This is former President Dwight D. Eisenhower."

Former President Eisenhower at that time was in the hospital —again—and had been in and out of the hospital several times in recent months.

Peter missed on his timing. He saw the end as only a matter of days or weeks. But then, so did a lot of other people. Eisenhower fooled them all by living many months longer than was expected. After spending the last months of his life continuously in Walter Reed Hospital, he died on March 28, 1969.

During this same series of televised demonstrations, Peter also gave fairly accurate, though less dramatic, readings on Governor Nelson Rockefeller, New York's Mayor John Lindsay, and a few other names in the news. But at the same time he picked the wrong presidential candidate to win the 1968 election. Peter expected Humphrey, not Nixon, to win. But he knew that Senator Robert F. Kennedy would not live to be nominated.

Early on the morning of June 5, 1968, my husband awakened me with the words, "Kennedy has been shot. You're wanted on the phone. It's the *Tribune*."

My assignment was to drop everything and join the pool of *Tribune* staff reporters and photographers from Washington and Chicago who were converging on Los Angeles to cover the story. I was only one of many reporters from all over the world assigned to cover the tragic death of Senator Kennedy. All day and throughout the long chilly evening I kept a shivering vigil beside an outdoor telephone booth opposite the ambulance entrance of Good Samaritan Hospital, reporting periodically to my office in Chicago.

The next day I watched the final farewell of thousands of mourners at the Los Angeles airport as the giant jet soared off with the body of Bobby Kennedy, the family and friends—and three women all widowed by assassins' bullets:—Mrs. Ethel Kennedy, Mrs. Jacqueline Kennedy, and Mrs. Coretta King.

It was only later, when my assignment was finished and my mind refreshed, that I permitted myself to think back to a little scene that had taken place around the bar in our home a few weeks earlier.

We had gathered there, my husband and I, Peter and Stephy, and a friend, Sylvia Siegman, who was assisting us with the tape recordings and transcriptions for this book, to drink a toast to Stephy, who had finally enrolled in cooking school and was learning to cook. In fact, she had brought over a gourmet fish dish that she had prepared as a surprise for us. Peter and I had just finished another long session with the tape recorder and Sylvia, while Stephy had been puttering about the kitchen. We all were teasing her about her cooking talents.

"Next thing you know you'll be learning to sew and clean house. . . ."

"You'll make a terrific hostess. . . . Look at the parties you can throw . . . and all the people you'll get to meet . . . celebrities and politicians. . . ."

"Next thing you know you'll be in politics. . . ."

"Ja, she stick her nose in there, too," Peter said, teasing.

"You mean maybe I'll be mingling with people like Bobby Kennedy?" Stephy quipped.

"Don't worry about Kennedy. He be knocked off next," said Peter.

He said it casually, with none of the histrionics of a crystal gazer, and at the time it had none of the awesome aura of a "prophecy." This was a social conversation, and we took it as such. Dr. Martin Luther King's death was still fresh in our minds. The political campaign was gathering steam. The Kennedy family name, as everyone knew, had become practically synonymous with tragedy of one sort or another. And after all, it had become a popular pastime for people to predict the death of Presidents and politicians. None of us gave a second thought to Peter's words at the time.

*"Don't worry about Kennedy. He be knocked off next."*

It was only after it happened, and so soon, that the words came back to haunt us.

But then, it was probably only coincidence. . . . Or was it?

At least six months before Senator Kennedy's death, Peter had psychometrized an envelope containing a picture of Ted Kennedy during one of his demonstrations. He had said then, not knowing the contents of the envelope, "This is a family that has had a lot of problems. I see many brothers and sisters. All die violent deaths. One brother has been killed. No, maybe two brothers already? [He didn't know for sure.] But another brother is going to be killed. Not this one. He escapes. I don't see him dying violently. [But he did escape death in a plane crash.] I see him going high, maybe in politics."

Could it have been only coincidence that he had predicted another Kennedy would meet violent death six months before the event, and then again only a few weeks before? The first time, though, he didn't know that he was "reading" the Kennedy family, which brings up the question, If he knew so much about them, why *didn't* he know whom he was talking about?

"I tell only what I see and hear, what the voice tells me," he says. "If the voice don't tell me it's Kennedy, how do I know?"

"What voice?" I asked.

"Jesus Christ, what you think? The voice that came back with my other mind."

"Oh."

Peter had told me in trying to explain how his "gift" works that sometimes he sees pictures and sometimes he hears the "voice," but he rarely spoke of the voice, and I was curious about it.

Auditory hallucinations, of course, are usually considered rather serious.

Whenever I questioned him about the voice, he seemed touchy about it. "What the hell! You think I gonna tell I hear voices? People think I am crazy. But I tell you the truth, the voice never lies, never."

I knew, of course, that Peter had heard "voices"—plural—soon after his accident while he was in his semiconscious states in the hospital, and for some time after. Sometimes, of course, the voices were real, though indistinct or blurred, as were those of his family and the hospital staff when he first regained consciousness. And sometimes they were imaginary, as on that long-ago fitful morning when he was roaming around a cemetery in Holland and all the voices of the dead seemed to rise up and run after him. . . .

But the "voice" that seems to sometimes turn on his psychic insight is different. I asked him to describe it.

"It is deep, like an old man," he said, "like this," and he demonstrated.

"Is it the voice of anyone you know, a voice you recognize?"

"No."

"Do you remember the first time you ever heard the voice?"

"Definitely. When I was with Dr. Peters in the hospital. The voice told me about the G D on the doctor's pajamas."

"Did the voice also tell you about Nurse Zelda's valise?" I asked.

"No. That was not the voice. That was the mental picture I saw. A picture." He was very definite about it.

"Are the pictures you see in black and white or in color?"

"No color. Only black and white. The only color I saw was when I was unconscious."

"Do you see pictures and hear voices at the same time?" I asked Peter.

"No, never. Sometimes it is pictures like on a TV screen. Sometimes only the voice."

"Is it always the same voice? All the time?"

"Always the same voice. It is the voice I hear in my other mind, dear. I told you I have two minds."

Yes, he had told me. Many times. And at this point I wasn't about to argue with him about it.

I did ask him, though, whether he could carry on a conversation with the voice.

"No, not ever. That is impossible, and I tell you why. I make no possible interruptions. Let's say he is talking to me and I interrupt and ask a question. Then I never get an answer. He is gone, just like that. Fast. So when he talks to me I listen, and when he is finished, he is gone. Maybe he tell me about a plane crash and all the people burned to death. This time I don't see it, no pictures. It's the voice that told me. I cannot talk back to him. It's not possible. It tells me. I just cannot call him and say, 'Tell me something.' It just comes . . . maybe in the middle of the night. Anytime. But the voice protects me. The voice never lies."

Between the visions and the "voice" I, for one, certainly wouldn't want to trade places with Peter.

I tried to understand his explanation of how he knew about the Kennedy family. Did he obtain this knowledge through his mental pictures or from the voice?

"It was all pictures," he said.

Then why did he say he didn't know he was talking about the Kennedys because the "voice" didn't tell him?

"It's the voice what tells me the name," he said. "Most times when I see pictures, I do not see the name too. That's for the voice."

Personally, it would seem to me that these fascinating mental phenomena—the strange voices and visions that flash on and off inside a human brain—would be only slightly less, if indeed any less, important to scientific researchers than the rock specimens brought back by our astronauts from the moon.

Meanwhile, paradoxically, on that memorable and historic day, July 20, 1969, when men first set foot on the moon, the biggest news story next to the lunar landing was Senator Edward M. Kennedy's car crash on Martha's Vineyard which killed a pretty blonde secretary who had once worked for the late Senator Robert Kennedy.

So far, Ted Kennedy was living up to Peter's prediction that, unlike his brothers, he would escape violent death.

Peter left right after the moon landing for Ann Arbor, Michigan, to begin work on the multiple murder case of the Ann Arbor-Ypsilanti coeds.

I asked him, as he was about to leave, what he thought of the Ted Kennedy incident.

"The guy's in a lot of trouble," he said. It of course didn't take any psychic sense to figure that out.

I also asked him whether he thought the incident would affect Ted Kennedy's political future, including his chances for the 1972 Presidential nomination.

"Definitely," he said. But again, his answer could have come from common sense rather than psychic sense.

The editor of an eastern publication tried to persuade Peter to come to Edgartown, the scene of the accident, and work on the case. He offered him an attractive fee in addition to his expenses. Peter refused. He said he had no wish to add to the Kennedy family's problems. Personally, I think his decision was a wise one.

Ordinarily Peter does not like to give anyone bad news of upcoming death or disaster unless it is in general terms, and not on a too personal level. If he sees an imminent tragedy in the family, he at least tries to soften the blow, although as I have said, he sometimes seems to have no control over what rushes out of his mouth, particularly when he has very strong psychic impressions.

Such was the case with Sylvia Siegman, whom I mentioned earlier in this chapter as the friend who was helping us with the tapes and transcriptions of our interview sessions for this book. During the first few months of working together, Sylvia was always present at our sessions. In addition to operating the tape recorder, she was also learning to be a court reporter and was practicing by taking down all our conversations on her stenotype machine. She then would type up all the transcriptions from both the tape recorder and her stenotype machine and bring them to me.

I might add that because she adored Peter, she did all this work for us at no cost. She wouldn't accept a single penny from either of us.

One evening as she was about to leave the house, I saw Peter take her over to a corner, out of our hearing, and begin talking to her rather excitedly. He seemed to be admonishing her about something. Then he walked out to her car with her, and I heard him say, "Please, please! Do me a favor. Listen to me."

She drove off. Peter came back in the house, looking very troubled. We asked him what was wrong.

"Jesus Christ, she won't listen," he said angrily. "I tell her she better not go out with that guy anymore. . . ."

"Are you trying to tell her who she can and can't date?" I asked. "Maybe she doesn't like to be told."

"But if she knew what I see! I say to her, 'Where are your brains? Listen to me.'"

"What do you see about her?"

"I see death around them—both of them," he told us. "No, I don't know which one, but I see death around them. She say she won't stop going out with him, so I tell her please do me a favor and don't drive in the car with that man for a month."

"Did you tell her you saw death around her?"

"I don't like to tell her about death, but I tell her I see an accident in that car with her boy friend and I ask her not to drive with him anymore, at least not for a month."

Sylvia showed up for our sessions for the next couple of weeks. Everything seemed to be going along normally, and so far as I knew, Peter said nothing more to her.

Then one day soon after, Stephy called to cancel Peter's interview session with me because—Sylvia couldn't come. She was in the hospital. She had been in an automobile accident with her boy friend. He was killed. Sylvia had a brain concussion, was hospitalized for five weeks, and as this is written is still undergoing treatment nearly a year later. (The accident occurred in January 1969.)

I have not seen her since. But I have talked to her by telephone. She still has not fully recovered from the shock of the experience but is undergoing psychotherapy to bring her out of her depression and encourage her to talk about it. She admits, "I attached no importance whatsoever to Peter's warning. He told me that my relationship with this man was no good, that it would end in some kind of violence or accident. But I didn't pay much attention, I never thought twice about it—until after it happened." (It was one of the weirdest, freakiest kind of California Freeway accidents involving a jackknifing truck and five cars; Sylvia was rescued from her car, which had burst into flames.)

The tragedy poses the question: Could she have prevented the accident either by refusing to go out with her boy friend for a month as Peter had pleaded with her to do (or would he have had the accident anyway, with someone else?), or by telling him of Peter's warning (which she hadn't done) and urging him to be careful?

This of course brings up again those metaphysical-philosophical conundrums that are inevitable in any discussion of psychic phenomena: Is the future predestined and unalterable? Is there an "Eternal Now" in which all events that ever have been, are now, or will be (J. W. Dunne's "experiment with time" theory), or can we change the course of events, which presumes the premise of free will?

I do not consider the answers to such questions within my province as a reporter. I can only report that the perplexing mind of a man such as Peter does give rise again and again to these questions and many, many more . . . and that Peter, in pleading with

Sylvia Siegman not to go driving with her boy friend, impatiently demanded, "Where are your brains?"

And I as impatiently might inquire the same of scientists who, having completed their conquest of the moon, continue to ignore the exploration of the human brain.

# · 12 ·

# The Ann Arbor Murders

As I was finishing writing this book, Peter became involved in
swift succession in two more crime cases, the Ypsilanti-Ann Arbor murders, and the fantastically brutal Sharon Tate–Jay Sebring case, which involved five murders. Both of these were more
bizarre and sensational than any others in his entire career. The
Ypsilanti-Ann Arbor coed slayings took place over a period of
two years in the college campus area of the University of Michigan and Eastern Michigan University at nearby Ypsilanti.
There were eight victims, six of whom were students at either
UM or EMU. Of the two others, one was a high school dropout
but killed in the area, and the youngest, Dawn Basom, thirteen,
of Ypsilanti, was last seen (April 15, 1969) hurrying home about a
half-mile from her house near the EMU campus, the same area
where some of the other victims were last seen.

As this is written, a twenty-two-year-old senior at EMU, John
Norman Collins, has been charged with first-degree murder in
the death of the seventh victim, Karen Sue Beineman, an
eighteen-year-old EMU coed, and is in jail in Ann Arbor awaiting
trial. Police are collecting evidence, which they expect will link
him to some of the other brutal sex slayings.

Peter startled veteran policemen and newsmen with some of
his preliminary discoveries that led them to John Collins.

Peter was called into the investigation of the Ann Arbor-

Ypsilanti slayings in late July, 1969, by a citizens' group, which raised a thousand dollars to cover his expenses. He had full cooperation of the police—much better cooperation, he said, than when he worked on the Boston Strangler murders.

His first contact with the case was on June 14, 1969, when he was visited at his home in Studio City by Arnold Rosenfeld, a Detroit *Free Press* reporter, who had brought with him some photographs of the victims (there were six then), a map of the area, and some articles and clothing belonging to the victims.

On this very first reading of the objects, and with no previous knowledge of the cases (remember, Peter doesn't read the newspapers, and though everyone in Michigan might have been talking about the murders, they didn't create a ripple in blasé Hollywood), he came up with a remarkably accurate description of young Collins, who wasn't arrested until weeks later.

"He is not an old man, about twenty-five–twenty-six [wrong]. . . . He is quite brilliant and quite a bit of education. . . . Young face, like a student [he was studying to be a teacher], like a baby face, beautiful face, not a stupid man, very intelligent, goes to school at night, a University have night classes. . . . I see a small school. Not a heavy person, I would say about 136 pounds. He drives a motor bike. . . . The farm I see here and behind the house further up is a creek. I see a water pit . . . a dry well. . . ."

He described the farmhouse where police believe that Dawn Basom was slain as the murderer's headquarters. At one point, touching a photograph of the farmhouse, he said:

"He operated in this house. Now there is no clue that the girl was in the house. This is where he operated from. In this house was a chair with broken legs, a chair and beer bottles, cans. And I see a lot of newspapers, newspapers, in that house. There was never. . . . that he killed the girl in that house is not true. . . . It was his headquarters. He watched here for a long time."

And later: "He is still active there [at the house]. In other words, he is not in the house anymore, but he drives around. In the area . . . on a motor bike. . . ."

Peter mentioned a motor bike several times in his first reading. Collins was later identified as the man on the motorcycle who had given Karen Sue Beineman a ride outside a wig shop, where

Karen Sue had just purchased a wig. Karen Sue told the woman who sold her the wig, "I've only done two foolish things in my life—buy this wig and accept a ride from a stranger on a motorcycle."

She was last seen alive riding a motorcycle with the man later identified as John Norman Collins. Her nude and sexually molested body was found three days later on an obscure road on the outskirts of Ann Arbor.

Ironically, police believe that Karen Sue Beineman's death might have been a deliberate test of Peter's psychic powers. She was the killer's—or killers'—seventh victim; and in fact she was killed soon after Peter arrived in Ann Arbor and began working with police on the six other cases. Almost immediately upon his arrival he had predicted that there would be another killing. Sure enough, a short time later he received an anonymous telephone call at his Ann Arbor motel ordering him to "get out of town or there'll be another killing." Police traced the call to a pay phone in an Ann Arbor bus station.

Peter also told police that Karen Sue's body would be found near the motel where he was staying. It was located less than a mile away. He also told police several facts about the body which proved true, although he did not visit the murder scene.

Peter had told police from the beginning that he believed the same person—or persons—was responsible for at least three of the six unsolved murders, and in television interviews he had stated that he was beginning to "visualize" the killer and predicted his arrest.

At almost the exact hour that Karen Sue was reported missing late Wednesday night, July 23, Peter was appearing on television (WWJ-TV, the Detroit *News*) saying: "I hope the killer is watching, because he'll be shocked by what I'm going to say about him." He gave a physical description of the suspect . . . "About six feet tall and with curly dark brown hair. . . . He sometimes dresses in women's clothes and sometimes in men's. . . . He is playing a very clever game with the police, but they are going to get him very soon. . . . I won't get him. The police will get him," he said.

It was Peter who led police to the wig shop and to the salesgirl who had sold Karen Sue the wig and saw her ride off with the man on the motorcycle. It was also Peter's persistence that paid off in eliciting for the police the name of John Collins from a girl who had once dated him. The girl came to Peter's motel at 1:30 A.M. after seeing him on television and voluntarily offered the information that she believed her friend was the suspect he visualized, but she at first would not reveal his name. The description of her boy friend, however, tallied with Peter's. She also confirmed that he had a motorcycle: "He just bought the motorcycle on Monday. . . ." There were three police detectives present during the time Peter talked with her, and it is clear from the transcriptions of tapes in our possession that the girl began to have second thoughts about fingering her boy friend as a suspect: "I don't think he is," she said. "He is not that interested in girls really. . . . [And then abruptly] His name is John Collins." She then asked that the tape recorder be shut off.

Collins had been picked up for questioning once and released. Three days after Peter's interview with the girl friend, he was arrested and charged with the murder of Karen Sue Beineman. Although he has been charged with only one murder, as this is written police are continuing their investigation for evidence to link him with some, if not all, of the others. Peter's theory is that three or four men comprising a religious cult or blood fraternity are responsible for the eight mutilation slayings of the Michigan coeds.

Among other items of note that Peter gave to the police about John Collins was that he had a trailer or was somehow associated with a trailer. A few weeks later police found a trailer near Phoenix, Arizona, that belonged to a male friend of Collins. The friend is still under investigation as a possible accomplice in the murders.

When Peter first arrived in Ann Arbor, the police were, as usual, understandably skeptical about working with a psychic, or a mystic, as they called him. "How do you work? What do you do?" they asked.

"Bring me to one of the graves, and I show you," Peter replied.

They took him to the grave of one of the victims who had been killed a year earlier. He knelt beside the small mound, touched the headstone, and then set out for a wooded rural area, accompanied by three investigators. He pinpointed the exact sites where the bodies of three murdered girls were found, and described how each one was killed. He also accurately described the position the bodies were lying in when they were discovered.

At one scene where a stabbing victim was found, Peter said he suddenly felt a "heavy pressure, like a thousand pounds," upon his chest, and immediately said, "She was stabbed from chest to navel. . . . There was internal bleeding. . . . But she was not killed here," he said. "She was brought here in a car trunk."

Police confirmed that it was their belief the victim had been killed in another location, her body kept hidden for about four days, and then moved to where it was found in a clump of trees near Ann Arbor.

In fact, only after Peter had demonstrated how he worked and actually had come up with so many accurate details of one of the murders a full year after it had happened, was he given the green light and full cooperation from the police force while working on the murders. Although not confirming all Peter's claims, Ann Arbor Police Chief Walter E. Krasny said: "It would have been impossible for him to have learned some of the things he has come up with from either police or news media sources."

Peter also astounded Detective Robert Scofield, who had been assigned to him as his bodyguard, by telling the officer about his camper truck.

It happened while Peter and the investigators were eating lunch. Peter suddenly turned to Scofield and said, "You have a camper and something is leaking in it."

Scofield was somewhat taken aback. He did own a camper but he had not told Peter about it. When the group returned to the motel where Peter was staying, Scofield telephoned his wife and asked her to check the camper. He was even more amazed when she came back on the phone and told him that the propane gas tank connected to the stove was leaking. It could have caused an explosion.

Scofield could only ask what many before him have asked, "How did you know?"

And Peter could only reply, "I don't know. But if you have a gift, you should use it."

Peter had just finished working on the Michigan coed murders and was returning to his home in Studio City, California, for a much-needed rest. No sooner had he walked into the house than the telephone started ringing—as indeed it had been all weekend. He was soon to become involved in what to date is the most sensational crime case of his career, the grisly Tate-Sebring murders.

At 8:30 A.M. on Saturday, August 9, a Negro maid reported for work at the sprawling hilltop home of actress Sharon Tate and her director-husband, Roman Polanski, at the end of Cielo Drive in the hills of Benedict Canyon. What she found sent her running to a neighbor's home in a state of shock, screaming, "There's bodies and blood all over the place!"

In a pool of blood, in front of a beige-green couch lay the horribly slashed and mutilated body of beautiful twenty-six-year-old Sharon Tate, a star of *Valley of the Dolls*. Polanski, her husband, is best known in America as director of *Rosemary's Baby*, the story of a young wife who becomes pregnant through witchcraft. Sharon was eight months pregnant. She was dressed in bra and panties. A bloodied nylon cord was around her neck. It ran over a beam in the open-beam ceiling and was tied around the neck of another victim, Jay Sebring, thirty-five, a famous Hollywood men's hair stylist, who was once Miss Tate's fiancé. There was a hood over Sebring's head.

Outside, on the lawn in front of the ranch-style home, was the body of Voityck Frokowski, thirty-seven, Polish refugee and friend of Polanski's, and Frokowski's girl friend, Abigail Folger, twenty-six, a Radcliffe graduate and heiress to the Folger coffee fortune. She had been stabbed repeatedly. The fifth victim in the massacre was eighteen-year-old Steven Parent, a student and friend of the caretaker who lived in the guest house on the property. He had been shot to death in his car in the driveway.

The bizarre and gruesome massacre, more macabre than anything ever dreamed up in the celluloid dream factory known as Hollywood, shocked the world and touched off one of the biggest man hunts in Hollywood history.

Peter was brought into the case by an attorney named Peter Knecht, who had been Jay Sebring's lawyer and was also a personal friend of Sebring's. It was Peter's first Hollywood case, and he swore it would be his last.

I was fortunate enough to be able to work with Peter—or to be present and observe how *he* worked—from the very beginning. I was with him during his original meetings with Roman Polanski at the home of John and Michelle Phillips of the Mamas and Papas. I was with him during his session with one of the principals in the investigation, an artist-informant who had told police he knew the killers. We have recordings of everything, including his meeting with Polanski in the murder house and the psychic impressions he received there as he psychometrized various objects and pieces of clothing.

As this is written, hippie cult leader Charles Manson has been charged with masterminding the murders, and is awaiting trial along with four other members of the cult, including one named Charles Watson.

With their trial still pending, the details of Peter's psychic detective work on the Tate-Sebring case cannot be revealed here (we're saving them for our next book), except to say that my own personal observations, notes, and transcriptions on this case reconfirm once again the amazing insight of a man I still find hard to believe. As I have followed the case and watched it unfold in the newspapers, I often find myself reading in disbelief and remembering—that's exactly the way Peter described it, even down to a bearded guy named Charlie.

# · 13 ·

# The Challenge

If Peter Hurkos is not a fraud, what is he?

Is he psychic—or psychotic? If psychotic, why is he not in a mental institution?

Is he a mental case, or does he really have a "sixth sense"? And if he does have a "sixth sense," how did he get it? How does it operate? Why does he have it? For what purpose? What is he supposed to do with it?

Is he a zombie, a discarnate spirit reanimating a dead body?

Is he a reincarnated person à la Bridey Murphy?

Is he a split personality à la Jekyll and Hyde, or a multiple personality as in *The Three Faces of Eve?*

Is his special kind of cerebral phenomenon more in the nature of the split-brain response reported by biological laboratories on the basis of their split-brain operations on monkeys? Or is it more in the nature of Dr. Wilder Penfield's theory of "double consciousness"—or two concurrent existences—which Penfield found could be evoked by implanting electrodes in the human brain? Is it really ESP or ESB, Electrical Stimulation of the Brain?

After working with Peter throughout this book, I believe I can say that he has neither the sophistry, the cunning, the intellectual wherewithal, or the inclination to be a charlatan. He is often wrong; he is far from infallible. And under tension and pressure to prove himself he may stubbornly stick to his story to a point of exaggeration, or belligerently assert his accuracy to the point of antagonizing his listeners. (This has happened on his television appearances.) But if he has used trickery or deception with me, then I must say he is a greater actor than all the Barrymores, Burtons, and Brando put together. And no one is going to believe this. It is easier simply to believe Peter.

But then, how do you explain him?

I am a reporter, not a scientist.

And unfortunately, the majority of scientists are either too apathetic about or hostile to the subject of psychic phenomena to bother to investigate or study the neurophysiological activity or brain wave patterns of a person who apparently somehow has acquired hypersensitive faculties. Although individual scientists, philosophers, and psychologists have recognized that psi (for psychic phenomena, *i.e.*, telepathy, clairvoyance, and precognition) must be regarded as a fact established by as great a weight of observation and experiment as that which supports the basic facts in other sciences, most of them still back away from it, possibly because of the word itself—"psychic." It is derived from the Greek word *psychikos,* meaning "of the soul or life, spiritual." It also means "sensitive to nonphysical forces."

In my opinion, it is an unfortunate word because of its association with the spiritual and the supernatural and the occult. With all due respects to Dr. J. B. Rhine, I believe that his choice of the term "extrasensory perception" also is unfortunate, for the same reason—its frequent association with the spiritual and the supernatural and the occult. (Dr. Rhine's early experiments with mediums and their so-called spirit communications did little to enhance ESP's scientific status.) Most physical scientists still refuse to accept the work of psychical researchers (parapsychologists) as scientific; they do not accept the phenomenon popularly known as extrasensory perception as having been scientifically established. And they are, moreover, distrustful of a phenomenon that throughout history has been an open sesame for fraud and trickery of the most ludicrous kind. The public's gullibility, the human urge to *believe* in supernatural powers, makes it easy for the ESP charlatans to have a field day, and I suppose it is asking too much of brain scientists—neurophysiologists—to consider the possibility of a *genuine* psychic.

Still, they must admit that there are certain genuine *mental* phenomena (psychic and/or nonpsychic) that though not yet explained nevertheless do exist.

Let's take a look at some of them for comparisons.

## YOGIS, RELIGIOUS MYSTICS, AND PRIMITIVES

There is widespread belief in the occult powers of the yogi. The belief is unfounded. The true yogi is not interested in occultism, magic, supernaturalism, or any aspects of psychic phenomena. But modern science has definitely established that many of the yogi's physiological and mental feats are indeed genuine and astounding, that the yogi is able to develop, through prolonged conditioning and practice, unusual voluntary control of certain physiological functions.

The true yogi is indifferent to the curiosity of scientists, but some have been reluctantly persuaded to be guinea pigs in the All India Institute of Medical Sciences in New Delhi, in its newly established yogic section of neurophysiological research. (The institute is supported largely by Rockefeller and Ford foundation grants for studying reproductive physiology in relation to India's overpopulation problem.) It has been scientifically established that some yogis are able voluntarily to influence their heartbeat—to stop the heart sounds, if not the heart itself, and actually to *slow* their heart rate, which is much more difficult to achieve than voluntary acceleration or quickening of the heart. It has been established too that brain wave patterns of meditative yogis are distinctly different from those of normal persons in repose. And in airtight-box tests in the laboratory, conducted with yogis who claim the ability to remain buried alive underground for long periods of time, it was found that yogi subjects could reduce their oxygen requirement by 45 to 50 per cent of the normal requirement; under similar conditions a normal person's oxygen would increase rather than decrease.

How is the yogi able to accomplish all this? Not through supernatural powers, as many think. Yoga training is a long and difficult process, and it involves several stages, including difficult and sometimes semiacrobatic meditative postures (*asanas*), complicated breathing exercises, and specialized mental exercises. These comprise:

1. *Pratyahara,* or sense withdrawal. The yogi learns to restrain the flow of external sense impressions to his mind.

2. *Dharana,* or concentration. This is not the same as "concentration" in the Western sense. Its final phase is characterized by the highest state of complete *thoughtlessness,* or a totally blank mind.

3. *Dhyana,* or contemplation. In *dhyana,* the yogi begins to perceive new and subtle aspects of the object of his contemplation.

4. *Samadhi,* or trance. The desire of all yogis is to reach this stage. Many fail. There are five stages of this trance, according to the manuals. In the final stages of *samadhi,* the yogi is supposed to achieve an ecstasy of the highest form attainable, sometimes characterized by "superconscious" or "supernormal" perception, transcending space and time. It is this more than anything else that has given rise to the widespread but mistaken belief in the yogi's powers of extrasensory perception.

In my research in India I could find no one of repute who would lend credence to the relationship between the hypersensitive perception of the yogis and ESP.

In the beautiful Pink City of Jaipur, I met Dr. K. Sampurnanda, governor of the state of Rajasthan, who for more than thirty years had been a scholar of both Sanskrit and Yoga. It was Dr. Sampurnanda who gave me one of the most meaningful interpretations of Yoga and its relationship to extrasensory perception.

"The yogi does not develop extrasensory perception," he said. "What is sometimes mistaken for *extra*sensory is purely sensory, a highly refined extension and development of the normal sensory organs and powers that are latent in everyone, if we wish to develop them. As for perception, the physiology of the yogi is no different from others. There is no new set of nerves involved. The yogi's perception is not different from ordinary perception except that some become hypersensitive.

"This can only be explained in the background of Yoga. According to the yogic way of thinking, the senses are much more powerful than we normally find them to be. Man has developed and evolved as he is today because he is subject to certain desires. His psychological and physiological apparatus is conditioned for the satisfaction of his desires; thus he makes a very limited and selected use of the power of his senses. There are things he does not wish to hear, things he does not wish to see. He uses his sensory organs only to the extent that they satisfy his desires.

"Nature is a great economist. She does not give what does not have to be used. In the practice of Yoga there are many restraints put upon man. He has to practice a strict self-discipline and subdue his desires as much as possible. Therefore, through great practice, and sometimes painfully, he may, little by little, gain use of these sensory powers that have lain dormant from disuse. Some of his sensory organs become hypersensitive. The powers of sight and sound come back automatically in greater force. Not that they were dead; they were there all along. But they are normally not used to their fullest capacity.

"The person who really comes to grips with these powers is the yogi. But the powers that come to him are not any added or *extra*sensory powers of perception, no sixth or seventh sense. They are his own normal sensory powers developed by self-discipline to higher stages of sensitivity than in most people."

Read this again and think about it. I have long been convinced, even before I met Dr. Sampurnanda, that what we call *extra*sensory perception is not at all an *extra* sense but a highly sharpened, hypersensitive development (extension?) of our own normal sensory powers.

The yogis develop this higher stage of sensory sensitivity through rigid self-discipline, self-control, self-denial, and various forms of sensory deprivation. (This can cause hallucinations and mystical or psychical experiences.) The word "Yoga" means, literally, "to yoke," and in ancient Hindu philosophy, Yoga can be described as a system of ascetic practice, abstract meditation, and mental concentration all aimed at spiritual purity and union with the supreme spirit. This latter hardly fits in with the Hurkos image, and this brings us to the question: How were Peter Hurkos' normal sensory powers developed to a higher stage of sensitivity than in most people?

Certainly not through rigid self-discipline, self-control, and self-denial as with the yogis.

Yet there is a faint trace of similarity; the sensory withdrawal during Peter's blindness at birth and the early years of his childhood; the *dharana, dhyana,* and *samadhi* (concentration, contemplation, and trance, which achieves the "superconscious" or "supernormal" perception) mental exercises which Peter does in fact employ during his psychic reading, though he would be the first to deny that his mental talents or techniques bear any relationship at all to Yoga.

As I have mentioned earlier, Peter always fasts before he works on a case. His simple explanation: "I see better on an empty stomach." One of the well-known facts of Yoga is that in some stages fasting is important to achieve supernormal perception.

The yogi's psychosomatic control of his body and breathing is a well-known fact, commonly referred to as mind over matter. Somewhat similarly, Peter achieves such intense states of concentration that he sometimes cuts off his breathing entirely—and passes out.

On one such occasion he had to be rushed to the hospital in an ambulance.

As I have pointed out in my book *The Other Side of the Mind* (with W. Clement Stone), such physical feats as "burial alive" and lying on a "bed of nails" are not part of genuine Yoga practice and are in fact frowned on by the true yogi philosophers. Nevertheless, it is true that some yogis who have deviated from the ascetic path for the sake of showmanship have been able, through autosuggestion, to induce states of extreme catalepsy for the purpose of burying themselves underground in coffins. Apparently a similar state of self-induced catalepsy or extreme autohypnotism is used for lying on a bed of nails, a feat that I personally saw demonstrated in Benares by a twenty-seven-year-old yogi named Shambhu Nath Yadava, a champion wrestler of the province of Uttar Pradesh.

Yadava had been studying Yoga for nine years, concentrating on a yogic exercise called *Kumbhak,* through which—he told me —he has learned to "stiffen" the body as well as the nerves for lying on the bed of nails. There was no doubt about the authenticity of his demonstration, or the sharpness of the long spikes that had been driven into the long board—sharp end up—on which he reclined. His bare back was splotched afterward with imprints from the spikes, but the skin was not punctured, he denied feeling any pain, and he said the spike marks would disappear in two or three hours. Yadava was not giving his demonstrations for entertainment. He started the *Kumbhak* stiffening exercises to keep physically fit and continued practicing fifteen or twenty minutes a day—performing the bed-of-nails feat just as a hobby!

Apparently some yogis have also learned the art of psychosomatic control of body temperature. For example, by a certain technique of breathing and by fixing their thoughts on cool scenes, such as mountain streams or snow-capped peaks, they are able to keep cool in even the hottest weather. (Oh, would that I could do likewise, say I, writing this in Palm Springs in August in 120-degree heat!) The lamas of Tibet do the same thing in reverse, concentrating their thoughts on the hot run or on fires, which helps them withstand frigid winters living in caves among snow-covered mountains and clad only in cotton garments —or completely naked.

It is clear that intense autosuggestion or self-hypnosis plays a leading role in the physical and mental disciplines of the oriental religious ascetics, although many yogi adepts are perhaps not aware of this.

By whatever name it is called—autosuggestion, self-hypnosis, mind over matter—a similar kind of mental activity must be going on inside the physical brain of the Fijian firewalker on the faraway island of Beqa and of the Australian aborigines who can will people to die by putting a curse on them—"pointing the bone" or having them "sung" to death.

I saw the Fijian firewalkers with my own eyes, and for those who must remind me that our eyes can deceive us, I will only report here (full details are in *The Other Side of the Mind*) that the Fijian firewalk—over hot stones, not embers—has been thoroughly investigated and found to be a genuine, authentic feat— no trickery or hocus-pocus. How they do it no one knows, but it is indisputably some form of what must be called mind power.

I also spent a month with the aborigines, the most archaic human race in existence, in the desolate, forbidden, outback bush country of northern Australia known as Arnhem Land. They still practice black magic and witchcraft and are superabundantly endowed with mysterious mental powers that are widely accepted as genuine and have defied scientific explanation. Anthropologists have written voluminously about the psychic powers of the Australian aborigines, so there is ample material for anyone who feels inclined to delve deeper into the subject—as well as a chapter in my aforementioned book.

Only a few points are relevant here. Primitive societies are generally considered to be more psychic or supersensitive than more civilized peoples. It is doubtful whether anyone could find a society more primitive than the Australian aborigines or any better subject for studies in genuine mental phenomena. They are undoubtedly the most hypersensitive race of people in the world, the most highly suggestible, the most nontalkative, and the most psychic in the truest literal sense of the word, that is: *sensitive to nonphysical forces.*

Besides being one of the most remote and isolated spots in the world, Arnhem Land is itself an impenetrable heart of darkness, with rugged escarpments, towering ranges, and terrain so inhospitable that much of it has never been seen by white men.

It would obviously require remarkable mental and sensory powers merely to survive in that primeval bushland. The aborigines have developed their superior sensory powers from sheer necessity. They cannot read or write, nor can they count above ten. But they can live for long periods in parts of the bush where white men would die of thirst and hunger.

The bush has sharpened their sense. Sights, sounds, smells, and touch sensations have special meanings for them. They have hypersensitive eyesight and acute hearing; they can easily distinguish between natural background sounds and those made by moving animals; and they can read footprints or tracks on the ground as other people read newspapers and books. As one of them told me, "My wife's footprint was the first thing I remembered about her."

Like the yogi in training, the Australian aborigines are given well-programed lessons in self-control and self-denial when they are youths and as they mature. (An aborigine, for instance, is never permitted to look at or speak to his mother-in-law.) The law is scrupulously observed and saves endless speech.

Moreover, immediately after the tribal initiation rites, the newly circumcised boy is forbidden to eat certain foods and talk to certain relatives (especially female)—not only for a month, two months, six months, but for two years!

The tribal speech taboo explains much of the reticence of the aborigines. A man who is half-dumb for two years is seldom garrulous thereafter. It also explains something of what most people take for granted about the aborigines—their system of so-called telepathy. The aborigines have developed the art of contemplation to a much greater degree than most people, as well as the art of dreaming. In fact, the whole secret of their silent communication system lies in their dream-time way of life. Whenever a problem arises, the aborigine sits and contemplates it, concentrating intensely, and then as he goes to sleep he concentrates on dreaming about it—and he does. In the aborigines' pagan mythology, animals, birds, and reptiles are all symbolic of some spirit preexistence before birth, and literally everything in an aborigine's dream has a special symbolic meaning that can be decoded and interpreted telepathically.

For example, while I was in Arnhem Land, an aborigine dog woman (one who takes care of her clan's dogs) named Queenie wandered into the superintendent's office of the Maningrida government settlement early one morning and said, "My brother bin properly-dead-finish." The superintendent knew that Queenie's brother was in Cape York, over two hundred miles away. "You've been dreaming again, Queenie," the superintendent said. Just then a wireless message came through: "If Queenie's still around, tell her that her brother died at five o'clock this morning." The superintendent turned to Queenie and asked, "How did you know that, Queenie?" "I just knew," said Queenie.

Fully verified reports of this kind are common in the aborigines' strange never-never land. I asked hundreds of them how they did it. The answers were always the same: "We just know." Or, "Dreamin'."

Most of my conversations with the aborigines, of course, were done through an interpreter, but I met one who could speak English well enough to tell me, "We have no radios or motor cars or telephones to pass on messages. So we do it with finger talk and dream time. When we are lonely we just sit by ourselves and contact our people, whatever their dreaming is. Maybe it's a tree, or the lily root, or the dingo, or the kangaroo. It's all in the dream time. We just know. . . ." Aborigines never know their age. "Age does not worry us. Everybody has a start and a finish. That is why we don't worry about anything. We always know when it's time for corroborees. We just *know.*"

Primitive peoples have more time for contemplation than those in modern civilized societies. Could it be that the aborigines' dream-time way of life has developed in them mental and sensory powers lost to non-Stone Age people through disuse? As the yogi philosopher said to me, "Nature is a great economist. She does not give what does not have to be used."

Could it be that the yogis, the religious mystics, and the primitives hold the secret to that missing link in the power of the human mind?

This is not merely metaphysical mishmash. Scientists cannot deny that the weight of evidence is there, that primitive peoples and religious mystics have indeed demonstrated—and still do— many forms of mental phenomena which cannot be attributed to the supernatural and which must have a physiological basis somewhere in the functioning of the physical human brain.

And if the yogis and aborigines can develop such mental faculties as have been authenticated and scientifically accepted as *fact* (though as yet unexplained), why not a Peter Hurkos or Edgar Cayce—or for that matter, others as well? What is the brain-mind mechanism that triggers or causes such phenomena?

Personally I find it a fascinating correlation that so much of the reputed psychic powers of the aborigines comes from their sacred dream-time, as did many of Edgar Cayce's great prophecies, medical cures, and life readings of previous reincarnations. For more on this I highly recommend Jess Stearn's book *Edgar Cayce, The Sleeping Prophet,* particularly his chapters on "The Dream World" and "Reincarnation." And as I have mentioned, dreams have played an important role in Peter's psychic demonstrations. Primitive peoples think in images—or pictures—rather than words. Both Edgar Cayce's and Peter's psychic impressions came to them in images, pictures—though, as mentioned earlier, Peter also sometimes hears voices, words.

There is an interesting comparison too between the modern psychic and the primitive or religious mystic and the emphasis each places on contemplation, concentration, self-control, self-denial, sensory deprivation, and sensory development.

I am not suggesting that Edgar Cayce or Peter Hurkos belongs in the same category with the aborigines or the yogis. But I am suggesting that somehow they might have developed or acquired a similar brain-mind mechanism that made them psychic.

The question is how?

And going back to my question: How were Peter Hurkos' normal sensory powers developed to a higher stage of sensitivity than in most people?

From a blow on the head?

There are those who believe that all genuine psychics must have suffered an injury to the pineal gland. This is an appendage of the brain which is said to be a remnant of an important sense organ in ancestral forms. (In some reptiles, it has the structure of an eye and is called the pineal eye.)

There are, of course, certain brain injuries that result in loss of memory and other faculties. Peter's injury, as we know, resulted in a loss of memory in some areas.

The brain is powered by a battery of electrical-chemical components. Is it possible that Peter's fall on the head, his brain injury, and the electrical-chemical collusion resulted not only in a partial loss of memory, or sensory deprivation in some areas, but in a sharpening of the sensory powers that are latent in all of us, but lie dormant from disuse?

REINCARNATION OR GENETIC MEMORY?

I have been here before,
But when or how I cannot tell. . . .
Sudden Light—D. G. Rossetti

Edgar Cayce fervently believed in the doctrine of reincarnation and as an earnest student of the Bible found much in that book to prove that it was not alien to Christianity, as many think. His ventures into lost continents and previous existences via his dream world form an important part of the Cayce legend. He once told a woman that she had lived ten thousand years ago in what is now New Mexico, and that she had made certain hieroglyphics that could still be found in a certain location. Later, the woman went there with friends and reported back to Cayce that she had found the marks, just as indicated, though neither Cayce nor the woman had ever been to New Mexico—in this life.

The doctrine of reincarnation has had a long and fascinating history, originating probably with the ancient sages of India. Among the Greeks it was taught by Pythagoras and Plato, and it has been accepted by many thoughtful men, notably poets and philosophers.

Many, including Raynor C. Johnson (*The Imprisoned Splendour*), believe that some form of preexistence may explain child geniuses, such as a Mozart or Chopin, as well as mathematical prodigies and others with outstanding gifts or talents that cannot be otherwise explained. The idea is that if we recognize preexistence, we therefore may reasonably suppose that such gifts represent an overflow into the present life of great achievement in particular fields in a previous life.

The most popular book on this subject to appear in recent years was the controversial but sensational best seller *The Search for Bridey Murphy*, by Morey Bernstein. As nearly everyone knows, it is the story of a young Pueblo, Colorado, housewife who under hypnosis was regressed to a previous life in Ireland. The original Bridey, Mrs. Virginia Tighe, admitted that she actually did not believe in reincarnation herself but attributed her remembrance of things past under hypnosis to genetic memory.

At this point, I think I should explain that I am neither a believer nor a disbeliever in reincarnation. My mind is still open. But for some time I have had a tentative theory that genetic memory, if there is such a thing, might explain not only that familiar phenomenon of *déjà vu*, but the widespread belief in reincarnation as well. (Jess Stearn says two thirds of the world accepts it, and I'll take his word for it.) It might also explain my friend Rose Wilder Lane's recurring prophetic dream of the walled city of Ragusa.

I have asked many brain scientists but have found none yet who would acknowledge (at least in print) the possibility of a genetic memory, although one top brain man at one of our leading medical universities did admit to me off the record that he believed that genetic memory would one day be proved a scientific fact. If a child can inherit *physical* features from his parents, why can't he inherit memory "engravings" from a long-distant past?

Whether the claims for reincarnation as yet have any factual basis is largely a matter of personal opinion, and mine is of no more value than anyone else's. I can only hope to combine critical caution with a tolerant spirit and accept the fact that one finds truth in many strange places.

Peter was talking:

"The moment I fall down I saw my whole life go by in one second and then boom-boom, everything was black. When I come out of the dark I want to go back where I was, when it was all beautiful. Beautiful flowers and beautiful music and everything changed. Even a tulip was different, more beautiful than a normal tulip. Yes, I saw flowers and mountains, beautiful mountains. This is what I paint now. All my painting is what I see in my mind from my accident. . . ."

I had known that Peter had started painting a few years ago and that he also had learned to play the organ. He does both quite well, but I hadn't considered this unusual until now. Many people take up painting and music in their later years. But Peter was telling me:

"I never painted before my fall. Only house painting. Then few years ago I start painting. Somebody said, 'Paint. Paint what you saw.' And I am painting."

"Who was the somebody who told you to start painting?"

"The voice," he said.

Oh.

He explained that he paints only the beautiful things he saw during those four days he was unconscious after his accident. He can't copy. He can't look upon a scene and paint it. "I cannot paint what I see. I paint only what was in my mind then, when I was unconscious. I paint right here on the floor, and I stare and I grab the paint. I don't even know the colors. I paint upside down—it doesn't matter. I sit on the floor and paint in the dark. I see it anyhow. . . ."

It is true. I have watched him paint. I have seen his paintings. In fact, I have three of them. He has sold many of them. His house is virtually wall-papered with his paintings. All are finger paintings done with great globs of paint, no brush and easel. Most are scenes of rather stark and brooding beauty—mountains and sea, desert and stream, a lonely path in the woods, skies of burnt orange and deep reds. All remembered from that time when he was in a world between living and dying. . . .

And that was when he heard the music, too.

"Yes, it was like a choir. Lot of people singing far away."

When did he start playing the organ? "After my fall. In Holland. When I was in theater in Holland I saw an organ for the first time. Somebody tell me, 'Peter, you play the organ,' so I play the organ. Same as I learn to paint."

The same voice?

"The same voice. I never have played piano in my whole life. I have never lessons. But I just feel it, and I was playing Ave Maria by Schubert and the Warsaw Concerto. . . . Listen, I don't know music, but the voice tell me the combination. You feel, you go, you mix it like the paint, and so I play. . . . What my eyes see in the mind, it makes my hands do. . . ."

"You've mentioned hearing this voice, Peter. Is it the same voice?"

"Yes, the same voice. Many times. I don't want to talk about it. People think I am crazy. . . . It is a deep voice like this [he did an imitation] . . . the old man voice, somebody else inside me."

"Peter, do you know anything about reincarnation?," I asked.

"Definitely. Because my father said I am not the same Peter anymore. He died and he came back. That's what my father said."

He stopped and then said suddenly, "But what I am fighting to know. Is it my mind that travels at night in places where we don't know, or is it that we were born before? Why can I wake up in the night and paint pictures of places where I have been? Is it my mind that travels while I am asleep, or have I been born before? I have not found the answer. . . ."

Almost as an afterthought he asked, quietly, "But then how you explain a fingerprint from so many millions people?"

And that was the extent of Peter's acquaintance with the subject. He had no remembrance of any previous existence. In fact, he scoffed at the idea. He had heard the word "reincarnation" bandied about, and he believed that he had been reborn because his father told him so—and because he knew himself that his accident had changed him. He had come back hearing the voice and seeing the pictures, and with the strange gift of perceiving glimpses of the past and the future. He had come back with suddenly acquired—not gradually developed—talents for painting and music which even though perhaps not exactly in a class with genius are really quite remarkable nevertheless. There is sometimes a fine line between genius and insanity, just as some psychic manifestations sometimes border on the psychotic.

What was happening within Peter's physiological brain-mind mechanisms during the four days he lay unconscious in the hospital? Edgar Cayce's omnivision into past, present, and future was said to come from what he called a universal consciousness but which psychologists would probably call his subconscious mind. What kind of subconscious world was Peter traveling in while he lay unconscious?

I do not mean to infer here another "venture into reincarnation" in the metaphysical sense. But there are many subconscious channels into the past—and the future: electrical brain stimulation, the mind-expanding drugs, hypnosis, meditation, psychic trances, sleep and dreams. . . . And possibly brain concussion?

Where did all the beautiful colors and pictures and music that Peter saw and heard while he was unconscious come from? From other worlds? From previous lives? Of whom? And how? They came from somewhere, and one thing seems fairly certain: They did somehow originate within the biological chemistry of his own physical brain and probably mainly within the complex mechanisms that control memory. When scientists find out how memory operates—how we remember and forget—they will have unlocked one of the most fascinating mysteries of the human mind.

Meanwhile, it is believed that all our experiences, every single impression from birth on, are permanently and indelibly recorded within our computer-like brain, much in the manner of a tape recorder. It's all there in our memory storehouse—whether we remember it or not. And many things can turn the memory valve on or off.

If this is true, why isn't it possible to inherit certain memories from our ancestors? And might such genetic memory help explain many of these metaphysical mysteries on a physical basis?

## ESB Versus ESP

Personally I think that some of the developments in our brain research centers are even more incredible than the mental feats of a Peter Hurkos or Edgar Cayce, and—quite unintentionally, I'm sure—they give credence to some forms of psychic phenomena as well as the brain's capacity to perform marvels as awesome and unreal as man's landing on the moon.

Most reports on brain research are reserved for scientific journals, and therefore the public unfortunately is not as familiar with them as with our astronauts' space flights—which everyone can watch on television.

This is no place for a scientific treatise, but I think it is relevant to mention especially the fascinating research being done on ESB—Electrical Stimulation of the Brain. This refers to the process of implanting electrodes deep in the brain and electronically amplifying the brain's own minute electrical impulses in order to investigate brain wave patterns. ESB already has brought scientists closer to finding the missing link between physical brain activity and nonphysical mind, thought, and behavior processes; closer to understanding the relationship between the physiological and psychological brain processes; closer to solving certain brain-mind mysteries that were once thought to be beyond the grasp of science.

For example, did you know that by putting electrodes in certain areas of the brain scientists can actually produce certain feelings in people and animals—love and hate, bliss and anger, rage and fear, pain and pleasure, thirst, hunger, drowsiness, sexual desire? These feelings can be turned on and off at will with an electrode —and some of them also with drugs. Scientists are using both electrical and chemical brain-stimulators in their research. They have also found that certain brain areas when electrically or chemically stimulated produce visible and auditory hallucinations similar to those frequently associated with psychotics—and sometimes with clairvoyants and psychics.

Electrical stimulation of the depths, the lowest parts, of the brain has created all sorts of visual images, and this is considered particularly important for research into the relationship between mental imagery and symbols and thoughts. It suggests, as I mentioned earlier, that primitive man did his thinking in pictures, or images, before words or language developed. And in our twentieth-century space age, the Stone Age Australian aborigines, the most archaic human race in existence, still do their thinking largely in symbolic mental images and still are so skilled in the art of nonverbal silent communication, including telepathy and clairvoyance, that this is why they are known as the world's most psychic people.

But to me the most fascinating development in ESB experimentation was the discovery by Dr. Wilder Penfield of the Montreal (Canada) Neurological Institute that electrical stimulation in the cortex can suddenly force into a patient's consciousness detailed recollections of past events long forgotten.

It can revive long-buried memories and can take a person backward through time in a form of "age regression" similar to that sometimes produced by hypnosis. These electrically induced experiences always appear to be real happenings out of the past but not recollections the patient has been consciously carrying in his memory. That is, he is living the experience rather than remembering it. According to Penfield, "The patients have never looked upon an experiential response as a remembering. Instead of that it is a hearing-again and seeing-again—a living-through moments of past time."

Nevertheless, the patient does not lose contact with the present: he seems to have two concurrent existences, one in the operating room and one in the portion of the past that he is reliving. This has led to the use of the term "double consciousness" to describe the sensation. It is far different from ordinary memory.

In Penfield's words:

"When, by chance the neurosurgeon's electrode activates past experience, that experience unfolds progressively, moment by moment. This is a little like the performance of a wire recorder or a strip of cinematographic film on which are registered all those things of which the individual was once aware—the things he selected for his attention in that interval of time. Absent from it are the sensations he ignored, the talk he did not heed.

"Time's strip of film runs forward, never backward, even when resurrected from the past. It seems to proceed again at time's own unchanged pace. It would seem once one section of the strip has come alive, that the response is protected by a functional all-or-nothing principle."

A regulating inhibitory mechanism must guard against activation of other portions of the film. As long as the electrode is held in place, the experience of a former day goes forward. There is no holding it still, no turning back, no crossing with other periods. When the electrode is withdrawn, it stops as suddenly as it began.

"A particular strip can sometimes be repeated by interrupting the stimulation and then shortly reapplying it at the same or a nearby point. In that case it begins at the same moment of time on each occasion. The threshold of evocation of that particular response has apparently been lowered for a time by the first stimulus. . . ."

One patient relived an episode of early childhood with such naturalness that she felt fear again as strongly as she had felt it at the time of the original event. Another seemed to be reliving everything associated with the event of giving birth to her child. One recalled a dream from early childhood, in vivid detail. Another seemed to be hearing an orchestra playing a number that she herself didn't know how to sing or play, and in her conscious memory she only vaguely recalled having heard it before. And another patient seemed to be reliving a Christmas Eve in church in Holland, where she had lived as a child.

All these cases are recorded in the book *Speech and Brain Mechanisms,* written by Wilder Penfield and Lamar Roberts.

I visited with Dr. Penfield in Montreal in the spring of 1964. Known as the granddaddy of neurophysiology and one of the world's leading neurologists, he was semiretired then but still active and eager to talk in general terms about the progress in brain research. But he was reluctant to comment on the psychic talents of Edgar Cayce or Peter Hurkos, saying only, "There are many things we do not know yet."

He made the same reply when I asked him about the possibility of a genetic memory. I sensed that he at least had an open mind about it.

He seemed very definite, however, that none of his patients had been age-regressed to a previous life, à la Bridey Murphy. He said he believed that some of his patients had been regressed to the age of two with ESB, but no younger—although some have claimed to have memory recall from infancy, six or eight months.

It should be explained that all of Penfield's patients were epileptics, and he made his ESB discovery of the age-regression and memory recall quite by accident during an operation on one of them.

Even though he shrugged off the notion of preexistence, as most medical scientists do, still Penfield's findings do lend a measure of scientific support to the hypnotic age-regression theme in *Bridey Murphy.* What Penfield did with electrodes, Morey Bernstein did with hypnosis, only a little more so.

Can Penfield's electrodes-in-the-head observations shed any light on Peter Hurkos' strange mental functioning? Could ESB provide the missing link between the metaphysical and physical aspects of the accident which gave Peter his "sixth sense"? Is it possible that he sometimes has two concurrent existences—a "double consciousness"—like Penfield's patients when he implants the electrodes in their brains?

Is it possible that the physical injury to Peter's brain could have caused what the great neurosurgeons lump together as "psychic effects"—illusions, hallucinations, and the eerie memory recall, the "living-through" moments of past time that can actually be triggered by planting electrodes in the brain?

That this much is scientific fact, not metaphysics, is something to ponder, isn't it? Is it possible that all those subconscious memories from the brain's warehouse that can be dredged up via ESB, drugs, or hypnosis, and particularly those purporting to be memories of past lives, might in fact be genetic memory?

Some memories, we know, are erased after a severe blow on the head (amnesia), and some old memory traces, strengthened with time, are peculiarly sharpened with such a blow. Memory is a fickle thing. Many old people seem to have exceptionally vivid recollections of long-past events but cannot remember recent events. When a young child with a total vocabulary of, say, fifty words suffers a brain concussion, he may lose half his vocabulary, and the words that are lost are always the last ones learned (*The Machinery of the Brain,* by Dean E. Wooldridge).

Is it possible that the remembering and forgetting—the blacking-out of some memory areas and the supernormal subconscious recall in others—was in Peter's case caused by physiological brain damage, a concussion? Is it possible that his backward and forward glance into time is due to a certain juxtaposition of brain cells, a mixup in the electrochemical energies of the brain because of his injury—but in the same manner or nature of the disturbance caused by implanting electrodes or drugs in the brain?

I'm only asking.

### SPLIT OR MULTIPLE PERSONALITY?

The way Peter's father puts it, "He came back with two minds."

And the way I understand it, one is the mind of the original Pieter van der Hurk and the other is the zombie mind that possesses him, like two men in one body.

When I was working some chapters back in this book, a charming and intelligent young lady, Diane MacAfee, who was typing parts of the manuscript, ventured cautiously, as though not wishing to offend me or question my judgment, "Do you mind if I ask you something? How could you possibly still be skeptical about Peter?"

I explained that both by birth (I'm from Missouri) and by the nature of my profession (as a reporter), it is my duty to doubt. Why did she ask?

"I don't see how you could not believe in him—especially after your own personal experiences with him." She hesitated, then asked, "Did you ever read *The Three Faces of Eve?*"

I had not only read it but had reviewed it and written some feature pieces about it.

"If there could be such a person as Eve, why can't there be a Peter Hurkos—with multiple personalities?," asked Diane.

And indeed why not?

*The Three Faces of Eve* is the fantastic true story of a housewife who was three women in one body, told by the two doctors who helped her find her real self, Dr. Corbett H. Thigpen and Dr. Hervey M. Cleckley of the Department of Psychiatry and Neurology at the University of Georgia.

The case of Eve White was thoroughly covered in medical journals and was considered one of the most remarkable cases of multiple personality in modern medical history. It was also made into a Hollywood movie which won an Oscar for Joanne Woodward in 1957.

There were at first only two distinct personalities, Eve White and Eve Black. Eve White was extremely shy and timid, reserved and proper, a married woman in her mid-twenties with a small child, who was her main interest in life. She first came to Dr. Thigpen, staff psychiatrist at the University Hospital in Augusta, suffering from agonizing headaches and blackouts. Several visits later, in the middle of an interview, she astounded the psychiatrist by suddenly changing from a demure housewife to a sexy, flirty girl who announced herself as Eve Black and denied being married or having a child.

Out of these two separate and conflicting personalities, always warring against each other, emerged a third personality, who called herself Jane, a more mature personality who impressed the doctors as being the bright light of hope. And finally, after extensive psychiatric treatment, including hypnotic age-regression, came the development of the fourth and wholly integrated personality known as Evelyn Lancaster. Her autobiographical story is told in *The Final Face of Eve*, (by Evelyn Lancaster with James Poling). This is her own story of her existence as three completely disassociated personalities, three completely different persons.

The opening sentence of the book carries an impact: "This is primarily the story of the three girls who had to die before I could be born."

As Evelyn Lancaster points out, multiple personality is one of the rarest maladies known to medical science, so rare that less than a hundred cases have been recorded in the medical literature of the past two centuries. The public has long been familiar with the phenomenon through Robert Louis Stevenson's popular fictional story *The Strange Case of Dr. Jekyll and Mr. Hyde*. But true multiple personality is an emotional illness that has little in common with fiction. In many ways, however, it is an even stranger phenomenon than it is in fiction, as Evelyn Lancaster learned. Perhaps the most celebrated case in psychiatric history was that of Sally Beauchamp. Sally was one of several personality manifestations of the famous Miss Beauchamp studied so thoroughly by Dr. Morton Prince half a century before *The Three Faces of Eve*. In many ways, the staid and proper Miss Christine Beauchamp who consulted Dr. Prince was like the original Eve White, and the frivolous Sally could have been a twin sister to Eve Black.

I mention all the Eves and Beauchamps here to remind readers that multiple personality is a very real, medically authenticated phenomenon and not merely a metaphysical mirage. And I wonder, is it possible that Peter, if he submitted himself and his so-called "two brains" to psychotherapy—which he has never felt the need of—would be categorized as a "multiple personality"? (It will be recalled that he did, of course, desperately seek treatment of some kind, any kind in the months immediately after his accident.)

It must be clarified, however, that the phenomenon of split personality (as manifested in the *Jekyll and Hyde* fiction), usually is synonymous or at least associated with schizophrenia, which is much more common than multiple personality. And they are not one and the same.

Split personality is a psychotic condition, medically known as schizophrenia, in which the person is "split off" from reality.

Multiple personality is a neurosis, which is not nearly as serious as psychosis, because the person still remains in contact with reality, even though reacting to it neurotically.

There are some interesting similarities between Eve with her three distinct personalities and Peter with his two minds.

Each had an unhappy childhood (though so do millions of others), but both were adults when their real problems started. Eve White heard a "voice," had blackouts and horrendous headaches. When one of her alter personalities was about to emerge she could feel a queasiness in her stomach. She would seemingly lose her strength and become short of breath, and she was unable to control these symptoms, which were not unlike those that Peter frequently has.

It is probably only coincidence, but I find it intriguing that both Eve White and Peter completely lost their memory for telephone numbers, even though Eve once worked as a telephone operator.

Eve White had a distinctive handwriting that changed when the "voice" or Eve Black would take over. The handwritings were completely dissimilar—just as Peter has the ability to talk in a different "voice" when he is at work, as he did on the Boston Strangler case.

There is no evidence that Eve was psychic, except for a precognitive dream or two, and there is nothing to indicate that Peter needs the type of intensive psychotherapy that she underwent for nearly five years. But the multiple-personality parallels evoke many unanswered questions. One is, If Peter would undergo hypnotic age-regression, could he relieve himself of his zombie?

One answer is, He's not about to try it. He doesn't believe in it. But the more important factor, which Peter probably isn't even aware of, is that his particular type of psychotherapeutic treatment (age regression under hypnosis) works best with traumatic *emotional* problems.

Thus, Eve found her real self only after she was led back through age-regression psychotherapy to remember and relive a terrifying event from early childhood—her grandmother's funeral. Although Peter had his share of terrifying traumatic events in his childhood (doesn't everyone?), I cannot believe that reliving them through psychotherapeutic hypnotic age regression would rid him of what haunts him, his alter personality or other mind that seems to know things no one can explain.

One final word here on hypnotic age regression: There are well-authenticated cases in which subjects were carried back to the age of one month in hypnotic age regression—but there are no authenticated cases of a subject's being regressed to a fetal existence or to some previous life, as the sensational *Bridey Murphy* story claimed.

But there are experiments going on in brain research laboratories that might indeed lend credence to the psychological phenomenon of either a split or multiple personality.

## SPLIT BRAIN

Multiple personality is a psychological phenomenon, but it has its biological counterpart in the rather spectacular split-brain experiments in some of the leading brain research centers.

Most of this research is being done with monkeys. The monkey is subjected to a split-brain operation in which its *corpus callosum* and optic nerve are cut. The *corpus callosum* is the fibrous band connecting the two symmetrical halves of the brain.

Then a frontal lobotomy is performed on one side of the monkey's brain, producing a relaxed, "I don't care" sort of animal. Monkeys are normally deathly afraid of snakes. The split-brain monkeys are no exception. But in these experiments the snakes are displayed so that they are seen first by one eye and then the other. The monkeys exhibit their usual fright and escape reactions when they see the snakes from one side of the brain. But when they are forced to use the eye connected with the hemisphere that had the lobotomy, the snakes hold no fear for them. The monkeys couldn't care less. It is as though two different animal personalities now inhabit the body that had formerly been occupied by one!

Dr. Dean Wooldridge, who has described (in *The Machinery*

of the Brain) the split-brain experiments in the biological laboratories of the California Institute of Technology, says there are plans to extend the techniques to permit cutting most of the brain stem as well as the cortex into disconnected symmetrical halves.

He says, "It is fascinating to contemplate the possibility of preparing an animal with essentially two separate brains, each capable of receiving its own sensations, recording its own memories, learning its own behavior patterns, developing its own emotional habits and personality attributes, and perhaps even sleeping and waking independently of the other.

"Fantastic though it seems, such a splitting of one into two separate individuals, both inhabiting and, from time to time, controlling the same body, may well be a consequence of the continuation of the exciting work that is underway in the biological laboratories of the California Institute of Technology!"

The split-brain monkeys, for example, respond differently depending upon which half of the brain they are using. Have they been provided with two different senses of consciousness that are turned on or off in accordance with which eye they look through? If so, and if the split-brain technique is extended all the way down through the brain stem, doesn't this definitely make possible the development of two clearly different personalities in the same body?

What is the significance of the remarkable fact, discovered by brain scientists, that the sense of consciousness can be turned on or off by the presence or absence of electric currents in the brain stem.

And how explain the peculiar phenomenon of "double consciousness" experienced by Penfield's patients under temporal-lobe stimulation, in which they had the subjective sensation of living concurrently in the past and the present?

Is it possible that Peter Hurkos' "two minds" is a phenomenon similar to Penfield's "double consciousness"—or a split personality akin to that of the split-brain monkeys?

# · 14 ·

## *Conclusions*

At this point I am inclined to go along with Peter's attitude toward cynics who demand that he prove his gift. Why is the burden of proof on him? Let those who doubt disprove it.

There is nothing unique about human minds going astray, for the brain is truly one of the great mysteries of man. Considering that very little brain research was done before World War II, and that it has come into its own only during the last ten years or so, it is understandable that there is no ready explanation of the *why* or *how* of the physiological brain processes of an Edgar Cayce or Peter Hurkos—or of an Eve White or Sally Beauchamp.

But what is not understandable is that brain scientists would turn down the opportunity now to study or test a brain such as Peter's in their brain research laboratories.

When I tried to get him admitted to UCLA's Brain Research Center, I was informed that all the institute's research subjects were either epileptics or schizophrenics and that it could not accept a so-called psychic. I got the usual double-talk about the pros and cons and "plausibility" of ESP and was referred to a psychologist who had an "interest" in ESP. This was not what we needed, or wanted. Peter had spent enough time with so-called ESP experts. He had taken tests for telepathy, clairvoyance, and general ESP. There was no question that he *had* it, by whatever name it was called. (His laboratory experiments with Dr. Andrija

Puharich proved that.) The question was how and why and by what physiological brain processes?

And this was a question for neurophysiologists, not psychologists.

But we got short shrift from the brain men.

A number of persons have expressed puzzlement or disappointment that Peter has not submitted himself to long-range research projects. As I have pointed out in earlier chapters, he has indeed submitted to long-range testing in Dr. Puharich's experimental laboratory in Glen Cove, Maine, but I am sure that Dr. Puharich would be the first to agree his tests were not as extensive or of the same nature as those that could be conducted in a recognized neurological institute such as the one connected with the University of Montreal and made famous by Dr. Wilder Penfield, or the Burden Institute in Bristol, England, headed by another pioneer neurophysiologist and cybernetician, Dr. W. Grey Walter, or, of course, the Brain Research Center at UCLA.

Peter is willing and ready to give his time and his brain to the brain scientists for research when they are willing and ready to accept him—and providing, of course, that someone pays the bills while he's being researched.

When I explained this to Hugh Lynn Cayce, who feels strongly that Peter should be tested further, he told me of several foundations with funds for this type of research. Peter's friend C. V. Wood and I had a meeting with the head executive officer of one of these foundations to try to arrange further research on Peter. Woody was willing to provide funds for Peter's personal expenses, to meet his housekeeping and family obligations, and he also offered to help meet the cost of the research if the foundation should require funds for this.

The response we got was somewhat discouraging. Here is an excerpt from the letter:

". . . Relative to Peter Hurkos . . . I discussed the suggestions made in our meeting with the people here. Although the possibilities of such an examination generated considerable interest within the group it soon became apparent that ours is not the Institution that ought to do the work. There are two good reasons for this decision.

"1. We are not geared (by professional specialty and facilities) to carry out as comprehensive an examination or evaluation as is desirable in this case.

"2. Such an examination, to carry the weight needed, should be conducted by an Institution more prestigiously recognized as authoritative in the field of neurophysiology (*e.g.* Grey Walter).

"I do hope that an evaluation of the sort we discussed will come about and thank you for giving us the opportunity to have been considered in this light."

In trying to follow up on an experience Peter had in a hospital in Hollywood, I met with even stronger and more peculiar resistance. According to the story Peter and Stephy told me—and you are about to see why I have only their word for it—Peter once passed out during one of his psychic consultations and had to be rushed to a hospital in an ambulance. As Stephy explains it unscientifically, "He has a hyperventilation problem. Sometimes when he's working, he concentrates so hard that he just forgets to breathe, so he passes out."

This time she thought he was dead. She first called the nearest fire department, and firemen administered oxygen but could not revive him. In the emergency wing of the hospital, doctors working over him at first believed that he had had a stroke.

Stephy, of course, was at his side and undoubtedly not endearing herself to the doctors any by rattling off her own diagnosis to them.

"It's his hyperventilation," she kept telling them. "He's psychic and he gets this way. . . ."

"What do you mean psychic?" one of the doctors asked.

"Psychic . . ." She tried to explain.

"You mean psychotic," they informed her, giving her an odd look.

Peter was out four hours. When he revived, the first thing he noticed was an unusual ring worn by one of the nurses attending him.

"Let me feel your ring," he said urgently.

"Why?" the nurse asked curiously.

"Give it to me." It was almost a command.

She took the ring off and gave it to him.

"The person this ring belonged to is dead," he began, and as specific descriptions and details of past events gushed from his mouth, the nurse first stood as though frozen in her tracks, and then suddenly ran from the room screaming.

Soon a battery of doctors and nurses surrounded Peter. One medic made what Peter took to be a disparaging comment on his psychic talent, and Peter sat up in bed and yelled, "What the hell, do I have to prove it to you on my deathbed?"

The upshot was that he began spieling off personal clairvoyant tidbits about some of the doctors and nurses that set them all back on their ears in amazement.

Peter says they then made some kind of test with him; he doesn't know what it was.

"They put little needles all over my head and hooked me up with a lot of wires to a big machine. And a little paper comes out with funny lines. I think these are my brain waves. The doctors say this is fantastic, they are so amazed . . ."

"What kind of lines?" I asked Peter.

"What the hell, how do I know what kind of lines? All I know is if you move it hurts, and I was there for two hours and they never did send me a bill."

It was probably an EEG test, though I got nowhere trying to verify this. Peter's own physician had been out of town at the time, and Stephy knew only the name of the doctor in charge of Peter's treatment in the hospital. I telephoned him at his office and asked whether Peter had been a patient of his at the hospital. He confirmed that he had. When I explained my interest and asked for an appointment with him to discuss the incident, he said he did not wish to discuss it. I told him that I would not use his name if he didn't want it used, but he simply repeated that he would not discuss the matter. When I asked why not, he very rudely said that was his business and hung up.

I telephoned the hospital's records department, and was fortunate enough to connect with a naïve clerk who did indeed find a record for Peter Hurkos and was reading it to me when she was abruptly interrupted.

"Oh, I'm sorry," she said, "we have no authority to give out information from our records without the doctor's permission."

Fat chance of that. But I had enough to know why I met a stone wall with the doctor. The clerk had just finished reading off two fascinating words on the written record when she was stopped. The words were "Psychic symptoms." I would venture a guess that the record was destroyed and the clerk lost her job. I tracked down the name of the nurse who had given Peter her ring. I talked to her once on the phone while she was on duty at the hospital. She told me then that she would be willing to meet with me and discuss the incident but that she couldn't talk about it on the phone. When she didn't show up at our appointed meeting hour, I called again and was told that she was no longer at the same hospital. She was at Good Samaritan. I left messages there for her several times, but she never returned my calls. Obviously something or someone had caused her to change her mind about talking to me about Peter, and I had no wish to endanger her job by pursuing her further.

*Since this was written I have obtained, with the* sub rosa *assistance of a medical doctor who for obvious reasons must remain nameless, photostatic copies of the hospital's records on Pieter van der Hurk, Case No. 64–11267, Adms 8/11/64; Disch: 8/14/64.*

EXCERPTS:

ADMITTING DIAGNOSIS: Coma.

DISCHARGE DIAGNOSIS: Hyperventilation syndrome.

HISTORY: The patient is a 53 yr. old Caucasian admitted from the Citizen's Emergency Hospital in "coma" state. . . . Then followed the Physical Examination, Laboratory Data, and Hospital Course. . . . "The patient was placed at bed rest . . . and then placed on Librium 10 mg. TID. It was felt that his acute episode at the time of hospitalization represented an acute hyperventilation syndrome with a secondary respiratory alkalosis. . . ."

*There was also attached a three-page electroencephalogram report showing Placement of Electrodes, Brain Wave recordings, and the official medical report, in summary:*

TECHNIQUE: 18 Electrode recording using scalp to scalp and scalp to ear leads. . . .

DESCRIPTION: The dominant frequency was 9.5 cps with amplitudes up to 20 microvolts. The alpha pattern appeared symmetrically over the posterior aspect of both hemispheres. During three minutes of hyperventilation occasional 4 cps rhythmic low voltage waves appeared over the left occipital region. . . .

COMMENT: When the photic stimulation was performed at 20 cps, the patient became "psychic" and gave the technician a number of historical features about her past although he had never seen her before. The EEG was entirely normal during this time.

*This is the report from one of the most prestigious hospitals in the film capital and signed by two medical doctors as well as a medical record librarian. Although neither the doctors nor the hospital wishes to be identified with a psychic, there it is. They already have been.*

It has not been my intent in this book to plead a cause, win converts, or make categorical assumptions about Peter's peculiar type of sensitivity, but rather to assemble, investigate, and report the fascinating story of a simple Dutchman who sincerely believes that he died and came back with two minds—and to raise certain questions that hopefully will one day be answered by scientific investigators.

In an age of test-tube babies, heart transplants, and lunar landings, it seems incredible that science should any longer ignore the genuine psychic aspects of man's mind. A genuine psychic such as, I believe, Edgar Cayce and Peter Hurkos, may be a rarity, but if his special gift is genuine, then I believe an explanation is called for; just as genius at an early age cannot be ignored because of its rarity. Some persons will remind you that, after all, probably 90 per cent of Peter's psychic talents are wasted on trivia—such as telling someone he needs a tooth filled. Peter has never claimed to be a benefactor of mankind, though Cayce most surely was, with his healing powers. It is not inconceivable that the collective scientific mind that figured out how to land our astronauts on the moon and get them back to earth might one day come up with a practical use for man's psychic talents—such as perhaps a whole new communications system through an extension of our own latent sensory powers? Remember, the communications system of animals is a wondrous world that should give us pause regarding our own capabilities.

Little by little the brain's mysteries are being unlocked. Peter's "gift"—whatever it is—seems to me no more or less incredible than other forms of mental phenomena, such as Wilder Penfield's double consciousness, age regression, and memory recall with electrodes; and the split-brain, split and multiple personality cases in our laboratories and medical records.

Brain damage has been known to render bright and capable people to a state of vegetation where they are untrainable and for all practical purposes useless. Might the reverse be true? Is it possible that an injury to a certain part of the brain could reverse this process and extend certain senses to a higher degree of development—as indeed they are in animals and primitives?

That the mind does at times transcend time and space there can be no question.

The questions are, Why? And How?

Is it perhaps a steppingstone in the ultimate revelation of what life is all about?

Men have conquered Mount Everest for no better reason than that it is there. But what better reason can there be? For the same reason men have conquered the moon. Scientists say that man's exploration of the moon will increase his understanding of himself. And so, they might say, would man's exploration of the mind.